Windows NT Automated Deployment and Customization

Richard Puckett

MTP
MACMILLAN
TECHNICAL
PUBLISHING
U·S·A

Windows NT Automated Deployment and Customization

By Richard Puckett

Published by:
Macmillan Technical Publishing
201 West 103rd Street
Indianapolis, IN 46290 USA

All rights reserved. No part of this book may be reproduced or transmitted in any form or by any means, electronic or mechanical, including photocopying, recording, or by any information storage and retrieval system, without written permission from the publisher, except for the inclusion of brief quotations in a review.

Copyright © 1998 by Macmillan Technical Publishing

Printed in the United States of America 1 2 3 4 5 6 7 8 9 0

Library of Congress Cataloging-in-Publication Number: 97-76476

ISBN: 1-57870-045-0

Warning and Disclaimer

This book is designed to provide information about Windows NT deployment. Every effort has been made to make this book as complete and accurate as possible, but no warranty or fitness is implied.

The information is provided on an "as is" basis. The authors and Macmillan Technical Publishing shall have neither liability nor responsibility to any person or entity with respect to any loss or damages arising from the information contained in this book or from the use of the discs or programs that may accompany it.

Publisher *Jim LeValley*

Executive Editor *Linda Ratts Engelman*

Managing Editor *Caroline Roop*

Acquisitions Editor
Jane Brownlow

Development Editor
Lisa M. Gebken

Project Editor
Brian Sweany

Copy Editors
Leah D. Williams
Susan Hobbs

Technical Editor
Robert Campbell

Technical Reviewers
Jeff Arnold
Scott Hublar
Scott Ladewig

Team Coordinator
Amy Lewis

Manufacturing Coordinator
Brook Farling

Book Designer
Gary Adair

Cover Designer
Aren Howell

Production Team
Kim Cofer
Daniela Raderstorf

Indexer
Ginny Bess
Sandra Henselmeir

About the Author

Richard Puckett is a computer systems engineer with the University of Virginia. He is currently part of a team of engineers tasked to migrate the existing NetWare systems on the academic grounds over to Windows NT. This team has spent the last six months researching the deployment options of Windows NT Workstation through Microsoft white papers, Web sites, UseNet groups, NT-related books and periodicals; testing and retesting deployment options and commands; and assisting various departments, labs, and schools in properly implementing Windows NT.

Trademark Acknowledgments

All terms mentioned in this book that are known to be trademarks or service marks have been appropriately capitalized. Macmillan Technical Publishing cannot attest to the accuracy of this information. Use of a term in this book should not be regarded as affecting the validity of any trademark or service mark.

About our technical reviewers...

These reviewers contributed their considerable practical, hands-on expertise to the entire development process for **Windows NT Automated Deployment and Customization.** *As the book was being written, they reviewed all of the material for technical content, organization, and flow. Their feedback was critical to ensuring that* **Windows NT Automated Deployment and Customization** *fits our reader's need for the highest quality technical information.*

Scott J. Ladewig received his B.S. in chemical engineering in 1990, and MBA and Master of Information Management (MIM) degrees in 1995, all from Washington University in St. Louis. While in graduate school, Scott worked at the Center for Engineering Computing (CEC) at Washington University as an assistant system administrator and was heavily involved in migrating CEC's online information from Gopher to the Web. Since 1994, Scott has been the manager of Information Systems for VisionAire Corporation, a business jet aircraft manufacturer based in Chesterfield, Missouri. At VisionAire, Scott is currently responsible for all aspects of VisionAire's corporate IT solutions, including its corporate Web site. He has developed broad experience in the design, installation, and administration of Windows NT networks and Exchange Server installations. Scott is also a member of AITP.

Scott Hublar graduated from Sullivan College with a bachelor's degree in business administration. He is currently employed at Jewish Hospital Healthcare Network where he works as a PC consultant, network administrator, and mainframe programmer. Scott's interests in computing and technology started at an early age. At age 12, he was awarded first place in his state for computer programming at the Accelerated Christian Education Convention. Since then, he has worked in IT departments ranging from banking to law to health care. Scott has been a featured speaker on technology topics at national conventions and symposiums. He is currently pursuing interests in 3D design and digital animation. Of all his accomplishments, Scott is most proud of being the father of his two-year-old son, Ian Scott Hublar.

Dedication

This book is dedicated to my wife, Allison, who patiently withstood my three-month absence from her life while I wrote this book.

Acknowledgments

Writing a book is probably one of the hardest things I've ever done, and it would not have been possible without the help of some extremely talented individuals to guide my way.

I would like to thank Linda Ratts Engelman for giving me the opportunity to write this book, editor Lisa Gebken for her consummate editorial skills, and editor Jane Brownlow for her excellent time management of this project and, more importantly, the fudge.

Kudos should also go to Scott Hublar and Scott Ladewig for their insightful review on how to make this a better book all around. Special thanks go to Bob Campbell, who has not only provided the necessary level-headed technical review for this book, but who has been a mentor without equal.

Thanks also go to the case study participants of this book, who patiently put up with my numerous queries for information. To Nate Ravid of Sikorsky Aircraft Financial Systems for his humor and insight in a tight spot—thanks Nate. To Marcus Brieden of ADA for breaking the language barrier and a few time zones to be in this book. To Paula Sillars of the University of Canterbury for her short course on library software and life in New Zealand. To Cliff McCollum for coming in late in the game with a great story. Thanks should also go out to Dan Robinson, Marcus Nelson, and Paul Revilla for their assistance in creating excellent case studies for this book.

Contents at a Glance

		Introduction	1
Part I		**Basic Configuration of an Unattended Installation**	**5**
	1	Why NT Workstation?	7
	2	Creating a Distribution Share Point (DSP)	19
	3	Creating Answer Files	35
	4	Customizing the Installation of NT	81
Part II		**Advanced Configuration of an Unattended Installation**	**129**
	5	Installing Additional Applications	131
	6	Securing Desktop Environments	159
	7	System Policies and User Profiles	185
	8	Maintaining the Environment	217
Part III		**Appendices**	**245**
	A	Native NT Tools	247
	B	Useful Registry Edits	269
	C	Windows NT Services and Protocols	275
	D	Cloning NT	281
		Glossary of Terms	285
		Index	291

Table of Contents

	Introduction	1
Part I	**Basic Configuration of an Unattended Installation**	**5**
1	**Why NT Workstation?**	**7**

    An Overview of NT Workstation 4.0 7
    What's Wrong with NT "Out-of-the-Box"? 9
        NT File System Permissions—The ACLs 10
        Securing the System Registry 10
        Service Packs and Hot Fixes 11
    Network Protocols and Services 12
    Deployment Planning and Methodology 14
        Case Study: Communication Difficulties and Planning Issues 14
        Common Deployment Mistakes 15
        Automating the Deployment Process 16
        Checklist: Planning a Deployment 17

2	**Creating a Distribution Share Point**	**19**

    What Is a Distribution Share Point? 19
        Creating a DSP 20
        Subdirectories Necessary for the Automated Install 21
        Case Study: ADA–Das SystemHaus GmbH 23
        Troubleshooting Directory Structures in the DSP 24
        Accessing the DSP Remotely 25
        Accessing DSPs in Windows NT Domains 25
        Accessing NetWare Networks 28
        Accessing UNIX Systems 28
    Push Installations of Windows NT 29
    Files Unique to an Automated Installation of Windows NT 32
        WINNT.EXE or WINNT32.EXE 32
        UNATTEND.TXT 32
        <FILENAME>.UDB, the Uniqueness Database File (UDF) 32
        CMDLINES.TXT 33
        $$RENAME.TXT 33
        SYSDIFF.EXE 33

3	**Creating Answer Files**	**35**

    The UNATTEND.TXT Explained 35
        Case Study: Sikorsky Aircraft Financial Systems 38
    Answer File Keys and Values 38
        [Unattended] 39
        [MassStorageDrivers] 46
        [DisplayDrivers] 47
        [KeyboardDrivers] 49

viii   Windows NT Automated Deployment and Customization

```
[PointingDeviceDrivers] ........................................................... 50
[OEMBootFiles] ..................................................................... 50
[OEM_Ads] ............................................................................ 51
[UserData] ............................................................................. 52
[GuiUnattended] ................................................................... 52
[Display] ................................................................................ 54
[Modem] ................................................................................ 56
[(modem config section)] ..................................................... 56
[Network] .............................................................................. 57
[(Detect Adapters Section)] ................................................. 59
[(netcard parameter section)] .............................................. 59
[(Protocols Section)] ............................................................ 60
[(NetBeui Parameters)] ........................................................ 61
[(IPX Parameters)] ............................................................... 61
[(Tcpip Parameters)] ............................................................ 61
[(DLC Parameters)] ............................................................. 62
[(RASPPTP)] ........................................................................ 62
[(STREAMS)] ....................................................................... 62
[(Services Section)] .............................................................. 62
[(NetWare Client Parameters)] ........................................... 64
[(Snmp Parameters)] ............................................................ 64
[(RasParameters)] ................................................................. 66
[(RAS Ports Section)] .......................................................... 68
Some Examples of Answer Files for Different Environments ............ 69
Options for Automating Deployments of NT Server ....................... 73
    AdvServerType= ................................................................ 73
    [LicenseFilePrintData] ..................................................... 74
    AutoMode= ....................................................................... 74
    AutoUsers=(decimal number) ......................................... 74
    InstallDC=(domain name) ............................................... 74
    InstallInternetServer=(IIS Parameters) ......................... 74
    [(IIS Parameters)] ............................................................. 74
    InstallINETSTP= .............................................................. 74
    InstallADMIN= ................................................................ 75
    InstallFTP= ........................................................................ 75
    FTPRoot=(ftp root directory) ......................................... 75
    InstallWWW= ................................................................... 75
    WWWRoot=(www root directory) ................................ 75
    InstallGOPHER= .............................................................. 75
    GopherRoot=(gopher root directory) ........................... 75
    InstallDir=(internet services install directory) ............ 75
    InstallW3SAMP= .............................................................. 76
    InstallHTMLA= ................................................................. 76
```

Contents   ix

	GuestAccountName=(name)	76
	GuestAccountPassword=(password string)	76
	Troubleshooting Answer Files	78
4	**Customizing the Installation of NT**	**81**
	Uniqueness Database Files	82
	Creating a .UDB File	82
	Contents of a Sample .UDB File	83
	Case Study: Fulbright & Jaworski, L.L.P.	85
	Installation Startup Parameters for Windows NT	86
	Adding OEM-Supplied Network Adapter Drivers	90
	Replacing Device Drivers from the NT CD-ROM with Those from the Manufacturer	102
	Scripting a Network Adapter .INF to be "Unattended-Aware"	105
	Summary of the Process	111
	Installing Specialized Video Adapters	113
	More on Use of the TXTSETUP.OEM File and Writing Custom Installation Files	115
	The [Disks] Section	115
	The [Defaults] Section	116
	The [Component] Section	116
	The [Files.component.ID] Section	117
	The [KeyName] Section	118
	The [Config.KeyName] Section	118
	More on Value Types and Corresponding Value Entries	119
	Adding and Removing NT's Accessories	120
	Removing Unnecessary Applications	123
	The Briefcase	123
	The Welcome Screen	124
	Disabling the Installation of MS Exchange and Explorer	125
	Troubleshooting UDBs, Startup Parameters, Specialized Adapter Errors, and Custom Scripts	126
Part II	**Advanced Configuration of an Unattended Installation**	**129**
5	**Installing Additional Applications**	**131**
	The CMDLINES.TXT File and How it Works	131
	Case Study: University of Canterbury Library, New Zealand	134
	Adding Applications to the Installation	135
	.REG Files	135
	MSOFFICE.BAT	137
	IntranetWare Client 32	139

Using SYSDIFF 145
    Direct Application of .IMG Files 147
    Expanding .IMG Files with /INF 147
    SYSDIFF Error Codes 148
Using REGEDIT.EXE 150
    BROWSER.REG 151
    NOSERVER.REG 151
    Testing .REG Files 152
Service Pack Updates 153
Applying Hotfixes 154
Installing and Configuring Printers...155

6 Securing Desktop Environments   159
Windows NT Security Options 159
    Case Study: Pinkerton Security Agency 160
NT's Default Security Settings 160
    Problems with the Everyone Group 161
    NT's Vulnerability to Intrusion 162
NTFS Permissions and the Group Everyone 163
    NT's Default NTFS Permissions 163
    Modifying File System Security During an Unattended
        Installation 165
    Setting File System Security During Deployment Using a
        .BAT File 166
CACLS.EXE 166
    Creating a CALCS.BAT File Using ZAK 169
User and Group Rights 173
    Modifying Default User and Group Permissions 174
    NTRIGHTS.EXE 177
Securing the System Registry 178
    Protecting the Registry from External Tampering 179
    Modifying Registry Permissions During an Unattended
        Installation 179
Service Pack 3 Installations 182

7 System Policies and User Profiles   185
The Role of System Policies 185
    The System Policy Editor, POLEDIT.EXE 186
    System Policy Templates 188
    Distributing System Policies 195
    Creating a Custom Policy File 196
    Using System Policies for Security 207
    Case Study: University of Victoria's Department of
        Computer Science 212
Modifying NT's Default User Profile 213
    Creating Custom User Profiles for Use During
        Unattended Installation 214

8 Maintaining the Environment 217

Maintenance Options for Windows NT 217
   Case Study: Instructional Design Lab, University of
   Virginia School of Law...219
Maintenance and Update Logistics..219
   The AT Command..220
   The SHUTDOWN Command..227
   Using the Network Install Tab..229
Controlling User Environments 232
   Securing a Workstation with System Policies.....................233
   Securing a Workstation via the Control Panel 235
   More on Defining User Settings...236
Restoring NT Workstation 238
   Diagnosing a Stop Event..238
   Modifying the BOOT.INI File...241
   Alternative Diagnosis Options 242

Part III Appendices 245

A Native NT Tools 247

CACLS.EXE...247
   Recognizing CACLS Output 248
SYSDIFF.EXE..249
REGEDIT.EXE and REGEDT32.EXE..251
AT.EXE 251
NET.EXE 255
   NET COMPUTER [*Option*]..257
   NET CONFIG SERVER [*Option*] 257
   NET CONFIG WORKSTATION [*Option*] 258
   NET CONTINUE [*Servicename*]..258
   NET FILE [*Option*]...258
   NET GROUP [*Option*]...259
   NET HELP [*Option*]...259
   NET HELPMSG [*Error Number*]..260
   NET LOCALGROUP [*Option*]...260
   NET NAME [*Option*]...261
   NET PAUSE [*Service*]..261
   NET PRINT [*Option*]...261
   NET SEND [*Option*] Message..261
   NET SESSION [*Option*]...262
   NET SHARE [*Option*] 262
   NET START [*Service*]..263
   NET STATISTICS [Workstation or Server].........................263
   NET STOP [*Service*]..263
   NET TIME [*Option*]..263

xii Windows NT Automated Deployment and Customization

	NET USE [*Option*]	264
	NET USER [*Options*]	265
	NET VIEW [*Option*]	267
	POLEDIT.EXE	267
B	**Useful Registry Edits**	**269**
	Chapter 5, "Installing Additional Applications"	269
	Chapter 6, "Securing Desktop Environments"	271
	Chapter 7, "System Policies and User Profiles"	273
	Chapter 8, "Maintaining the Environment"	273
C	**Windows NT Services and Protocols**	**275**
	Windows NT Workstation's Default Services	275
	Windows NT Protocols	277
	AppleTalk	278
	Data Link Control (DLC)	278
	NetBIOS Extended User Interface (NetBEUI)	278
	NWLink IPX/SPX Compatible Transport	278
	NWLink NetBIOS	278
	Point-to-Point Tunneling Protocol (PPTP)	278
	STREAMS Protocol	279
	Transmission Control Protocol/Internet Protocol (TCP/IP)	279
D	**Cloning NT**	**281**
	The Security ID (SID)	281
	Cloning NT After Text-Mode	282
	GHOST	283
	Tips for Using Cloned Disk Images	284
	Glossary of Terms	**285**
	Index	**291**

Introduction

This book covers the process of planning, creating and deploying automated installations of Windows NT Workstation, and to a lesser extent, NT Server. Designed to augment any currently available information from Microsoft on the unattended process, it presents an administrator with some of the more advanced techniques required to further customize their automated installations of NT.

It is also designed to provide answers to some of the more common questions about the automation process, touching on subjects such as advanced distribution methodology, desktop security and customization, and automating system maintenance.

The impetus for this book came as a response to the many thousands of postings found in the NT newsgroups on the subject of unattended installations of Windows NT. Since NT 4.0's release, that natural conduit for shared information—the newsgroups—has been inundated with requests too numerous to count on the subject of automating and customizing installations of Windows NT.

This flood of queries in the newsgroups has been perpetuated by the surprising lack of reliable, advanced information on the subject. Microsoft released an extremely useful white paper on the subject called *The Guide to Automating Windows NT Setup*, but it did not answer some of the more advanced questions that administrators had about securing their desktop environments or configuring some of NT's more complex features. Seasoned administrators who were familiar with earlier versions of NT or operating system deployments in general were left to search or test for solutions on how to customize their automated installations of NT 4.0. Much of this discussion, questioning, and frustration ended up in the newsgroups.

The heart of the discussion lies within the operating system itself. Windows NT 4.0 represents something of a paradox from the standpoint of its current installation process. NT's rich features and configuration options make it an excellent desktop operating system for a variety of different environments. But this is a curse as well as a blessing. Because these configurable options exist, many administrators would like to modify them to suit their needs during the

2 Introduction

course of an automated installation. But the deployment tools that are currently shipped with the operating system, while extremely useful, possess only limited configuration capabilities, leaving many of NT's more advanced features unconfigurable during the unattended process.

As the operating system has matured, so have the tools available for deploying Windows NT. Microsoft has to date released resource kits for both NT Workstation and Server 4.0, along with two NT Server Resource Kit supplements.

In addition to their value for administering NT systems, these resource kits also possess numerous tools that are extremely useful when developing an automated installation of Windows NT.

The Contents

This book is broken down into three parts. Part I covers the basic configuration of an unattended installation of Windows NT. Part II covers some of the more advanced configuration options available, and Part III contains the appendices for the book.

The first three chapters are designed to look at the basic elements of the deployment process with a fresh eye, making the whole process of deploying NT more readily comprehensible. If you are familiar with the unattended setup process already, I would recommend skipping ahead to Chapter 4, "Customizing the Installation of NT," and beyond because these chapters contain information on the more advanced techniques used in creating a customized unattended installation of Windows NT.

Part I: Basic Configuration of an Unattended Installation

Chapter 1, "Why NT Workstation?" introduces the reader to planning strategies and to the pitfalls that can be encountered along the deployment path. This chapter can be extremely helpful to readers new to the deployment process who are looking for some helpful guidelines to follow.

Chapter 2, "Setting Up a Distribution Share Point," covers the steps needed to create a network Distribution Share Point (DSP) and includes descriptions of the principal files that are key to the unattended process.

Chapter 3, "Creating Answer Files," defines the keys and values used to create answer files for Windows NT. This chapter provides the reader with examples of UNATTEND.TXT files under various networking environments and includes separate information on automating NT Server installations.

Chapter 4, "Customizing the Installation of NT," covers adding, customizing, or removing the accessories included with the NT operating system. It provides the reader with the information necessary to add custom device driver files for specific hardware needs.

Part II: Advanced Configuration of an Unattended Installation

Chapter 5, "Installing Additional Applications," looks at the various options available for adding applications to the unattended installation process. These applications include those not capable of a "silent" installation method, such as service packs and printers.

Chapter 6, "Securing Desktop Environments," shows the reader how to automate security changes to the operating system and user environment during the course of unattended installation. This chapter provides the reader with a brief overview of the possible security risks under NT 4.0 and how they can be secured through a series of registry edits, NTFS, and Registry and User permission changes.

Chapter 7, "System Policies and User Profiles," describes how to augment security through custom System Policies and modified default User profiles. This chapter also gives you instructions on how to create custom policy templates for use in your own network environments.

Chapter 8, "Maintaining the Environment," covers automating and scheduling the maintenance and update options available under NT, as well as some simple troubleshooting and diagnostics steps.

Part III: Appendices

The appendices contain useful referential data for use during the deployment process.

Appendix A, "Native NT Tools," provides a handy reference for the tools native to Windows NT that can be used during the deployment process.

Appendix B, "Useful Registry Edits," gives the reader a comprehensive listing of all of the Registry modifications covered in this book.

Appendix C, "Windows NT Services and Protocols," describes NT's default services so that the reader can decide whether to keep, remove, or disable them.

Appendix D, "Cloning NT," covers the cloning process of NT. It describes the approved methods of deploying NT through the use of cloning technologies.

The glossary consists of terms and definitions used in the context of unattended installations of NT. It includes some of the more cryptic NT terms concerning the operating system itself.

On the Web

Many of the files and examples found in this book can be accessed on MTP's web site at http: macmillantech.com.

Conventions Used in this Book

The following conventions are used in this book:

> *Tip*
>
> Tips provide you with helpful ways of completing a task.

> *Troubleshooting Tip*
>
> Troubleshooting tips provide resolutions of some problems you may encounter during deployment.

> *Warning*
>
> Warnings provide you with information you need to know to avoid damage to data, hardware, or software, or to avoid error messages that tell you that you are unable to complete a task.

> *Author's Note*
>
> In these areas, I relate to you personal experiences I've encountered that give you a real-life understanding of a topic.

Part **I**

Basic Configuration of an Unattended Installation

1 Why NT Workstation?

2 Creating a Distribution Share Point (DSP)

3 Creating Answer Files

4 Customizing the Installation of NT

Chapter 1

Why NT Workstation?

This chapter covers:
- An overview of Windows NT Workstation 4.0
- What's wrong with NT "out-of-the-box"
- Deployment planning and methodology
- Common mistakes made when deploying NT Workstation
- The automated deployment process

After reading this chapter, you should be able to do the following:
- Identify NT's strengths and weaknesses
- Understand how to use NT in your work environment
- Be able to develop a working deployment plan
- Avoid the common pitfalls of most deployment plans
- Have a general understanding of the automation process

An Overview of NT Workstation 4.0

Too often users, management, or entire organizations fall prey to the computing industry's marketing efforts, believing that an upgrade to the newest or next release of an operating system will solve their current user and maintenance issues. Sometimes it is true, but more often than not, new technologies may bring only partial solutions to an organization's current needs, while introducing a host of new, often unlooked-for problems in the process.

Windows NT Workstation, when deployed correctly and for the right reasons, can greatly enhance a user or network environment. However, when improperly or cavalierly applied, Windows NT can be a major headache for any NT administrator.

8   Part I: Basic Configuration of an Unattended Installation

Windows NT Workstation 4.0 is the very latest 32-bit desktop operating system from Microsoft. It provides users with the stability, security, and processing power to move ahead with the latest software technology. Currently, Windows NT Workstation is creeping into many facets of business and industry, and much of the newest software is being written to run with Microsoft's 32-bit operating system specifications. Many corporations have opted to upgrade directly from Windows 3.1x to Windows NT 4.0 because of its many advanced features and native security, thus bypassing the alternative desktop of Windows 95 altogether.

Before making the decision to go with Windows NT Workstation, you must consider and weigh its many pros and cons. To start with, as a desktop operating system, NT requires much more horsepower in terms of RAM, processor, and disk space than Windows 95 or 3.1x. Tables 1.1 and 1.2 compare the minimum hardware requirements and the recommended requirements of 95 and NT:

Table 1.1.   Minimum Requirements

Windows 95	Windows NT
386DX or better processor	486DX/66 or better processor
8MB of RAM	16MB of RAM
40–45MB of disk space	120MB of disk space
VGA or higher resolution	VGA or higher resolution

Table 1.2.   Recommended Requirements

Windows 95	Windows NT 4.0
486DX or better	Pentium 75 or better
16MB of RAM	16MB of RAM
(24MB recommended)	(32MB recommended)
300MB of disk space	540MB of disk space

The minimum requirements presented here are nowhere near the actual acceptable level of performance standards for running NT Workstation. A more acceptable minimum hardware specification might be a 486DX2/66 with 32MB of RAM and a minimum of 500MB of free disk space.

In addition to its hardware needs, NT possesses a much smaller Hardware Compatibility List, or HCL (which is growing rapidly as developers write new code for their hardware), and it has only limited Plug and Play capabilities, mainly in its video, net card, and modem categories.

Windows NT is also a much more complex OS to administer. Though it shares a common user interface with the friendlier Windows 95, underneath it is very different. Windows NT Workstation has numerous network, security, and user-interface configuration options available, many of which can have adverse effects on the local system—as well as on the network—if they are misconfigured.

This leads us to another concern over migrating to Windows NT—troubleshooting. Even though Windows NT represents a major improvement in desktop stability, troubleshooting and maintenance of an NT desktop environment can be extremely difficult. What's more, there is currently very little documentation available on troubleshooting the OS. Of major significance is the limited support for many older legacy applications, which in certain cases do not function properly under NT.

In its defense, NT is extremely capable when configured correctly and run on a higher-end system. Its security functionality is great for tailoring access to the file system and to the configuration tools at the workstation level. Its Remote Access Server (RAS) is a fantastic tool for allowing remote use of your network. Its companion, NT Server, brings out the full potential of NT Workstation, expanding the security seamlessly to fit into Microsoft's Network Administration model. When running many of the latest 32-bit software, NT's performance and stability have been excellent, and in certain cases have outstripped other desktop environments. Windows NT can run on RISC-based systems (Alpha, MIPS, and PowerPCs), and it contains support for multiprocessor configurations.

But where does NT Workstation fit into your computing environment? NT is an excellent choice as a desktop OS if you are concerned about user access. Its security system allows for individual or group-defined permissions to files, directories, and applications. Its performance on lower-end systems is not stellar, so it should be restricted only to newer, faster PCs that meet NT's HCL. It is a good choice if you are planning to use the latest 32-bit software in your organization but not if you intend for it to continue supporting legacy applications.

What's Wrong with NT "Out-of-the-Box"?

NT works right out of the box with a default installation, but it does not work as well as it could. With the completion of a standard setup, NT appears to be ready to go to work, and administrators can be lulled into thinking that nothing more is left to configure. Depending on your current environment, that may or may not be true. If ignored, these defaults can develop into real network problems and security issues. Even though NT possesses excellent security capabilities, the defaults are not configured right out of the box. This was intentional on the part of Microsoft because they initially believed that average users might not want to incorporate highly secure systems on their desktops.

Many of the topics presented in this chapter are covered in more detail later in the book. In brief, when developing a proper deployment, the highlights that undoubtedly will affect your deployment planning and that will require some thought and possibly immediate attention are the following:

- The Everyone group and how it relates to NTFS permissions (when NTFS volumes are used) and Registry security
- Service packs and hot fixes
- NT's protocols and services
- The default browser settings

NT File System Permissions—The ACLs

NT's security for NTFS volumes and the system Registry contains the group Everyone, where the Internet and guest accounts reside, which grants excessive permissions and presents a grave security risk. For starters, the group Everyone has change access in the root of the volume, which can cause trouble if the user intentionally or inadvertently deletes files from the root of the volume where NT is installed. The group Everyone also possesses change access in the System32 subdirectory, which houses NT's dynamic-link libraries and system support files, which are necessary for accessing fonts and programs such as Internet Explorer but which present an additional risk for potential deletion and/or modification.

> *Tip*
>
> *Alterations to the permission sets must be made with caution because rash changes to the Access Control List (ACL) could inadvertently lock users out of the OS. Securing the file system could be important if you are a network or workstation administrator who does not want to allow your user community to inadvertently or intentionally change network settings or services, or even to install programs. These kinds of concerns apply to the next section as well.*

Securing the System Registry

Another standard regarding the installation of Windows NT is the security of the Registry and its vulnerability to unwanted changes from both internal and remote sources. The system Registry is the brain of NT; it stores a user's settings, installed application data, operating system variables, and environment settings. Access to the system Registry is by default very low because it was intended to give administrators the ability to manipulate settings remotely.

But the default security can represent a security risk, enabling users to view, copy, and change the settings that govern their environment with native editing tools. And the capability to edit system Registries does not merely apply to the system they are using. Both of Windows NT's registry editors can permit a user to access certain portions of another workstation's Registry.

This capability can represent a grave problem for administrators, who may be faced with a failing workstation and not know that its failure is caused by a registry edit performed remotely. Even worse, portions of the Registry containing sensitive data regarding the workstation's security can be copied and, with the proper tools, exploited, granting an intruder access to the secured information.

Therefore, it is highly recommended that the system Registry be secured from harm. A few Registry settings you should be immediately aware of are those regarding the group Everyone, which possesses Full Control or Change access in certain areas.

> **Tip**
>
> *If you are interested in a more secure Registry, consider removing the Everyone group from the Registry entirely and replacing it with the group Users or Authenticated Users (post-SP3).*

In order for enhanced security to be enabled on the Registry, several keys need to be added. These can be scripted into an automated deployment with great care to ensure that the registry edits created use the proper syntax.

> **Troubleshooting Tip**
>
> *An incorrect or improperly written Registry update can have devastating effects on a workstation. Take great care when using updates during an unattended installation of Windows NT.*

Service Packs and Hot Fixes

Microsoft periodically releases service packs and hot fixes for Windows NT Server and Workstation. These fixes can be installed to add specific functionality to NT or to correct some after-distribution problems detected within the OS, many of which are security-related. With the latest discovery of NT's vulnerability to attacks such as the GETADMIN or SMB Protocol downgrade hacks, as well as its rising popularity as a target for hackers, service packs and hot fixes are a much-needed inclusion to the deployment process.

As new service packs and hot fixes become available, a mechanism must be in place that enables administrators to install and update systems on their networks. The kinds of functionality needed to accomplish these updates can be scripted into an automated installation process.

Network Protocols and Services

Most users unfamiliar with NT tend to overinstall some of the peripheral options for the operating system during installation, bogging it down with a host of unnecessary protocols and services. Remember that for each protocol installed, Windows NT maintains a separate browse list. Unnecessary protocols can steal system resources that are vital to running the operating system and any installed applications. Such protocols can also further complicate the diagnoses of problems as they arise.

As for services, NT automatically installs both the Workstation and Server service during installation, which is often undesirable when deploying NT on a large scale. The Server service under NT Workstation is necessary if users share files and printers through logins to one another's systems or if you use Microsoft's System Management Server. You may want to consider whether this service is beneficial. Running it can translate into additional overhead for your network if left in its default configuration. The Server service also brings with it two potentially undesirable functions, LM Announcements and browse list replication.

The first potentially undesirable aspect of the Server service is its use of LM Announce packets. The Server service-enabled workstation uses the packets to announce itself to the Master Browser for its domain or workgroup. The Master Browser under NT networks is the primary domain controller, but under non–NT Server environments, such as NetWare, that list is left to the most powerful NT workstation running the Server service for the longest period of time. This packet is used to let the Master Browser on the network know that another server has come onto the network and that the browse list maintained by the Master Browser should be updated with the workstation's name.

Traffic of this nature can begin to fill up the browse list that appears in the Network Neighborhood because every NT workstation runs the Server service. This kind of buildup leads us to the second potentially undesirable aspect: browser traffic and browser elections. By default, Server-service-enabled NT workstations generate a great deal of browser traffic on a network in the form of browse-list replication and browser elections. *Browser traffic* on a network is due to the maintenance and distribution of the browse list that contains networked resources that have "announced" themselves to the Master Browser. Browser traffic is no small matter under NT because such traffic constitutes approximately 31 percent of all startup traffic on an NT network.

After a Server-service-enabled workstation has announced itself to the network, it attempts to contact the Master Browser for the most recent browse list. If that request is timed out or fails, it forces an *election* for Master Browser status. This is a broadcast election packet that sends out a request to all of the resources connected to the network. The request asks for their current values with respect to their electoral status as potential Master Browsers. These packets are passed around, and the resource with the highest election criteria is promoted to the position of Master Browser. It remains Master Browser until it goes offline or until another election is forced, which occurs when a new workstation or server comes online that possesses a higher Master Browser criteria value.

You can imagine what would happen if 1,000 NT workstations were installed with the server and related browser services enabled—all of them in constant contact with one another, updating and maintaining possibly multiple browse lists for each protocol loaded. Periodically, they would even force browser elections (especially in non–NT Server environments) between them as a Master Browser came up and down on the network.

Therefore, patterns of access and browse list maintenance should be well thought out before deploying NT. Take into consideration the needs of your user community and your network capacity. It's usually best to identify which systems actually require the Server service before deploying NT, which diminishes the actual size of the browse list that is passed around between systems on your network.

Next, decide where you want your backup and potential browsers to be located on your network and then disable the process on all of the other systems. Careful consideration should also be given to deployments of NT that may require access to other systems across WAN links or over routers. Understanding browser architecture and its requirements is a necessity when planning deployments of NT Workstation on a large scale. These services, which can be disabled during an automated deployment of Windows NT, are covered in detail later in this book.

Deployment Planning and Methodology

Case Study: Communication Difficulties and Planning Issues

Two consulting groups are retained to deploy several NT servers and 1,000 NT workstations for a major company. Each consulting firm is well-versed in the customization and deployment methods and strategies used to integrate Windows NT in the enterprise. Approaching their respective responsibilities diligently and thoughtfully, both groups plan out the process as it pertains to their piece of the operation.

The group responsible for deploying NT Workstation devised a highly specialized installation incorporating the custom scripts, configuration files, and automated application installations that the client had requested. They also selected a unique method of attaching to an NT server using bootable disks that incorporated the MS-DOS Client and TCP/IP in order to access the custom installation files for NT Workstation stored there. The IP address dynamically assigned to the system by a DHCP server could then be used to identify the workstation so that the appropriate unique workstation configuration data could be applied during the installation process.

What this group was not aware of was that the consulting group responsible for the server portion of the installation had been required to configure the network frame type for the system using 802.2 during the process of setting up the servers and the network. This unique requirement was mainly due to the constraints of the older existing equipment used on the network. The MS-DOS Client version of TCP/IP uses the 802.3 frame type, so the installation group encountered an enormous number of frame errors on the routers when they attempted to start their automated installations of NT Workstation over the network.

Several other concerns over deployment methodology began to arise between the two groups as some of the more subtle differences between their respective plans became apparent. The two groups followed separate planning paths in order to use the increased functionality between Windows NT Server and Workstation and to use the unique network constraints. Using these separate paths exacerbated these concerns.

This is an excellent example of some of the toughest issues regarding large-scale deployments of Windows NT—planning, communication, and coordination. The two groups involved on this project are well-respected in the consulting community, each with years of experience in effectively deploying and administering NT environments, and yet communication issues still arose between them.

Keep this example in mind. The issues the two groups encountered, as well as other issues, both technical and non-technical, should be well thought out prior to the actual deployment. Planning represents a critical part of any deployment process because so many unforeseeable events can occur along the way.

Common Deployment Mistakes

If one had to specify the single most critical flaw in most Windows NT deployment plans, it would reside in the testing phase. Most administrators are under a great deal of pressure to provide their user community with the latest technology, and for much of that new technology, the learning curve seems to be getting steeper with each new release or upgrade. Many of the mistakes occur from a rush to deploy. Overlooked issues can make for a longer road when such issues must be tackled as late as the rollout process. Confidence in your work is one thing, but experience tells you that a backup or contingency plan is vital in case something goes wrong.

Following are some simple steps that can assist you in designing a solid deployment strategy:

1. Develop a deployment plan.
2. Identify the desirable configuration requirements for NT.
3. Test deployment options and related methodology.
4. Develop a timetable for deployment.
5. Deploy according to plan.
6. Assess progress of deployment.

Also, the amount of troubleshooting required when diagnosing installation difficulties is often underestimated under NT. As was stated earlier, Windows NT possesses a number of different configuration options that can be automated. However, diagnosing problems when these configuration settings are being automated is another thing entirely.

For example, consider improper or incorrect security alterations during an unattended installation. The Registry, the ACL for NTFS partitions, users' rights, System Policies, and Share permissions all govern access to files, directories, applications, and services, so you can imagine the kinds of problems created when more than one is set incorrectly and an error message is received. Tracking down the changes can become an administrative headache. Say a user logs on to an NT workstation for the first time and everything seems to be functioning properly. A few days later, the user discovers for the first time that she cannot save changes she has made to the printer settings for the network printer. Is that a user rights issue? Is it the system policy that's in use? Or could an intentional Registry alteration have inadvertently caused this problem? Only through a proper and thorough testing phase can these kinds of problems and others like them be discovered and corrected.

Automating the Deployment Process

After considering just a few of the issues associated with NT Workstation and its installation and maintenance, you can see how properly planning a deployment of NT can seem a little daunting. Each element must be considered fully and weighed against your desired outcome. Is it possible to automate all of the changes you want to make to your deployments? Yes. But the real question is, is it worth the effort?

Automating NT installations can be as simple or as complex as you want, depending on the tools at hand, the creativity of the deployer, and the amount of time available for testing. It's important to develop a deployment that is maintainable—that is, one that presents solutions for upgrading and restoring NT, as well as serving your initial installation needs.

This section briefly highlights the automation process before delving into the technical documentation involved in each part of the process.

Automating the installation of Windows NT Workstation involves creating a series of scripts tailored to answer the configuration options asked during the installation process, to set security for the operating system, and to apply any additional software necessary. These scripts also customize the look and feel of the desktop environment you want to use. Each script references the next in some fashion, winding its way toward further customization of the setup process.

Each script may also reference a particular type of executable file or program, which is called upon to perform a specific function related to the install process. Some of the executables assist the installation in updating the target system's Registry, kicking off a service pack installation, resetting NTFS permissions of files and directories, or even applying groups of customized application data.

The installation process is really centered on the *Answer file*, which is the principal script file that responds to the various installation queries contained within NT's setup. The next section explores the various elements contained within an Answer file, the options available, and how to further customize them to meet the needs of your installation.

Checklist: Planning a Deployment

1. Identify the scope of the deployment

    - How many workstations do you plan to deploy?
    - What is the time frame of the deployment?
    - How many machines are upgrades? How many are new?
    - Are hardware upgrades necessary?
    - Do you require multiple client configurations?
    - Do the applications that the users need have to be upgraded or changed?
    - What kinds of security do you require?
    - Do certain network issues exist?
    - What kind of desktop environment do you require?
    - What kinds of end-user training are necessary?
    - How do you plan to manage the desktop environments?
    - What special scope details exist in your environment?

2. Develop a deployment strategy

    - How many people need to be involved?
    - What method do you plan to use to deploy the OS to the desktop?
    - What special circumstances exist, such as critical workstation backups prior to installation?
    - What kinds of applications do you want to be integrated into the install?
    - What kinds of testing are necessary to ensure a smooth deployment?

3. Test your deployment of NT Workstation

    - Does your initial build meet the criteria you've made? Can it be improved?
    - Is the build friendly to your user community? (Use the lowest common denominator method in developing a single build. Tailor it to your least capable users or create multiple builds for different user types.)
    - Are there bugs in your deployment?

- Is it easy to maintain?
- Do all of your new and legacy applications function properly?

4. Conduct an initial assessment rollout

    - Choose a select cross-section of your user community. Have them evaluate performance, ease of use, security, and reliability. Remember that change is usually resisted, so be careful about responding to feedback.

5. Tweak the deployment (or rebuild, if necessary, returning to Step 3).

    - After improvements are made, retest. Be sure that your tweaking is well-documented and does not stray too far from your established criteria. Don't lose sight of the big picture.

6. Conduct your full deployment

    - Make sure the time frame has been established well in advance.
    - If possible, have end-user training begin *before* deployment so that they are prepared for their new desktop.
    - Ensure that a backup plan exists in the event of a service failure—for example, when a network-based distribution becomes inaccessible because of an outage—and have a CD-based installation handy.
    - Conduct a post-deployment survey.
    - Establish maintenance teams and train them on the methods of troubleshooting and repairing your rollout.

Chapter 2

Creating a Distribution Share Point

This chapter covers:

- What a Distribution Share Point (DSP) is
- Directories needed to create a DSP
- How to access network-based DSPs
- Files specific to an automated installation

After reading this chapter, you should be able to do the following:

- Understand the proper directory structure for a DSP
- Create the installation startup disk for a variety of different network platforms
- Know the key installation files used for an automated deployment of NT

What Is a Distribution Share Point?

In order to take full advantage of an automated installation, you must configure the files and directories used in the setup process in a particular manner, preferably on a network-accessible distribution point, such as a file server. This configuration of files and directories is known as a Distribution Share Point, or DSP. DSPs can exist on a variety of different platforms, not just on Windows NT Server. Therefore, with NT you can include Windows 3.11 or 95 with file-sharing enabled, UNIX servers, and NetWare servers, to name a few.

DSP is usually a network-accessible directory containing the Windows NT distribution CD files for installation on the processor platform, which is accessed during a network logon session. However, a DSP can also be a custom-made

CD-ROM, containing the OS setup files along with any additional files and directories needed to further customize an installation. The number and type of DSPs available should be determined by your desired method of distribution and whatever other special considerations play into your unique situation.

Creating a DSP

Follow these steps to create a network-based installation of Windows NT:

1. Insert the Windows NT Distribution CD-ROM into a network-capable system.

2. Connect to a network server with a login ID that possesses sufficient rights to create a directory. Create the directory that will house your installation of NT on the server you want to use as your distribution system. Ensure that sufficient privileges are given to the ID or IDs that are used so that they can connect to the installation server, and access the setup files necessary to begin an installation session.

3. Copy the contents of the directory on the distribution CD that pertains to the type of workstation you will be installing to. For Intel processor-based workstations, it is helpful to copy the contents of the retail CD-ROM directory's I386 directory to the DSP. Doing so enables you to copy more than one processor platform installation set into the same directory in case you require multiple processor platform installations (see Table 2.1).

Table 2.1. Processor Types and Their Corresponding Installation Directories on the Windows NT Retail Distribution CD

Processor Platform	Corresponding Directory
Intel-based processor	I386
Alpha-based processor	Alpha
Power PC	Ppc
MIPs-based processor	Mips

Tip

To diminish the amount of disk space taken up by the installation directory, remove the INETSRV subdirectory from within the I386 directory. It contains optional Personal Web Server install files that may be unwanted in many environments.

Chapter 2: Creating a Distribution Share Point   21

> **Tip**
>
> *To further diminish the amount of disk space used by the installation file set, remove the DRVLIB.NIC from the DSP, leaving only the corresponding subdirectories that are needed by the network interface cards used on your network.*

With the installation files copied over to the distribution server, you can now create the necessary subdirectories required for customizing an automated NT deployment.

Subdirectories Necessary for the Automated Install

Within the DSP directory on the server, you need to create several additional subdirectories. If you have multiple-processor platform installation file sets in your DSP directory, you need to create additional subdirectories in each of them. These subdirectories are meant to house the customization files that are used in an automated deployment. Each directory exists to provide a specific installation purpose, such as housing specialized network or video drivers, updating existing system files, or installing additional applications. Figure 2.1 shows a graphical display of a basic directory structure on a DSP.

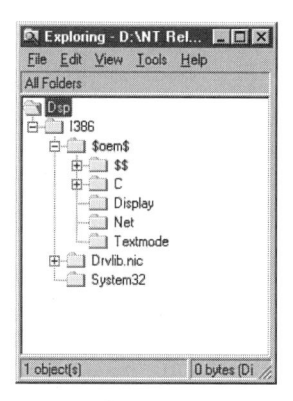

Figure 2.1. *Sample directory structure of a DSP.*

Following are the descriptions of each specialized subdirectory, both necessary and optional, that you should create on the DSP.

OEM

This is the first subdirectory you need to create within the DSP directory. It is used to house all of the additional subdirectories that may or may not be needed for the installation. It also houses the CMDLINES.TXT file, which is responsible for defining customization parameters referenced during the installation process. Any additional tools that you may use and reference in the CMDLINES.TXT file are also in this subdirectory. The additional optional subdirectories that should be housed within the OEM directory are $$, C, DISPLAY, NET, and TEXTMODE.

$$

This subdirectory contains any files that you copy to the %SYSTEMROOT% on the target workstation or its subdirectories within your new install. It can be especially useful if you want to copy files into the \WINNT directory (or whatever you choose to call it). Additional files can be copied deeper into the directory tree of the target system by creating a \SYSTEM32 subdirectory within the $$ directory on the DSP. You can then copy whatever files you want to this subdirectory, and they will be copied into the WINNT\SYSTEM32 subdirectory during the installation process.

Files and directories that exceed the DOS 8.3 naming convention need to be referenced in the $$RENAME.TXT file. This file is used to translate DOS naming convention files and directories into long file names again after they have been copied over to the target system.

> *Troubleshooting Tip*
>
> *Files placed in this directory and its subdirectories overwrite any system file installed or duplicated in the referenced directory during the setup process.*

Drive Letter (such as C, D, E, and so on)

Files and directories stored in this drive are copied over to the drive letter on the target system that bears the same name. This optional directory can be very useful if you choose to copy the installation files of a specific program over to the target system and then reference them later in the setup process.

> *Troubleshooting Tip*
>
> *Files placed in this directory and its subdirectories overwrite any system file installed or duplicated in the referenced directory during the setup process.*

DISPLAY

This optional subdirectory is used for storing OEM-supplied or updated video adapter files that are referenced in the [Display] section of the Answer file.

NET

This subdirectory is used solely for housing special network-related files (NIC drivers, protocols, and so on) that are referenced in the [Network] section of the Answer file.

> *Tip*
>
> *Network and video drivers can also be copied over to the target system by using the TEXTMODE subdirectory.*

TEXTMODE

This subdirectory contains driver or miscellaneous files that you want to be copied over during the TEXTMODE portion. These files can then be used later in the installation process in the Answer file. Some examples of files that may be placed in this subdirectory are an OEM-supplied or updated Hardware Abstraction Layer (HAL), a custom mass storage driver, a special keyboard driver, or other hardware-dependent files.

After your directory structure is in place, you can copy the files that may be needed to customize your installation of Windows NT. It is important to not only ensure that the appropriate files are in the correct directories, but also to ensure that the installation process has properly referenced them.

Case Study: ADA–Das SystemHaus GmbH

ADA–Das SystemHaus GmbH is a consulting firm specialized in providing computing and network support for corporations, including hardware and software installation and repair. ADA provides end-user training up to full organizational computing support. The firm has offices in several cities in Germany, including a training division of 70 members and 50 trainers located in Neuss (near Düsseldorf) that provides computer-based training sessions for the cities of Duisburg, Dortmund, Cologne, Krefeld, Mönchengladbach, and the surrounding region.

The training division in Neuss has 10 computer-based training classrooms with 80 PCs. These PCs are required to be completely re-created each week using Microsoft's classroom specifications for their related coursework. These specifications dictate how the systems are to be configured. These continual redeployments can be further complicated by the coursework requirements of the instructor and the training calendar for that week, as well as by whether or not the classes being offered are taught in English or in German.

The training division staff has responded to these requirements by automating the installation process of Windows NT. The installation is initiated from a bootable disk, which connects the system to an NT server. A menu then prompts the installer for information on the classroom number, the workstation number, the desired language, and the course number. This information is used to generate a Uniqueness Database File, or UDF, which is used to enter the custom data into the installation process of NT. After the installation of the core OS is complete, the corresponding data sets required for each course are copied over to the target workstation along with additional commands run from batch files.

This particular deployment of Windows NT in the training classrooms takes advantage of NT's File & Print Services for NetWare, an add-on service for mixed network environments that allows an NT server to emulate a NetWare server. In this way, the clients of both NetWare and NT environments can have access to files and services on an NT server. Using Novell's DOS Requester, the training support staff can access NT's installation files in order to set up the custom configurations of NT Workstation on the target systems in the training classroom. This method of accessing and installing NT is one of the many options available to administrators who are looking for ways to access and distribute installations of Windows NT Workstation.

Troubleshooting Directory Structures in the DSP

Few errors are directly associated with the DSP. They are usually caused by a misnamed subdirectory, an incorrect reference to the directory in an installation script, or insufficient rights possessed by the installer to access all of the files and subdirectories in the DSP. The last issue, insufficient rights, may not be a problem if the computing staff is handling the installation of Windows NT and logging in with administrator or high-level access user IDs.

But in situations in which a push installation is used, the directory structures containing the setup files for Windows NT should be protected from user tampering. (Push installation options are covered later in the chapter.) Table 2.2 shows the minimum amounts of permissions necessary to access a network-based DSP.

Table 2.2. *Minimum Permission Sets Needed to Use a Network-Based DSP*

Network Platform	Minimum Permissions Needed
NT	Read (on files and directories)
NetWare	Read and file scan
UNIX	Read (execute on subdirectories)

Chapter 2: Creating a Distribution Share Point   25

Accessing the DSP Remotely

After the DSP has been created, it is important for you to explore the method in which the DSP must be accessed for an automated deployment to be run. The most popular method is to use a network-capable boot disk that contains an automated login and startup script to start the target system. You can then use executables to perform any necessary disk functions (FDISK, FORMAT, and so on), auto-connect to the DSP, and then kick off the installation.

Accessing DSPs in Windows NT Domains

Windows NT Server contains a good program or utility called the *Network Client Administrator* that walks an administrator through the creation process of a network-capable floppy that can be used to access a DSP and start an installation. Following is a step-by-step example of how to use this Client Administrator:

1. From the server console, select Start, Programs, Administrative Tools (Common). From the list of options, click on Network Client Administrator. The Client Administrator window should appear.

2. Select the Make Network Installation Startup Disk option, then Continue (see Figure 2.2).

> *Tip*
>
> *Make sure that the floppy disk you are using is bootable. Unfortunately, the Client Administrator does not make the disk bootable during the process; the installation prompts you to make the disk bootable if it detects that it is not.*

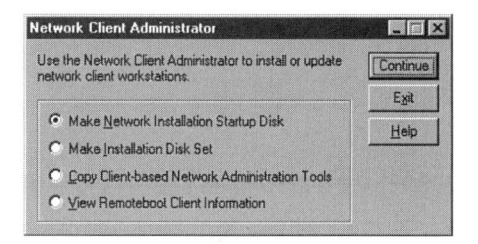

Figure 2.2. *Network Client Administrator startup screen.*

3. Next, the Client Administrator prompts you for the location of your installation directory on the server (see Figure 2.3). It is important that the files needed to install NT are on the server before you initiate this process; otherwise, the Client Administrator fails, stating that it was unable to locate the files needed to create the installation disk.

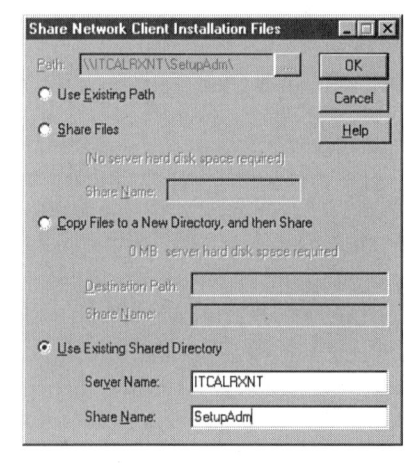

26   Part I: Basic Configuration of an Unattended Installation

Figure 2.3. The NCA share path.

4. After determining the installation type to use, select OK. The next screen appears, prompting you to choose the disk type, the network card, and the networking client platform that will be used to attach to the server (see Figure 2.4). In this figure, a 3.5-inch floppy has been selected to create a DOS bootable disk for a 3Com's EtherLink adapter card, the 3C509.

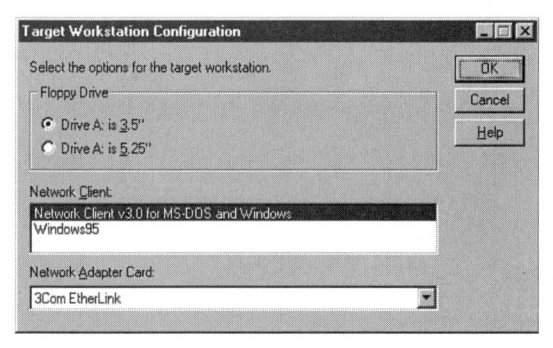

Figure 2.4. NCA Target Workstation Configuration screen.

5. After the appropriate settings have been defined, press OK. The next screen that appears prompts you for additional network configuration information, including the computer name, the username, the domain you log into, the network protocol you use to connect to the domain, and the destination of the floppy (see Figure 2.5). Remember that the server from which you access the Client Administrator dictates the network protocol choices for your boot disk. This is to ensure that the disk contains the protocols that allow it to connect to the target server.

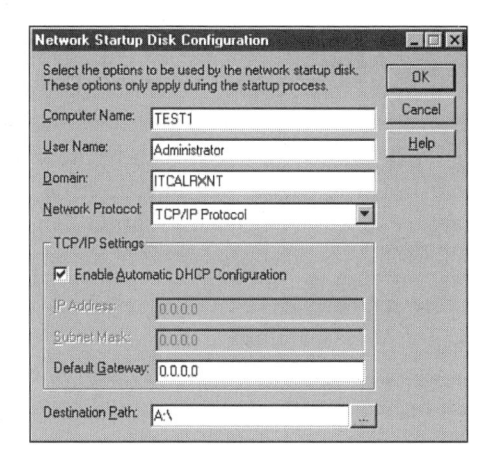

Chapter 2: Creating a Distribution Share Point   27

Figure 2.5. NCA *Startup Disk Configuration screen.*

6. After you press OK, a confirmation screen appears to verify the data inputted from the earlier screens (see Figure 2.6).

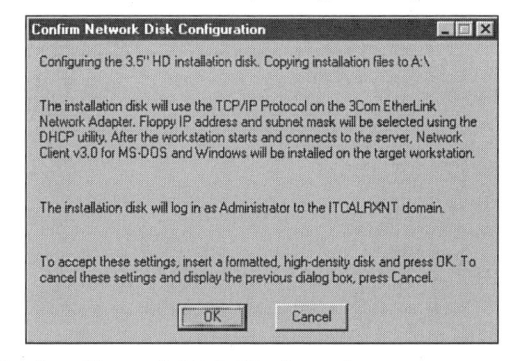

Figure 2.6. NCA *Confirm Network Disk Configuration screen.*

7. After pressing OK, the disk is checked to determine whether it is currently a system disk. If it is not, the Client warns the user that the disk is not bootable and then prompts the user to decide whether it should continue or halt the process. If the disk needs to be converted, simply remove it from the drive, take it to a DOS workstation, and covert it into a system disk. Reinsert the disk into the floppy drive and press OK. If the disk is already a system disk, the Client continues without prompting, copying over the files needed to boot to the server.

After the process has completed copying the appropriate files to the disk, the installation returns to the starting screen, at which point it can be closed.

28   Part I: Basic Configuration of an Unattended Installation

Accessing NetWare Networks

Many network adapters are shipped with an installation disk, which often contains the latest drivers needed to attach to NetWare networks from DOS. But if you are without such a disk, a DOS driver set can be created from the NetWare server itself. Most installations of NetWare 3.12 have the option of creating a network-capable disk. Network installation files can be found under SYS:\PUBLIC\CLIENT\DOSWIN on most NetWare servers.

Ensure that you correctly reference the NetWare Distribution server in the NET.CFG of the boot disk. The installation disk can also contain within its AUTOEXEC.BAT file the information necessary to automatically connect to the NetWare server, map the appropriate drives, and begin the automated installation of Windows NT.

Following is an example AUTOEXEC.BAT file that could be used with a bootable disk to boot to a NetWare server on a system using a 3Com 3C509 (Figure 2.7).

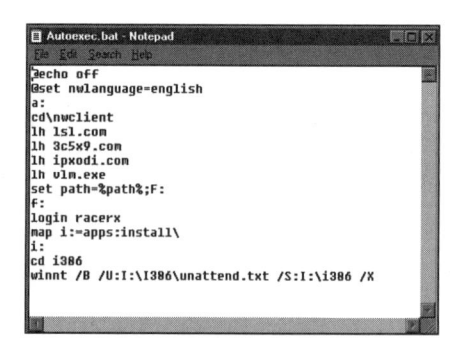

```
@echo off
@set nwlanguage=english
a:
cd\nwclient
lh lsl.com
lh 3c5x9.com
lh ipxodi.com
lh vlm.exe
set path=%path%;F:
F:
login racerx
map i:=apps:install\
i:
cd i386
winnt /B /U:I:\I386\unattend.txt /S:I:\I386 /X
```

Figure 2.7. *Sample AUTOEXEC.BAT used to install NT under NetWare.*

Tip

The batch file is using a login account that does not require a password. After the login, the code maps a network drive, switches to the distribution directory, and begins the installation process.

Accessing UNIX Systems

You cannot access most UNIX environments using a bootable disk. The files required to mount UNIX volumes cannot fit onto a single disk, and it is not feasible to use multiple disks. But if a server service known as SAMBA were installed in a UNIX environment, the volume containing the DSP could be accessed using a simple DOS bootable disk and TCP/IP. SAMBA is a free UNIX server service that makes UNIX volumes appear as NT-accessible drives.

The MS Client for DOS should enable installers to connect with a boot disk to a UNIX server running SAMBA and begin the installation of Windows NT. The beauty of SAMBA is that it is completely free. It can be obtained from its creator's Web site at **http://lake.canberra.edu.au/pub/samba/**.

Figure 2.8 illustrates how the AUTOEXEC.BAT file might look if you used a bootable disk with the MS-DOS Client to connect to a SAMBA server and begin an installation of Windows NT.

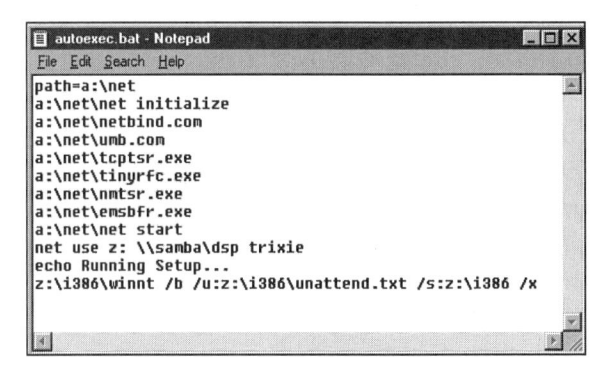

```
path=a:\net
a:\net\net initialize
a:\net\netbind.com
a:\net\umb.com
a:\net\tcptsr.exe
a:\net\tinyrfc.exe
a:\net\nmtsr.exe
a:\net\emsbfr.exe
a:\net\net start
net use z: \\samba\dsp trixie
echo Running Setup...
z:\i386\winnt /b /u:z:\i386\unattend.txt /s:z:\i386 /x
```

Figure 2.8. *Sample AUTOEXEC.BAT for installing NT under UNIX.*

The preceding file uses TCP/IP to connect to the SAMBA server and then uses a NET USE command to attach to a password-protected volume. It then runs the startup switches needed to kick off an installation of NT Workstation.

An additional solution for distributing Windows NT in a UNIX environment is to set up a single NT workstation running the server service and to run the installations from that system. The drawback of this solution is the limit of 10 simultaneous connections to an NT workstation; only 10 installations could be running at any given time.

Push Installations of Windows NT

Push installations are remotely triggered installations of an OS, a program, or a system update. Push installations of Windows NT are normally used when upgrading an existing network-aware OS because some form of rudimentary connectivity must exist in order for a server-initiated installation to occur. In some instances, the login script capabilities of the network OS can detect an existing platform type. This script capability can be used to upgrade an existing system by determining the platform type during the network boot sequence and then initiating an installation if a platform type other than Windows NT is detected.

30   Part I: Basic Configuration of an Unattended Installation

Following is a login script example for a NetWare system:

```
REM NetWare Login Script Installation of Windows NT Begin

IF OS NOT EQUAL TO "Windows_NT" THEN BEGIN
DOS SET INST_NAME = "%LOGIN_NAME"
BREAK ON
MAP I:=VOLUME:DIRECTORY\
WRITE "This PC will be upgraded to Windows NT 4.0"
WRITE "to halt this process hit any key to continue or CTRL-C to abort"
#PAUSE

#C:\COMMAND /C I:\DSP\INSTALL
ENDIF

REM End Installation Sequence
```

If you use this particular sequence in the NetWare login script, workstations that are currently running or have recently upgraded to Windows NT 4.0 are not affected, but other platform types are given the option to upgrade to NT 4.0 as they log in. This login script can be expanded to exclude certain platform or machine types and can even include or exclude specific network addresses.

Troubleshooting

Under 3.12 servers, calling a batch file in a login script can fail during the sequence, with either a system hang on the workstation or an error message. Use of the # in 3.12 login script and not placing the .BAT extension on the filename in the script ensure that the batch file functions properly during the boot sequence. Under NetWare 4.1, servers can use the following script:

```
REM NetWare Login Script Installation of Windows NT Begin

IF OS NOT EQUAL TO "Windows_NT" THEN BEGIN
DOS SET INST_NAME = "%LOGIN_NAME"
BREAK ON
MAP I:=SYS:PUBLIC\
WRITE "This PC will be upgraded to Windows NT 4.0"
WRITE "to halt this process hit any key to continue or CTRL-C to abort"
#PAUSE

C:\COMMAND /C DSP\INSTALL.BAT
ENDIF

REM End Installation Sequence
```

When opened, the INSTALL.BAT file might look something like the following:

```
REM Begin NT Installation

CD I:
WINNT.EXE /B /U:I:\DSP\UNATTEND.TXT /UDF:%INST_NAME%, I:\DSP\IDENTITY.UDB
/S:I:\DSP /X
EXIT

REM End NT Installation
```

The DOS variable %INST_NAME% is actually using the %LOGIN_NAME taken from the DOS SET command issued earlier in the NetWare login script. It applies the user's login name to the installation startup parameters in order to identify it to the UDF. Identifying it to the UDF allows custom settings to be applied to the setup process.

The second example of a login script-based installation is under NT. The options used in the NetWare example are very similar to those used in the NT login script, which is by default housed in the NETLOGON share of the logon server.

```
REM Begin NT Installation

@ECHO TYPE "This PC will be upgraded to Windows NT 4.0"
@ECHO TYPE "to halt this process hit any key
@ECHO TYPE "to continue or CTRL-C to abort"
PAUSE

SET UNAME = %USERNAME%
CMD /C NET USE J: \\SERVERNAME\SHARENAME /YES
WINNT.EXE /B /U:J:\UNATTEND.TXT /UDF:%UNAME%, J:\IDENTITY.UDB /S:J:\ /X
EXIT

END NT Installation
```

As you can see, this example is very similar to the NetWare example. Again, the batch file can be as complex as is needed; it can be used to detect processor architecture, the current OS, and even the processor revision to differentiate between installations of NT you may want to deploy.

Both of these examples are not true push installations because they both require a login sequence to initiate them. Each one is, however, an example of how installations of Windows NT can be remotely triggered, removing the requirement of traveling from workstation to workstation to boot from a floppy or manually kick off the install process.

Most true push installations require a service to be running on each client. This service must allow remote access and enable control of the local workstation to come from the server. The most common such server among Windows-based networks is Systems Management Server (SMS). In certain cases, push installations can be made without purchasing any additional software. Upgrades from previous versions of NT can use its native scheduling tool, AT.EXE, to schedule periodic checking of a network server for updates. A batch file in the login script can be used to activate this scheduler, instructing the service to periodically check a server for new instructions contained in a file called UPDATE.BAT, for example. These instructions can also include the information required to log the system on to the server, check a directory for the existence of a particular file, then log off when completed.

Files Unique to an Automated Installation of Windows NT

This section does not cover in detail all of the files used to customize installations of NT. Each file is covered fully in the upcoming chapters. This section merely familiarizes you with the general purpose of each of these native NT setup tools and their roles in the installation process relative to their locations on the DSP.

WINNT.EXE or WINNT32.EXE

These two files are used to begin the installation of Windows NT. WINNT.EXE is used for new installations of NT, including upgrades from Windows 3.1, 3.1x, and Windows 95. WINNT32.EXE is used solely for upgrading from previous versions of NT. By default, both files are found on the retail CD in the same directory as the installation files for the specific processor platform, so a CD-to-server copy should place them in the proper directory.

UNATTEND.TXT

The UNATTEND.TXT, in its various incarnations, is the principal file used to programmatically respond to the various configuration queries for the OS during the setup process. The UNATTEND.TXT file can be called anything you want, so long as it conforms to the 8.3 naming convention and is a standard DOS text file with a .TXT extension.

Multiple Answer files can be stored on the same DSP, enabling administrators to select a specific Answer file for custom installs using the same set of installation files. It is by default found in the same directory as the installation files for each processor platform, but it can exist anywhere, as long as it is referenced correctly in the startup parameters of the installation and is accessible.

<FILENAME>.UDB, the Uniqueness Database File (UDF)

This file, when used in conjunction with UNATTEND.TXT and referenced using the WINNT.EXE or WINNT32.EXE files, is used to specify multiple configuration additions to the UNATTEND.TXT file in order to allow simultaneous installations to occur. It does not exist by default, so it must be manually created. It can be called anything, but it must retain the DOS 8.3 naming convention and have the file extension .UDB. Like the UNATTEND.TXT file, it can exist anywhere, as long as it is referenced correctly in the startup parameters of the installation and is accessible.

CMDLINES.TXT

Next to the UNATTEND.TXT file, this file is the most important for some of the advanced configuration options that can be set up to run during an automated installation of Windows NT. This file can contain multiple commands that process registry edits, install service packs, and even set up multiple applications. When referenced using the key OemPreinstall = yes in the UNATTEND.TXT file, the installation process looks for the CMDLINES.TXT file in the root of the OEM subdirectory on the DSP. By default, this file is not created, so it must be manually constructed and placed in the OEM subdirectory.

$$RENAME.TXT

This file is used to translate short filenames into long filenames after they have been copied over to the target system during setup. This file must exist in each directory and subdirectory on the DSP in which this type of translation is necessary. This file is automatically generated when using the System Difference Tool, SYSDIFF.EXE, but can be manually created using a standard text editor.

The proper syntax for the $$RENAME.TXT file is as follows:

```
[Directory Name_1]
DOS_NAME_1 = "LONG_FILENAME_1"
DOS_NAME_2 = "LONG_FILENAME_2"
DOS_NAME_3 = "LONG_FILENAME_3"
DOS_NAME_4 = "LONG_FILENAME_4"
```

[DIRECTORY_NAME_1] is used to specify the path and name of the directory that contains the files that need to be converted. If no name exists in brackets or if a \ is present, then the installation looks for the files on the root of the drive.

DOS_NAME_1 is used to specify the file or directory that should be renamed. If the DOS_NAME_1 appears in quotes, the renaming process fails.

LONG_NAME_1 is used to specify the new long filename for the corresponding file or directory. This name must appear in quotes. If a space or comma is to be used in the long filename, double quotes must be present. For example, see the following output:

```
[\WINNT]
MYFILE~1.TXT="Thisismyfile.txt"
YOURFI~1.TXT=""This is your file.txt""
OURDIR~1=""Our Directory""
```

SYSDIFF.EXE

The *System Difference Tool* is an optional tool used to create and apply application data, programs, and environment settings to installations of Windows

NT, further augmenting the automation process. SYSDIFF can often be used to install applications that are incapable of running in "silent" or unattended mode during an installation and which may require further configuration. This file is referenced by the CMDLINES.TXT. It should be copied from the \SUPPORT\DEPTOOLS or \SUPPORT\OPK\ directory on the NT retail CD to the OEM subdirectory on the DSP.

With these files and directories in place, the next chapter covers the UNATTEND.TXT file and all of the various options that can be configured during an automated installation.

Chapter 3

Creating Answer Files

This chapter covers:

- What is an UNATTEND.TXT, or Answer file?
- Available options in an UNATTEND.TXT file
- Automation options for Windows NT Server
- Example Answer files for use under NetWare, Windows NT, and UNIX

After reading this chapter, you should be able to do the following:

- Effectively create an unattended Answer script for Windows NT.
- Understand the optional components for automating NT Server deployments.

The UNATTEND.TXT Explained

An *Answer file*, or UNATTEND.TXT, is Microsoft's name for the scripted text file that can be created to perform an automated installation of Windows NT. The Answer file is scripted to respond to the various dialog boxes that appear during the course of the installation. Because the file answers the setup questions for you, no user intervention is required during installation.

The term *UNATTEND.TXT* is used rather loosely in this book to refer to Answer files. The file itself can be called anything you want, just as long as the name you choose complies with the 8.3 (DOS) naming convention, retains the .TXT extension, and is referenced correctly in the deployment startup options.

> *Tip*
>
> *Multiple Answer files can reside within the same Distribution Share Point (DSP) directory, making it possible for several different types of OS deployment templates to exist using the same set of installation files.*

To generate Answer files, Microsoft provides an excellent GUI utility in both the Windows NT Workstation and Server Resource Kits. This utility is called the *Windows NT Setup Manager*, or *SETUPMGR.EXE*. Figure 3.1 displays the user interface for the Setup Manager.

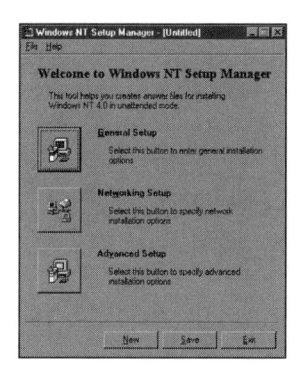

Figure 3.1. *Windows NT's Setup Manager.*

The Setup Manager is designed to assist administrators in developing custom Answer files to meet the needs of their deployment scheme. The tool leads the users through the painstaking task of generating a unique, textually correct Answer file.

But if you use the Windows NT Setup Manager to automate your installations of Windows NT, you will find that it is limited in its capabilities. When you are using the Setup Manager to generate Answer files during installation, certain standard queries still appear that require user intervention, most notable of which is the End-User License Agreement, or EULA. Therefore, the automation process is still incomplete. If you have a well-crafted Answer file created with this tool, you still need someone on hand to click Yes to the EULA screen. Only with additional manual editing can the installation process truly become automated.

If you do not have the NT Workstation Resource Kit 4.0, any standard text editor works, such as DOS's Edit or Windows Notepad. Microsoft provides a sample Answer file called UNATTEND.TXT in the I386 subdirectory on the NT Distribution CD. If you open the file using a text editor, it looks like the following:

```
; Microsoft Windows NT Workstation Version 4.0 and
; Windows NT Server Version 4.0
; (c) 1994 - 1996 Microsoft Corporation. All rights reserved.
;
; Sample Unattended Setup Answer File
;
```

Chapter 3: Creating Answer Files 37

```
; This file contains information about how to automate the
; installation or upgrade of Windows NT Workstation and Windows
; NT Server so the Setup program runs without requiring user
; input.
;
; For information on how to use this file, read the appropriate
; sections of the Windows NT 4.0 Resource Kit.

[Unattended]
OemPreinstall = no
ConfirmHardware = no
NtUpgrade = no
Win31Upgrade = no
TargetPath = WINNT
OverwriteOemFilesOnUpgrade = no

[UserData]
FullName = "Your User Name"
OrgName = "Your Organization Name"
ComputerName = COMPUTER_NAME

[GuiUnattended]
TimeZone = "(GMT-08:00) Pacific Time (US & Canada); Tijuana"

[Display]
ConfigureAtLogon = 0
BitsPerPel = 16
XResolution = 640
YResolution = 480
VRefresh = 70
AutoConfirm = 1

[Network]
Attend = yes
DetectAdapters = ""
InstallProtocols = ProtocolsSection
JoinDomain = Domain_To_Join

[ProtocolsSection]
TC = TCParameters

[TCParameters]
DHCP = yes
```

If you are familiar with script languages, you may not find this output too difficult to understand. But if you're not familiar with script languages, it may look a little daunting. This particular script is fairly generic. It can apply to most deployments for NT domains because it uses the setup options most likely to occur in an NT domain. But what if you are using NT Workstation in an environment in which NetWare is the network platform? how about UNIX? or maybe Windows 95 Peer-to-Peer Networking? The answer is to tailor the UNATTEND.TXT and related installation files to create a custom installation that fits your deployment needs.

Microsoft provides a guide for developing automated installations of Windows NT Workstation called the "Guide to Automating Windows NT Setup." It can be downloaded from the Microsoft Web site at **http://www.microsoft.com/ntworkstation /info/deployguide.htm**. This document can be an extremely handy reference tool. However, at last look, the document did not provide a very user-friendly explanation of certain processes and solutions for deploying Windows NT. It was limited mainly to certain issues regarding automating the OS installation and to some customizing.

Case Study: Sikorsky Aircraft Financial Systems

Sikorsky Aircraft Financial Systems consists of a team of three administrators who provide support for approximately 300 clients. These administrators are researching the use of unattended installations in order to convert approximately 25 OS/2 clients to Windows NT Workstation by the end of 1997 and another 50–75 clients from Windows 3.1 to NT by early 1998.

The finance department currently has desktop systems from several different vendors that range from 486DX33s with 24MB of RAM to Pentium 200s with upwards of 64MB of RAM. The various styles of machines have different video chip sets, disk configurations, and 3Com Ethernet cards. The 486DX33 machines will remain on a Windows 3.1 platform until newer hardware becomes available. The mixed hardware environment complicates the deployment planning process because the unattended installation requires options for the mixed platforms involved.

The NT workstations will be configured similarly, in that all will run TCP/IP and NetBEUI network protocols, with NT networking configured so that the workstations participate in workgroups.

Switching to Windows NT Workstation, along with the multitude of hardware and software platforms, precludes a "cloning" of machines, as was done in the past with Windows 3.1. This cloning created a necessity for scripting unique Answer files for the various machine- and hardware-specific configurations in their network environment.

Answer File Keys and Values

This section covers many of the documented (and some undocumented) switches you can use to create a multitude of different Answer files for any number of network environments.

As explained earlier, you can use any standard text editor to generate an Answer file. After you open it, you can use the following comprehensive listing of variables to create a custom Answer file for your deployment.

[Unattended]

This header within the Answer file informs the installation engine of an unattended installation. If this header is not present, the installation process ignores the rest of the file.

OemPreinstall =
Responses:

- yes. Looks for additional installation instructions on the DSP.
- no. Ignores any additional instruction and installs the OS only.

An answer of yes tells the installation process that the custom options that need to be applied are contained within the UNATTEND.TXT file. This file can include specified hardware or operating custom applications, files, and directories located on the DSP. These directories also need to be copied and set up on the target workstation during the installation. For automated deployments in which SYSDIFF is used to configure additional software, a value of yes is necessary. An answer of no tells the system to ignore any additional directories contained within the DSP and to copy only the referenced files with the DRVLIB.NIC, INETSRV, and SYSTEM32 subdirectories.

OemSkipEULA =
Responses:

- yes. Skips the display of the End-User License Agreement (EULA).
- no. Displays the EULA.

This is an undocumented key that effectively skips the EULA.

> *Tip*
>
> *If this key is used, a copy of the EULA agreement must be printed out and distributed to users to sign. A value of* no *causes the install to include the EULA pop-up screen.*

NoWaitAfterTextMode =
Responses:

- 0. Halts the installation process after completing the text mode of the setup.
- 1. Automatically reboots system to begin GUI mode of the setup.

This key automatically reboots the server after it completes the text mode portion of the installation. A value of 0 causes the install to stop after completing the text mode section. This key is valid only when OEMPreinstall = is set to yes.

> **Tip**
>
> *This key can be extremely useful if you are planning to use a disk duplication method of deploying NT Workstation. Halting the install after text mode permits an installer to reboot the workstation using a bootable, network-capable floppy and to copy the disk image to a DSP using any amount of disk duplication software. (See Appendix D, "Cloning NT," for more on disk duplication methods.)*

NoWaitAfterGUIMode =

Responses:

- 0. Halts the installation process after completing the GUI mode of the setup.
- 1. Automatically reboots system after completing the installation.

This key performs the same function as the previous one for the GUI portion of the install. A value of 0 causes the install to stop after completing the GUI section. The default is to halt the installation after it completes the GUI phase of the installation. But if you are planning to install additional software or further customize your deployments, a response of 1 is necessary in order to ensure that a reboot occurs and to allow any automated login processes to continue your installation. This key is only valid when OEMPreinstall= is set to yes.

FileSystem =

Responses:

- LeaveAlone. Leaves the file system intact.
- ConvertNTFS. Converts the current file system to an NTFS partition.

This key tells the installation to either leave any file system it detects intact or change to an NTFS partition with the value ConvertNTFS. NTFS partitions are useful if you want to implement a higher standard of security on your workstations because they allow for further security options that cannot exist on FAT volumes. The downside of NTFS partitions is their lack of recoverability options; they are inaccessible from a DOS boot disk.

> **Troubleshooting Tip**
>
> *When using FAT partitions, it is generally considered prudent to use partition sizes of 512MB or less because partitions larger than this size suffer from poor disk and storage performance.*

Chapter 3: Creating Answer Files 41

> *Tip*
>
> *When using automated deployments, it's usually best to set up NT using the* `LeaveAlone` *option initially and then to convert the file system to NTFS at a later point in the installation or after a few days. If an install fails after converting the file system to NTFS, it might be difficult to diagnose the failure or the access files copied to the disk because the partition is inaccessible from DOS (unless you are using an NTFS partition-reading utility, such as NTFS DOS).*

ExtendOEMPartition =
Responses:

- 0. Extend the installation partition to more than 2GB.
- 1. Use only the existing installation partition.

This key is used to install NT onto disk drives larger than 2GB. A setting of 1 tells the installation to extend the partition into any existing unpartitioned space during the text mode phase of the install. A value of 0 cannot perform this function.

> *Troubleshooting Tip*
>
> *The temporary install directory created must be located on the primary partition, and the hard-drive parameters must be limited to 1,024 cylinders. Disks larger than 1,024 cylinders cause the installation to halt.*

ConfirmHardware =
Responses:

- yes. Prompts the installer to confirm detected hardware.
- no. Automatically installs detected hardware.

This key sets whether the installation prompts the installer to confirm detected hardware. A value of yes causes the system to halt and to prompt the user for confirmation. A value of no causes the installation to attempt to detect and install hardware without user intervention. In order for an unattended installation of Windows NT to occur, this value should be set to no.

NtUpgrade =
Responses:

- yes. Upgrades the first detected version of NT discovered.
- no. Halts the installation process if a previous version of NT is detected. Use this value during an unattended installation of NT when `OEMPreinstall` = has been set to yes.

- `manual`. Halts the installation process and then prompts the installer to confirm an upgrade.

- `single`. Upgrades the first version of NT discovered. If multiple versions of Windows NT are detected, the installation prompts the installer to confirm which one should be upgraded.

This key determines whether the install process looks for and upgrades any previously installed versions of Windows NT. A value of `yes` upgrades the first detected version of NT. A value of `no` causes the install process to halt when an existing version of NT is located. A value of `manual` stops the installation and prompts the user to manually specify whether the previous version should be upgraded or ignored. And, finally, a value of `single` causes the install process to continue on the condition that only one pre-existing copy of NT is found. If multiple copies exist on a single system, NT prompts the user to determine which installation of NT should be upgraded.

Win31Upgrade =
Responses:

- `yes`. Upgrade a detected version of Windows 3.1 or 3.11.

- `no`. Do not upgrade a detected, previous version of Windows 3.1 or 3.11.

This key determines whether any existing copies of files contained within Windows 3.1 or 3.11 installations are *overwritten* if detected. This key is only useful if you are upgrading a previous installation of Windows; if not, set the value to `no`. A value of `yes` preserves those files from being overwritten.

TargetPath =
Responses:

- `*`. Generates a unique installation directory name.

- `(user choice)`. User defines the directory name.

- `manual`. Halts the installation and awaits user intervention for a directory name.

The `TargetPath` option determines which directory Windows NT is installed to on the target system. The `*` value causes the installation engine to generate a unique name for the Windows NT directory on the target system. If you want to provide the installation with a predetermined name for the Windows NT directory, provide the name without using a drive letter path, such as \WINDOWSNT or \JOESNT, not C:\JOESNT. A value of `manual` halts the install process for user intervention.

Chapter 3: Creating Answer Files 43

> *Tip*
>
> *If you want to install NT onto a drive other than C:, use the* /T:(*drive letter*) *with the WINNT startup process.*

OverwriteOemFilesOnUpgrade =
Responses:

- yes. Overwrites any OEM files that are detected during the installation process (default).
- no. Leaves any OEM-detected files in place.

This key determines whether the install overwrites any existing files with the same name it detects during the installation. A value of yes means that the installation overwrites detected files of the same name. The default value of no means that the system skips detected duplicate files on the target workstation.

ComputerType = HAL TYPE [,OEM ¦ Retail]
Responses:

- (NT CD-Supplied HAL), Retail. HAL types located in the [Computer] section of the TXTSETUP.SIF.
- (OEM-Supplied HAL), OEM. An OEM-supplied HAL using a custom TXTSETUP.OEM file.

You can use this optional key to manually set the Hardware Abstraction Layer (HAL) type that is used on the target systems. This key is usually not placed in an Answer file because the installation process autodetects the HAL type and installs it without user intervention. If, however, the installation fails to autodetect the HAL type or a custom HAL will be used, one can be manually defined. In order for a user-defined HAL to be properly installed during an automated deployment, several other steps must first be taken:

- If a HAL type will be user defined, regardless of whether it is a Retail or OEM version of the HAL, the key and the value OemPreinstall = yes must be present in the Answer file.

- If the predefined HAL is a Retail version—that is, one provided on the installation CD—then the additional value of "RETAIL" must appear after the HAL definition. This key is valid only when OEMPreinstall = is set to yes. Following is a listing of the available Retail HAL types found on the installation CD:

```
ComputerType = "AST Manhattan SMP","RETAIL"
ComputerType = "Compaq SystemPro Multiprocessor or 100% Compatible","RETAIL"
ComputerType = "Corollary C-bus Architecture","RETAIL"
ComputerType = "Corollary C-bus Micro Channel Architecture","RETAIL"
```

44   Part I: Basic Configuration of an Unattended Installation

```
ComputerType = "IBM PS/2 or other Micro Channel-based PC","RETAIL"
ComputerType = "MPS Uniprocessor PC","RETAIL"
ComputerType = "MPS Multiprocessor PC","RETAIL"
ComputerType = "MPS Multiprocessor Micro Channel PC","RETAIL"
ComputerType = "NCR System 3000 Model 3360/3450/3550","RETAIL"
ComputerType = "Olivetti LSX5030/40","RETAIL"
ComputerType = "Standard PC","RETAIL"
ComputerType = "Standard PC with C-Step i486","RETAIL"
ComputerType = "Wyse Series 7000i Model 740MP/760MP","RETAIL"
```

- If the predefined HAL is an OEM version—that is, one *not* provided with the installation CD—then the additional value of `"OEM"` must appear after the HAL definition. Following is an example of an OEM HAL description:

  ```
  ComputerType = "BetaHAL", "OEM"
  ```

In addition to the previous key and value, which are used when defining an OEM HAL type, the user must also provide the actual driver name in another section of the Answer file, called the [OEMBootFiles]. In this section, the user must define both the driver name, such as BetaHAL_UP, and the installation file, or .INF, in an automated format that the installation process can understand. Therefore, the .INF must be renamed TXTSETUP.OEM and must also be named in the [OEMBootFiles] section. The files themselves must be copied to the TXTMODE subdirectory of your DSP. Following is an example showing a section of an Answer file containing an OEM-supplied HAL:

```
[Unattended]
OemPreinstall = no
ConfirmHardware = no
NtUpgrade = no
Win31Upgrade = no
TargetPath = WINNT
OverwriteOemFilesOnUpgrade = no
CompterType = "BetaHAL", "OEM"
[OEMBootFiles]
BetaHAL_up
Txtsetup.oem
```

KeyboardLayout = Keyboard Layout
Responses:

- (NT CD-Supplied Keyboard Layouts). Keyboard layouts located in the [KeyboardLayout] section of the TXTSETUP.SIF.

- (OEM-Supplied HAL), OEM. An OEM-supplied keyboard layout using a custom TXTSETUP.OEM file.

The code appearing before each keyboard type in the following output can be used to identify the corresponding keyboard driver file in the TXTSETUP.SIF file in the [Files.KeyboardLayout] section. Following are Windows NT Retail CD-ROM supplied keyboard layouts:

```
["Keyboard Layout"]
0000041C = "Albanian"
00000423 = "Belarusian"
00000813 = "Belgian Dutch"
0000080C = "Belgian French"
00000416 = "Brazilian (ABNT)"
00000402 = "Bulgarian"
00010402 = "Bulgarian Latin"
00001009 = "Canadian English (Multilingual)"
00000C0C = "Canadian French"
00010C0C = "Canadian French (Multilingual)"
0000041a = "Croatian"
00000405 = "Czech"
00010405 = "Czech (QWERTY)"
00000406 = "Danish"
00000413 = "Dutch"
00000425 = "Estonian"
0000040B = "Finnish"
0000040C = "French"
00000407 = "German"
00010407 = "German (IBM)"
00000408 = "Greek"
00050408 = "Greek Latin"
00010408 = "Greek (220)"
00030408 = "Greek (220) Latin"
00020408 = "Greek (319)"
00040408 = "Greek (319) Latin"
0000040E = "Hungarian"
0001040E = "Hungarian 101-key"
0000040F = "Icelandic"
00001809 = "Irish"
00000410 = "Italian"
00010410 = "Italian (142)"
0000080A = "Latin American"
00000426 = "Latvian"
00010426 = "Latvian (QWERTY)"
00000427 = "Lithuanian"
00000414 = "Norwegian"
00000415 = "Polish (Programmers)"
00010415 = "Polish (214)"
00000816 = "Portuguese"
00000418 = "Romanian"
00000419 = "Russian"
00010419 = "Russian (Typewriter)"
00000C1A = "Serbian Cyrillic"
00010C1A = "Serbian Latin"
0000041B = "Slovak"
0001041B = "Slovak (QWERTY)"
00000424 = "Slovenian"
0000040A = "Spanish"
0001040A = "Spanish variation"
0000041D = "Swedish"
0000100C = "Swiss French"
00000807 = "Swiss German"
```

46 Part I: Basic Configuration of an Unattended Installation

```
0001041F = "Turkish F"
0000041F = "Turkish Q"
00000422 = "Ukrainian"
00000809 = "United Kingdom"
00000409 = "US"
00010409 = "US-Dvorak"
00030409 = "US-Dvorak for left hand"
00040409 = "US-Dvorak for right hand"
00020409 = "US-International"
```

This optional setting determines which keyboard layout is installed. If this key is not present, the installation process autodetects the layout type. The KeyBoardLayout key must match one of the previously defined keyboard types, as in the following example:

```
KeyBoardLayout = "US-Dvorak for the left hand"
```

If a keyboard type will be user defined, regardless of whether it is a Retail or OEM version of the keyboard layout, the key and the value OemPreinstall = yes must be present in the Answer file.

[MassStorageDrivers]

This section header within the Answer file informs the installation engine that SCSI device drivers are being defined in the unattended installation. If this header is not present, the installation process ignores the rest of the file and attempts to autodetect the SCSI devices. Just as with the installation of a user-defined HAL, SCSI device drivers appear beneath the [MassStorageDrivers] heading by their description and not by the driver filename.

"Storage Driver Description" = "OEM" or "Retail"
If the device driver is a Retail driver, the installation engine pulls the correct driver from the driver library on the DSP. Following is a listing of the Retail versions that are provided with the installation CD. They are located in the TXTSETUP.SIF file:

```
"Adaptec AHA-151X/AHA-152X/AIC-6X60 SCSI Adapter" = "RETAIL"
"Adaptec AHA-154X/AHA-164X SCSI Host Adapter" = "RETAIL"
"Adaptec AHA-174X EISA SCSI Host Adapter" = "RETAIL"
"Adaptec AHA-274X/AHA-284X/AIC-777X SCSI Adapter" = "RETAIL"
"Adaptec AHA-294X/AHA-394X/AIC-78XX SCSI Controller" = "RETAIL"
"AMD PCI SCSI Controller/Ethernet Adapter" = "RETAIL"
"AMIscsi SCSI Host Adapter" = "RETAIL"
"BusLogic SCSI Host Adapter" = "RETAIL"
"BusLogic FlashPoint" = "RETAIL"
"Compaq 32-Bit Fast-Wide SCSI-2/E" = "RETAIL"
"Compaq Drive Array" = "RETAIL"
"Dell Drive Array" = "RETAIL"
"DPT SCSI Host Adapter" = "RETAIL"
"Future Domain TMC-7000EX EISA SCSI Host Adapter" = "RETAIL"
"Future Domain 8XX SCSI Host Adapter" = "RETAIL"
```

Chapter 3: Creating Answer Files 47

```
"Adaptec 2920/2905 / Future Domain 16XX/PCI/SCSI2Go" = "RETAIL"
"IBM MCA SCSI Host Adapter" = "RETAIL"
"IDE CD-ROM (ATAPI 1.2)/PCI IDE Controller" = "RETAIL"
"Mitsumi CD-ROM Controller" = "RETAIL"
"Mylex DAC960/Digital SWXCR-Ex Raid Controller" = "RETAIL"
"NCR 53C9X SCSI Host Adapter" = "RETAIL"
"NCR C700 SCSI Host Adapter" = "RETAIL"
"NCR 53C710 SCSI Host Adapter" = "RETAIL"
"Symbios Logic C810 PCI SCSI Host Adapter" = "RETAIL"
"Olivetti ESC-1/ESC-2 SCSI Host Adapter" = "RETAIL"
"QLogic PCI SCSI Host Adapter" = "RETAIL"
"MKEPanasonic CD-ROM Controller" = "RETAIL"
"Sony Proprietary CD-ROM Controller" = "RETAIL"
"UltraStor 14F/14FB/34F/34FA/34FB SCSI Host Adapter" = "RETAIL"
"UltraStor 24F/24FA SCSI Host Adapter" = "RETAIL"
```

If the supplied driver is an OEM version, it must be additionally defined in the Answer file, with the driver filename and TXTSETUP.OEM file appearing in the [OEMBootFiles] section and the actual files copied to the TXTMODE subdirectory on the DSP. More than one SCSI device may be defined in this section.

If the Mass Storage Device type will be user defined, regardless of whether it is a Retail or OEM version of the storage device, the key and the value OemPreinstall = yes must be present in the Answer file.

[DisplayDrivers]

This section header within the Answer file informs the installation engine that display drivers are being defined in the unattended installation. If this header is not present, the installation process ignores the rest of the file and attempts to autodetect any display adapters by using the standard VGA driver. Just as with the installation of a user-defined HAL, display drivers appear beneath the [DisplayDrivers] heading by their description and not by the driver filename.

If the display type will be user defined, regardless of whether it is a Retail or OEM version of the display device, the key and the value OemPreinstall = yes must be present within the Answer file. The options present within the TXTSETUP.SIF file are as follows:

```
forcevga = "Standard VGA (640x480, 16 colors)",files.none
vga      = "Auto Detect",files.video
```

The autodection process, by default, looks for compatible adapter files from the following manufacturers:

Std	Standard Display Types
Actix	Actix
Ati	ATI Technologies

continues

continued

Std	Standard Display Types
Cardex	Cardex
Chips	Chips & Technologies
Cirrus	Cirrus Logic
Compaq	Compaq Computer
Dell	Dell
Diamond	Diamond Multimedia
Digital	Digital
Elsa	Elsa
FirePower	FirePower
Genoa	Genoa
Hercules	Hercules
IBM	IBM
LeadTek	LeadTek
Matrox	Matrox
MediaVision	MediaVision
Metheus	Metheus
Micronics	Micronics
Mips	Mips
Miro	Miro
Motorola	Motorola
NCR	NCR
NEC	NEC
NeoMagic	NeoMagic
#9	Number Nine Visual Technologies
Orchid	Orchid Technologies
Paradise	Paradise
ProLink	ProLink
S3	S3
Siemens	Siemens Nixdorf
SixGraph	Six Graph
STB	STB
Tseng	Tseng Labs

Chapter 3: Creating Answer Files   49

Std	Standard Display Types
Trident	Trident
V7	Video 7
WD	Western Digital
Weitek	Weitek

The following driver types are not autodetected and are therefore not recommended for use during an unattended installation of NT (except for the [DetectServices] of the DISPLAY.INF file):

Driver Type	Recommendation
; 8514a	Don't detect because you generally want to use ATI.
; trident	Don't detect trident because of old driver crashes on new chips.
; vga	Never need to detect vga because of vga save.

Tip

The DISPLAY.INF file can be expanded and searched for the appropriate card type beneath the manufacturer's name.

If the supplied driver is an OEM version, then it must be additionally defined in the Answer file. The driver file name and TXTSETUP.OEM file must appear in the [OEMBootFiles] section and the actual files must be copied to the TXTMODE subdirectory on the DSP. More than one display device may be defined in this section.

[KeyboardDrivers]

This section header within the Answer file informs the installation engine that keyboard drivers are being defined in the unattended installation. If this header is not present, the installation process ignores the rest of the file and attempts to autodetect the keyboard type by using the standard keyboard interface driver. Just as with the installation of a user-defined HAL, keyboard drivers appear beneath the [KeyboardDrivers] heading by their description and not by the driver filename.

If the Keyboard type will be user defined, regardless of whether it is a Retail or OEM version of the keyboard device, the key and the value OemProinotall = yes must be present within the Answer file. The sole option within the TXTSETUP.SIF file is as follows:

```
STANDARD = "XT, AT, or Enhanced Keyboard (83-104 keys)",files.i8042,i8042prt
```

If the supplied driver is an OEM version, then it must be additionally defined in the Answer file. The value must be followed by the "OEM" identifier, the driver filename, and the TXTSETUP.OEM file that appears in the [OEMBootFiles] section. The actual files copied to the TXTMODE subdirectory on the DSP must follow the value as well. More than one keyboard device may be defined in this section.

[PointingDeviceDrivers]

This section header within the Answer file informs the installation engine that pointing device drivers (mouse drivers) are being defined in the unattended installation. If this header is not present, the installation process ignores the rest of the file and attempts to autodetect the pointing device type by using a standard pointing device interface driver. Just as with the installation of a user-defined HAL, mouse drivers appear beneath the [PointingDeviceDrivers] heading by their description and not by the driver filename.

If the Mouse type is to be user defined, regardless of whether it is a Retail or OEM version of the pointing device, the key and the value OemPreinstall = yes must be present within the Answer file. The options within the TXTSETUP.SIF file are as follows:

```
"Microsoft Mouse Port Mouse (includes BallPoint)" = "RETAIL"
"Logitech Mouse Port Mouse" = "RETAIL"
"Microsoft InPort Bus Mouse" = "RETAIL"
"Microsoft Serial Mouse" = "RETAIL"
"Microsoft BallPoint Serial Mouse" = "RETAIL"
"Logitech Serial Mouse" = "RETAIL"
"Microsoft (Green Buttons) or Logitech Bus Mouse" = "RETAIL"
"No Mouse or Other Pointing Device" = "RETAIL"
"Microsoft Mouse Port Mouse (includes BallPoint)" = "RETAIL"
```

If the supplied driver is an OEM version, then it must be additionally defined in the Answer file. The value must be followed by the "OEM" identifier, the driver filename, and the TXTSETUP.OEM file that appears in the [OEMBootFiles] section. The actual files copied to the TXTMODE subdirectory on the DSP must follow the value as well. The following is an example of the an OEM-supplied mouse driver entry:

```
"Mickey Mouse Uniball" = "OEM"
```

More than one pointing device may be defined in this section.

[OEMBootFiles]

This section of the Answer file is used to copy user-defined device driver files from the OEM\Textmode subdirectory of the DSP to the target workstation. As mentioned previously, the actual names of each specified type of device driver must be present under this heading and must be properly referenced in the TXTSETUP.OEM in order for their installation to occur properly. More than one device driver can be scripted within the TXTSETUP.OEM file so that if you have special OEM-supplied device drivers for your SCSI devices and video adapters, for example, both can be referenced within the same TXTSETUP.OEM file.

[OEM_Ads]

This optional section enables you to customize the look of the GUI portion of the NT installation process as it runs on the target system.

Banner = "Your Organization's Installation*of Windows NT Workstation"

This key determines what text is displayed during the GUI portion of the setup. Two important things to remember are that the words Windows NT must appear somewhere in your text string, and that the use of an * serves as a hard return for your supplied text line.

Logo = Logo.bmp

This key enables the user to define the logo that appears in the top-right corner of the screen during the GUI phase of the installation. Usually, a .BMP is used and stored in the OEM subdirectory on the DSP, but .DLL files may be substituted as long as the bitmap within the .DLL file is defined by its base-10 resource ID number as a second value in the same line that contains the .DLL filename.

Background = Back.bmp

This key enables the user to define a background image that appears as a tinted blue backdrop screen during the GUI phase of the installation. Usually, a .BMP is used and stored in the OEM subdirectory on the DSP, but .DLL files may be substituted as long as the bitmap within the .DLL file is defined by its base-10 resource ID number as a second value in the same line that contains the .DLL filename.

> *Tip*
>
> *When using a .BMP image as a background for your installations, choose images that look good under a blue tint. It is usually best to create your background as an indexed grayscale image. Also, make the background as small as possible (that is, actual file size) to conserve memory during the installation process.*

[UserData]

This section heading, which defines the user information, is fairly self-explanatory. If this heading is not present, the installation ignores the presented data.

- FullName = "User Name Here". Your user's name.
- OrgName = "Your Organization Here". Your organization's name.
- ComputerName = (Computer Name). The target workstation's name.
- ProductId = "*xxxxx*-oem-*xxxxxxx*-*xxxxx*" or "*xxx*-*xxxxxxx*". The product ID can be either the OEM type number or the 10-digit retail number, depending on your installation CD type. When you define the 20-digit product ID, ensure that the variable oem appears in lowercase. Otherwise, the installation halts and prompts the user for a corrected product identifier. If the product identifier is left blank, the user is prompted to enter the appropriate information.

> *Tip*
>
> *For large-scale deployments of NT, a UDF (Uniqueness Database file) can be generated to provide the installation process with unique user/machine names, as well as with special protocol and service needs.*

[GuiUnattended]

This section deals with the GUI portion of the NT installation process. Again, if this header is missing, the installation ignores the data presented.

OemSkipWelcome =
Response:

- 0. Displays the Microsoft welcome page during setup.
- 1. Bypasses the welcome page.

This key determines whether the install skips the Windows NT welcome page. The install's behavior is again determined numerically by either a 0 or a 1, with the former showing the welcome page and the latter skipping the page.

OEMBlankAdminPassword =
Response:

- 0. Prompts the installer to enter a password for the default administrator's account.
- 1. Leaves the administrator password blank.

Chapter 3: Creating Answer Files 53

The value of 0 returns a response from the installation prompting the installer to enter a password for the local administrator's account on the target system. The value of 1 leaves the password blank.

> **Tip**
>
> *This key can be extremely useful when using a fully automated install. Later in the process, a .REG file is called upon to create an autologon for the installation to the target system and to begin an installation of any predetermined applications, such as MS Office. The blank password and logon sequence is used only once, after which the administrator's password can be changed to accommodate more adequate security measures.*

TimeZone = "(GMT-05:00) Eastern Time (US & Canada)"

This key presets the time zone for the target system. The following is a complete listing of the available time zones:

```
(GMT) Greenwich Mean Time; Dublin, Edinburgh, London
(GMT+01:00) Lisbon, Warsaw
(GMT+01:00) Paris, Madrid
(GMT+01:00) Berlin, Stockholm, Rome, Bern, Brussels, Vienna
(GMT+02:00) Eastern Europe
(GMT+01:00) Prague
(GMT+02:00) Athens, Helsinki, Istanbul
(GMT-03:00) Rio de Janeiro
(GMT-04:00) Atlantic Time (Canada)
(GMT-05:00) Eastern Time (US & Canada)
(GMT-06:00) Central Time (US & Canada)
(GMT-07:00) Mountain Time (US & Canada)
(GMT-08:00) Pacific Time (US & Canada); Tijuana
(GMT-09:00) Alaska
(GMT-10:00) Hawaii
(GMT-11:00) Midway Island, Samoa
(GMT+12:00) Wellington
(GMT+10:00) Brisbane, Melbourne, Sydney
(GMT+09:30) Adelaide
(GMT+09:00) Tokyo, Osaka, Sapporo, Seoul, Yakutsk
(GMT+08:00) Hong Kong, Perth, Singapore, Taipei
(GMT+07:00) Bangkok, Jakarta, Hanoi
(GMT+05:30) Bombay, Calcutta, Madras, New Delhi, Colombo
(GMT+04:00) Abu Dhabi, Muscat, Tbilisi, Kazan, Volgograd
(GMT+03:30) Tehran
(GMT+03:00) Baghdad, Kuwait, Nairobi, Riyadh
(GMT+02:00) Israel
(GMT-03:30) Newfoundland
(GMT-01:00) Azores, Cape Verde Is.
(GMT-02:00) Mid-Atlantic
(GMT) Monrovia, Casablanca
(GMT-03:00) Buenos Aires, Georgetown
(GMT-04:00) Caracas, La Paz
(GMT-05:00) Indiana (East)
```

```
(GMT-05:00) Bogota, Lima
(GMT-06:00) Saskatchewan
(GMT-06:00) Mexico City, Tegucigalpa
(GMT-07:00) Arizona
(GMT-12:00) Enewetak, Kwajalein
(GMT+12:00) Fiji, Kamchatka, Marshall Is.
(GMT+11:00) Magadan, Soloman Is., New Caledonia
(GMT+10:00) Hobart
(GMT+10:00) Guam, Port Moresby, Vladivostok
(GMT+09:30) Darwin
(GMT+08:00) Beijing, Chongqing, Urumqi
(GMT+06:00) Alma Ata, Dhaka
(GMT+05:00) Islamabad, Karachi, Sverdlovsk, Tashkent
(GMT+04:30) Kabul
(GMT+02:00) Cairo
(GMT+02:00) Harare, Pretoria
(GMT+03:00) Moscow, St. Petersburg
```

DetachedProgram=(detached program string)

This key is used to define any custom program you want to run along with the setup program. Note that using this particular method of installation may result in failure when certain types of installation programs are run concurrently with the Windows NT setup. The concurrent processes of installing an operating system and dealing with an application that wants to install itself (and possibly even attempts to update sections of the Registry that do not currently exist) cause this failure. This key should be used only with installation programs tested thoroughly with this option.

Arguments=(arguments string)

This additional key is used in conjunction with the `DetachedProgram` key to provide additional options for the program selected to run. Included might be options to run the program silently or to write a log file for the separately installed program.

[Display]

This section determines the display adapter settings that need to be configured during the installation process. The Windows "vanilla" display setting of 640×480 at 16 colors can be used so that all display adapters respond to the installation process. This setting can be extremely useful if you are installing NT onto mixed machine types with different video adapter types. You can opt to customize your adapter settings for your environment by using the information in earlier sections of this chapter that discuss display adapters or by using the following techniques. If this heading is not present, the installation ignores the corresponding data.

ConfigureAtLogon =
Responses:

- `0`. Confirms the video adapter settings during the GUI phase of the installation.
- `1`. Confirms the adapter settings after the first login.

This key determines when the display adapter is configured. A value of 0 configures the adapter during the install process, and a value of 1 indicates that the user should configure the adapter during the first logon. Do not use 1 if you are intending to fully automate your installations of NT with a specific driver in mind. Instead, use the `AutoConfirm` option to automatically confirm your selected driver type and settings.

BitsPerPel = 8, XResolution = 640, YResolution = 480, VRefresh = 60

The previous four settings determine, in order, the bits per pixel (8, 16, 24, and so on), X and Y resolution (640×480, 800×600, 1024×768, and so on), and vertical refresh rate (60, 65, 70, or a specified custom setting). If you know ahead of time the type of standard display/monitor types, these settings can be further specialized to suit your needs.

AutoConfirm =
Responses:

- `0`. Does not autoconfirm the display adapter settings in the Answer file.
- `1`. Automatically confirms the adapter settings without user intervention.

This key either determines whether the defined preset adapter settings should be used automatically or prompts the user for confirmation. A value of 0 prompts the user for action; a value of 1 automatically uses the settings defined previously.

If the video card installed cannot use the defined settings or if they appear invalid, the defaults of 16 colors, 640×480, and refresh rate of 60 are used for install.

InstallDriver =
Responses:

- `0`. Do not install the referenced display adapter.
- `1`. Install the referenced display adapter.

This key exists as an alternative to using the `[DisplayDriver]` option defined earlier in this chapter. A value of 0 states that the additional values of `InfFile` and `InfOption` should be ignored. A value of 1 processes the additional keys. Here you can simply denote that a user-defined display driver will be used.

InfFile = (filename.inf)
This key is used to define the installation .INF, which is used for the display adapter driver setup. If more than one adapter is installed, a corresponding .INF must exist for each adapter, unlike the TXTSETUP.OEM file, in which many adapter settings can appear for multiple configurations.

InfOption = (option)
This key defines any existing optional parameters within the installation .INF, which was previously referenced to, allow for further identification/customization of the adapter type. Many OEM .INF files are used to install and configure their display adapters' numerous chip types, and their installation .INFs contain that data within.

An adapter .INF can be opened and searched with a standard text editor for these options (if they are present). They may be located by first searching for the manufacturer's name, which must be enclosed with percent signs, such as `%manufacturer%`. The variable to the right of the enclosed name points to another heading within the .INF, under which are the installation options for the particular device. It is important to consult the documentation on the adapter for which you want to install the driver to ensure that you use the correct option in the automated install.

> **Note**
>
> *Both the .INF and the driver file for the display adapter used in this installation option must be stored in the OEM\Display subdirectory on the DSP.*

[Modem]
This optional section heading is used when a modem is installed during an unattended installation. If this heading is not present, the installation ignores the corresponding data.

InstallModem = (modem config section)
This key defines the modem specification section that contains the information on which COM port the modem is installed to, the modem manufacturer/model, and speed.

[(modem config section)]
This section contains the information necessary to install a modem using a predetermined COM port. If this section is left empty, the RAS installation

attempts to detect the presence of a modem on its installed ports and to configure any detected devices.

(COM port)=(Modem Type) [, (Manufacturer), (Provider)]
The (COM port) key determines which port the referenced modem is installed to. If RAS is used, the referenced COM port must match the COM port being configured for RAS. The (Modem Type) is the modem's description, which is contained in the modem's .INF file.

Contained within the Windows NT installation set are many of the .INF files used for the installation of common modem types under NT. You can extract the files, which are denoted by MDM*****.INF, from their compressed state to view and, if necessary, modify their contents. You can also use an existing NT workstation that has a similar modem already installed to discover the correct settings. Check in the %SYSTEMROOT%/INF/ subdirectory for the MDM*****.INF file and read the file's contents.

The values of (Manufacturer) and (Provider) are components of the install that are required only if a particular .INF file is used for the installation of several different modem types.

[Network]

This section of the Answer file is used to generate responses for installing the network services on the target system. If this heading is not present, the installation ignores the corresponding data.

Attended=
Responses:

- yes. Halts the setup for user intervention during the networking component of the installation.

- no. Automatically installs the networking component according to the defined settings in the Answer file, which is highly desirable for those who want a fully automated installation.

JoinWorkgroup=(Workgroup Name)
If the target system participates in a workgroup, use this key to specify the workgroup's name.

JoinDomain=(Domain Name)
If the target system participates in a domain, use this key to specify the domain name.

CreateComputerAccount=(Username,Password)

This key is used in conjunction with the JoinDomain option to create an account for the new computer in an existing domain. A username and password placed here must possess the rights within the domain to create new accounts.

> **Tip**
>
> *If a username and a password are placed within an Answer file, they will exist in clear text and may therefore present a security risk. Alternatives to using this method of creating accounts are to either create the new computer accounts beforehand or create an ID to use within the Answer file that possesses the capability to add new accounts only to the domain.*

DetectAdapters=

Responses:

- (detect adapters section). Refers to a section of network adapters where the installation should search.
- "". The installation automatically searches for and installs the first adapter it finds.

This key, which is used to enable network adapter detection during the unattended process, can be used to detect a specified range of adapters that are defined later in the [Network] section.

> **Tip**
>
> *Only adapters that have been scripted to be unattended aware—that is, the device driver installation file has been scripted to respond to information contained in an UNATTEND.TXT file—can be used with this key. If the value of this key is set to "", the first network adapter detected is installed.*

InstallAdapters=(install adapters section)

This key may be used in place of the detection option for installing network adapters onto NT systems. It can be extremely useful to include the type of network card if you are deploying NT into an environment in which the hardware platforms are identical.

InstallProtocols=(protocols section)

This key is used to call the section in which the desired network protocols are referenced for installation.

InstallServices=(services section)
This key is used to call the section in which the desired network services are referenced for installation.

[(Detect Adapters Section)]
This section is referred to earlier in the Answer file by the key `DetectAdapters=(Detect Adapters Section)`.

DetectCount=(number of detection attempts)
This key sets the number of attempts the installation makes to detect the network adapter.

LimitTo=(netcard inf option)
`LimitTo` is used to define the adapters the installation should attempt to locate and install. The defined adapters that appear as the value for this key must be taken from the [Options] section of the .INF used to install the card. These may be found in the OEMNAD**.INF in the DSP or in Appendix B of this book.

(Netcard Inf option)=(netcard parameter section)
This key is used by the installation as a pointer to the designated network card's additional parameters, which you may want to define during setup. The network card's .INF options, which are used for the key (Netcard Inf Option), are found in the OEMNAD**.INF file for the corresponding network card being installed.

[(netcard parameter section)]
This section is used to define the network card parameters for the user-designated network adapters specified in either the [Detect Adapters Section] or the [Install Adapters Section]. The additional parameters for a specific card can be found in a number of different ways, depending on the card type.

For drivers located on the Windows NT Distribution CD (RETAIL), the information on the card's parameters can be found in the OEMNAD**.INF file that corresponds to the card. If the card is new and its corresponding .INF does not exist on the NT CD, then the manufacturer's driver file, or OEMSETUP.INF, can be opened and read to determine the correct settings.

Finally, if the card is currently installed on a system running Windows NT, the Registry may be opened and the card's settings may be read from there. Open REGEDIT or REGEDT32 and search for the network adapter. The card's settings may be located at HKEY_LOCAL_MACHINE\System\CurrentControlSet\Services\. Look for the network adapter name, which should be followed by a number. The number represents the order in which the adapter was installed. The key should appear as follows:

    HKEY_LOCAL_MACHINE\System\CurrentControlSet\Services\Ieepro1

The right side of the screen within REGEDT32 contains the network adapter options that can be copied and inserted into an Answer file that uses the same network adapter type. Following is an excerpt from an Answer file using the `DetectAdapters` option:

```
DetectAdapters=[MyListOfAdapters]

[MyListOfAdapters]
DetectCount=3
LimitTo=ELNKII, EE16
ELNKII=ELNKIIParams
EE16=EE16Params

[ELNKIIParams]
Transceiver=0
InterruptNumber=5
IoBaseAddress=768

[EE16]
Transceiver=0
InterruptNumber=5
IoBaseAddress=768
BusType=1
BusNumber=0
```

You can see how the `DetectAdapters` key points to `MyListOfAdapters`, which in turn represents a section heading of its own. The [MyListOfAdapters] section enumerates the scope of the adapters to which the installation is limited. Each of these adapters has a corresponding section heading of its own.

> **Tip**
>
> *The numerical values appearing in an Answer file that are used to represent a network adapter's settings must appear in decimal format, even though they are translated into hex after they are installed. For example, say the IO address of a network adapter is 0x300. If the referenced value plans to be installed to that same address using an Answer file, it must appear as* 768, *the decimal equivalent to 0x300.*

[(Protocols Section)]

This section houses the user-defined protocols and the corresponding options that are installed on the target system. For each protocol installed, the section referenced by the protocol's key must be created within the Answer file or the installation fails.

Chapter 3: Creating Answer Files 61

NBF=(Netbeui Parameters)
This key is used to install the protocol NetBEUI.

NWLNKIPX=(IPX Parameters)
This key is used to install the protocol NWLNKIPX.

TC=(Tcpip Parameters)
This key is used to install the protocol TC.

DLC=(DLC Parameters)
This key is used to install the protocol DLC.

RASPPTP=(Ras PTPP Parameters)
This key is used to install the protocol RAPPPTP.

STREAMS=(Streams Parameters)
This key is used to install the protocol STREAMS.

ATALK=(ATALK Parameters)
This key is used to install the protocol ATALK.

[(NetBeui Parameters)]

Nothing but the section header is required to install this protocol.

[(IPX Parameters)]

Nothing but the section header is required to install this protocol.

[(Tcpip Parameters)]

The following keys are used within the [(Tcpip Parameters)] section.

DHCP=Yes | No
This key determines whether DHCP should be used to assign IP addresses. If DHCP is set to yes, no additional information should be needed to configure TCP/IP. If the response is no, additional information is required to configure the target system so that it can function using the TCP/IP protocol and include a static IP address, subnet mask, default gateway, DNS server, WINS, and DNS domain name.

> *Tip*
>
> *Even if DHCP is set to* yes, *the additional settings under TCP/IP may be used to further define the appropriate parameters for the TCP/IP stack. Addresses use standard dotted decimal format.*

ScopeID=(scope ID)
This key determines the target system's scope identifier if it is being installed onto a network that is using NetBIOS over TCP/IP.

IPAddress=(Ip address)
This key specifies the IP address for the computer.

Subnet=(subnet address)
This key specifies the subnet mask address.

Gateway=(gateway address)
This key identifies the computer's default gateway address.

DNSServer=(IP Addresses)
This key identifies up to three DNS servers.

WINSPrimary=(IP Address)
This key specifies the IP address of the primary WINS server.

WINSSecondary=(IP address)
This key specifies the IP address of the secondary WINS server.

DNSName=(DNS domain name)
This key specifies the DNS domain name.

[(DLC Parameters)]

Only the section header is required to install this protocol.

[(RASPPTP)]

Only the section header is required to install this protocol.

[(STREAMS)]

Only the section header is required to install this protocol.

[(Services Section)]

The following services can be installed using an Answer file:

- *DHCP.* Dynamic Host Configuration Protocol (NT Server only).
- *DNS.* Domain Name Service (NT Server only).
- *INETSTP.* Install Internet Information Server (NT Server only).
- *NETMON.* Network Monitor.

- *NWWKSTA*. Client Service for NetWare.
- *RAS*. Remote Access Service.
- *SAP*. SAP Service.
- *SNMP*. SMP Service.
- *STCPIP*. Simple TCP/IP.
- *TCPPRINT*. TCP/IP Printing Service.
- *WINS*. Windows Internet Name Server (NT Server only).

NETMON=(Netmon Parameters section)
This key exists as a pointer for the installation to the designated service's additional parameters, which are needed for installation.

STCPIP=(Simple TCPIP parameters section)
This key exists as a pointer for the installation to the designated service's additional parameters, which are needed for installation.

TCPPRINT=(TCPIP Printing Parameters section)
This key exists as a pointer for the installation to the designated service's additional parameters, which are needed for installation.

INETSTP=(Internet server parameters section)
This key exists as a pointer for the installation to the designated service's additional parameters, which are needed for installation.

SAP=(SAP Parameters section)
This key exists as a pointer for the installation to the designated service's additional parameters, which are needed for installation.

SNMP=(Snmp Parameters)
This key exists as a pointer for the installation to the designated service's additional parameters, which are needed for installation.

RAS=(Ras Parameters)
This key exists as a pointer for the installation to the designated service's additional parameters, which are needed for installation.

NWWKSTA=(NetWare Client Parameters)
This key exists as a pointer for the installation to the designated service's additional parameters, which are needed for installation.

> **Tip**
>
> *Of the previously mentioned services, the option keynames* NETMON, STCPIP, TCPPRINT, *and* SAP *only require their corresponding section headers to exist in order to be installed during an unattended installation. No additional information is required. Following is an example of each required section heading:*
>
>   [Netmon Parameters section]
>   [Simple TCPIP parameters section]
>   TCPIP Printing Parameters section]
>   [SAP Prameters section]
>
> *For the services* INETSTP *(NT Server only),* NWWKSTA, RAS, *and* SNMP, *additional configuration options are required to configure the service.*

[(NetWare Client Parameters)]

The following keys are used within the [(NetWare Client Parameters)] section.

DefaultLocation

The DefaultLocation key is used to identify the default NetWare server for the NetWare client:

    [(NetWare Client Parameters)]
    !DefaultLocation=(Netware Server Name)

!DefaultScriptOptions=

Responses:

- 0. Do not process login scripts.
- 1. Process only NetWare 3.1x login scripts.
- 3. Process either NetWare 3.1x or 4.x scripts.

This key defines the default action to perform with scripts. The option 0 implies that no scripts are run, 1 indicates that only NetWare 3.x-level scripts are run, and 3 implies that either NetWare 3.x or NetWare 4.x-level scripts can be run.

[(Snmp Parameters)]

The SNMPTRAP service is installed as a service that must be started manually. In order for it to be started automatically, the service must be enabled using a registry edit during the unattended installation:

    REGEDIT4
    HKEY_LOCAL_MACHINE\SYSTEM\CurrentControlSet\Services\SNMPTRAP
    "START"= dword:00000002

See Chapter 5, "Installing Additional Applications," to learn how to apply this and other registry edits during an unattended installation.

Accept_CommunityName=(community names)
This key is used to specify a maximum of three community names. The computer the SNMP service is running on accepts traps from these names. The (community names) are separated by commas.

Send_Authentication=
Responses:

- yes. Send an authentication trap when an authorized host requests information.

- no. Do not send an authentication trap.

Any_Host=
Responses:

- yes. Accept SNMP packets from any host.

- no. Do not accept SNMP packets.

Limit_Host=(host names)
This key identifies the acceptable hosts from which an SNMP-enabled system can accept packets. A total of three SNMP hosts can be identified, which must be separated by commas. The key is valid only when the key Any_Host=No is present.

Community_Name=(community name)
This key identifies the SNMP community to which the system belongs.

Traps=(IP addresses) | (IPX addresses)
This key specifies a maximum of three IP or IPX addresses to which traps should be sent.

Contact_Name=(name)
This key specifies the SNMP-enabled system's name.

Location=(computer location)
This key specifies the location of the computer.

Service=(Service Type)
Responses:

- physical (default)

- applications (default)

- datalink
- internet (default)
- end-to-end

Any of these services can be used separately or in conjunction with one another, but they must be separated by commas if multiple services are selected.

[(RasParameters)]

The following keys are used in the [(RasParameters)] section.

PortSections=(RAS Ports Section)

This key points the installation to the RAS Ports section. More than one ports section can exist if multiple ports are installed, provided a comma separates them.

DialoutProtocols=

Responses:

- TCP/IP. Installs TCP/IP as an RAS Dialout protocol.
- IPX. Installs IPX as an RAS Dialout protocol.
- NETBEUI. Installs NetBEUI as an RAS Dialout protocol.
- ALL. Installs all of the preceding protocols as RAS Dialout protocols.

The remaining parameters in this (RasParameters) section apply only to RAS server installation.

DialinProtocols=

Responses:

- TCP/IP. Installs TCP/IP as an RAS Dialout protocol.
- IPX. Installs IPX as an RAS Dialout protocol.
- NETBEUI. Installs NetBEUI as an RAS Dialout protocol.
- ALL. Installs all of the preceding protocols as RAS Dialout protocols.

NetBEUIClientAccess=

Responses:

- Network (default). Grants a dialin user access to the network.
- ThisComputer. Grants a dialin user access to the RAS server only.

TcpIpClientAccess=
Responses:

- `Network` (default). Grants a dialin user access to the network.
- `ThisComputer`. Grants a dialin user access to the RAS server only.

UseDHCP=
Responses:

- yes(default). Use DHCP to assign an IP address for the dialin user.
- no. Do not use DHCP.

StaticAddressBegin=(BeginIPAddress)
Assign a beginning static IP address for the dialin user. This key is only necessary if the `UseDHCP` key is set to `no`.

StaticAddressEnd=(EndIPAddress)
Assign an ending static IP address for the dialin user. This key is only necessary if the `UseDHCP` key is set to `no`.

ExcludeAddress=(IPRangeStart - IPRangeEnd)
This key can be used to exclude a range of IP addresses usable by the RAS server for remote clients. It requires that the `StaticAddressBegin` and `StaticAddressEnd` keys be defined.

ClientCanRequestIPAddress=
Responses:

- yes. Allows a remote client to request a specific IP address.
- no (default). Denies the remote client requests for a specific IP address.

IpxClientAccess=
Responses:

- `Network` (default). Grants a dialin user access to the network.
- `ThisComputer`. Grants a dialin user access to the RAS server only.

AutomaticNetworkNumbers=
Responses:

- yes (default). Automatically assigns an IPX number to the remote client.
- no. Manually specifies the IPX number of the remote client.

NetworkNumberFrom=(IPX_net_number)
Responses:

- IPX Range of Addresses (1 to 0xFFFFFFFE). This key is used if the AutomaticNetworkNumber is set to no.

AssignSameNetworkNumber=
Responses:

- yes (default). Use the same network number for all RAS clients.

- no. Assign unique network numbers for each RAS client.

ClientsCanRequestIpxNodeNumber=
Responses:

- yes. Allow remote clients to request specific IPX node numbers.

- no (default). Deny remote clients the capability to request specific IPX node numbers.

[(RAS Ports Section)]

The following keys are used in the [(RAS Ports Section)] section.

PortName=
Responses:

- COM1 through COM25

This key is used to identify the ports used by the RAS server.

DeviceType=Modem
This key defines the device used by RAS. The device type "modem" is currently the only device designed to work with RAS.

PortUsage=
Responses:

- DialOut. This value assigns dialout privileges to the defined RAS port. If the defined RAS port is COM1 and a Hayes-compatible modem has been installed, then the DialOut privilege has been granted to the Hayes-compatible modem installed on COM1.

- DialIn. This value assigns dialin privileges to the defined RAS port.

- DialInOut. This value assigns both dialin and dialout privileges to the defined RAS port.

Chapter 3: Creating Answer Files   69

The following is an example of an unattended RAS installation. To install RAS using one dialin/ dialout port that implements DHCP for IP for network access, use this code:

```
[Network]
InstallServices = ServiceParamsSection

[ServiceParamsSection]
RAS = RASParamsSection

[RASParamsSection]
PortSections = COMPortParams
DialinOutProtocols = TCP/IP
TcpIPClientAccess = Network
UseDHCP = YES
ClientCanRequestIPAddress = NO

[ComPortParams]
PortName = COM1
DeviceType = Modem
DeviceName = "Courier V. Everthing Internal"
PortUsage = DialinOut
```

Some Examples of Answer Files for Different Environments

This kind of Answer file might be used in an NT environment that uses DHCP to obtain an IP and that has users logging into a domain. You may notice the `JoinDomain` line and the `CreateComputerAccount` line that immediately follows it. These two keys are both used to add the workstation to the domain at installation time, but they require that an ID and password with the rights to create computer accounts on a domain are written clearly in the Answer file. The best approach is to create the computer accounts prior to the installation so that an administrator's password is not left vulnerable in a clear text file.

```
[Unattended]
OemPreinstall = yes
OemSkipEULA = yes
NoWaitAfterTextMode = 1
NoWaitAfterGUIMode = 1
FileSystem = LeaveAlone
ExtendOEMPartition = 0
ConfirmHardware = no
NtUpgrade = no
Win31Upgrade = no
TargetPath = WINNT
OverwriteOemFilesOnUpgrade = yes
```

70 Part I: Basic Configuration of an Unattended Installation

```
[OEM_Ads]
Banner = "The XYZ Corporation's Installation*of Windows NT Workstation"
Background = setup.bmp

[UserData]
FullName = "XYZ"
OrgName = "XYZ Organization"
ComputerName = NTTEST
ProductId = "xxxxx-oem-xxxxxxx-xxxxx"

[GuiUnattended]
OemSkipWelcome = 1
OEMBlankAdminPassword = 1
TimeZone = "(GMT-05:00) Eastern Time (US & Canada)"

[Display]
ConfigureAtLogon = 0
BitsPerPel = 8
XResolution = 640
YResolution = 480
VRefresh = 60
AutoConfirm = 1

[Network]
DetectAdapters = ""
InstallProtocols = ProtocolsSection
InstallServices = ServicesSection
JoinDomain = XYZDomain
CreateComputerAccount = Installer, Password

[ProtocolsSection]
TC = TCParamSection

[TCParamSection]
DHCP = yes

[ServicesSection]
```

Following is another example of an Answer file. The output that follows is used to connect to a 3.1x NetWare server:

```
[Unattended]
OemPreinstall = yes
OemSkipEULA = yes
NoWaitAfterTextMode = 1
NoWaitAfterGUIMode = 1
FileSystem = ConvertNTFS
ExtendOEMPartition = 1
ConfirmHardware = no
NtUpgrade = no
Win31Upgrade = no
TargetPath = WINNT
OverwriteOemFilesOnUpgrade = yes
```

Chapter 3: Creating Answer Files 71

```
[OEM_Ads]
Banner = "Big Red Corp's Installation*of Windows NT Workstation"
Background = setup.bmp

[UserData]
FullName = "BigRed"
OrgName = "Big Red Corporation"
ComputerName = BR1
ProductId = "xxx-xxxxxxx"

[GuiUnattended]
OemSkipWelcome = 1
OEMBlankAdminPassword = 1
TimeZone = "(GMT-05:00) Eastern Time (US & Canada)"

[Display]
ConfigureAtLogon = 0
BitsPerPel = 16
XResolution = 1024
YResolution = 768
VRefresh = 70
AutoConfirm = 1

[Network]
DetectAdapters = ""
InstallProtocols = ProtocolsSection
InstallServices = ServicesSection
JoinWorkgroup = Workgroup

[ProtocolsSection]
TC = TCParamSection
NWLNKIPX = NWLNKIPXParamSection

[TCParamSection]
DHCP = No
IPAddress = x.x.x.x
Subnet = x.x.x.x
Gateway = x.x.x.x
DNSServer = x.x.x.x
WINSPrimary = x.x.x.x
WINSSecondary = x.x.x.x
DNSName = bigred.com

[NWLNKIPXParamSection]

[ServicesSection]
NWWKSTA = NWWKSTAParamSection

[NWWKSTAParamSection]
!DefaultLocation = BIGRED1
!DefaultScriptOptions = 1
```

72   Part I: Basic Configuration of an Unattended Installation

In this installation of Windows NT, the Answer file is designed to install both the TCP/IP protocol—by using a static IP address (the *x.x.x.x* can be replaced with a proper IP address)—and the IPX/SPX protocols needed to connect to NetWare networks. When static IPs are used, additional configuration information may be required in the Answer file, including the default gateway and any DNS or WINS servers. The IPX/SPX protocol sections are NWLNKIPX = NWLNKIPXParamSection and [NWLNKIPXParamSection]. These sections tell the installation to add the appropriate protocols needed to attach to NetWare servers.

For NWLINK to work properly under NetWare, the MS Client for NetWare must be installed. Simply add the NWWKSTA = NWWKSTAParamSection line to the [ServicesSection] and then add the [NWWKSTAParamSection] with the preceding output, replacing BIGRED1 with the name of your Novell server.

Following is an example of an Answer file that could be used to deploy Windows NT in a UNIX environment:

```
[Unattended]
OemPreinstall = yes
OemSkipEULA = yes
NoWaitAfterTextMode = 1
NoWaitAfterGUIMode = 1
FileSystem = ConvertNTFS
ExtendOEMPartition = 0
ConfirmHardware = no
NtUpgrade = no
Win31Upgrade = no
TargetPath = WINNT
OverwriteOemFilesOnUpgrade = yes

[OEM_Ads]
Banner = "UNIXland's Installation*of Windows NT Workstation"
Background = notms.bmp

[UserData]
FullName = "CHMOD12"
OrgName = "UNIXland"
ComputerName = CHMOD12
ProductId = "xxxxx-oem-xxxxxxx-xxxxx"

[GuiUnattended]
OemSkipWelcome = 1
OEMBlankAdminPassword = 1
TimeZone = "(GMT-05:00) Eastern Time (US & Canada)"

[Display]
ConfigureAtLogon = 0
BitsPerPel = 8
XResolution = 640
YResolution = 480
VRefresh = 60
AutoConfirm = 1
```

```
[Network]
DetectAdapters = ""
netwareInstallProtocols = ProtocolsSection
InstallServices = ServicesSection
JoinWorkgroup = "UNIX1"

[ProtocolsSection]
TC = TCParamSection

[TCParamSection]
DHCP = yes

[ServicesSection]
NETMON=NetmonParams
TCPPRINT=TCPIPPrintParams
[NetmonParams]
[TCPIPPrintParams]
```

This particular example shows an NT deployment that takes advantage of IP under UNIX, incorporating UNIX DHCP to assign the IP address for the workstation, and installs TCP/IP Printing.

Options for Automating Deployments of NT Server

In addition to scripting installations for NT Workstation, Answer files can also be used to automate installations of NT Server. However, automating NT Server is not a highly recommended process, mainly due to the number and importance of additional configuration options that installations of NT Server require. You should be absolutely comfortable with the automation process and have a specific installation plan in mind before using unattended scripts for server deployments.

AdvServerType=

Responses:

- SERVERNT. Use for installing a standalone NT server.
- LANMANNT. Use for installing a primary domain controller (PDC).
- LANSECNT. Use for installing a backup domain controller (BDC).

This key is valid only when installing Windows NT Server. SERVERNT indicates that the computer is a standalone server. LANMANNT indicates that the computer serves as a PDC. LANSECNT indicates that the computer is a BDC.

[LicenseFilePrintData]

This section is valid only when installing Windows NT Server.

AutoMode=

Responses:

- PerSeat. Used to specify the client-managed licensing scheme, in which each client attaching to the NT server requires an individual license.

- PerServer. Used to specify the server-managed licensing scheme, in which the server manages the client licenses and connections. If the PerServer option is used, the additional key of AutoUsers must be specified.

AutoUsers=(decimal number)

Used with the PerServer option of AutoMode, this key indicates the number of client licenses purchased for that particular server, which translates into the amount of concurrent connections the server allows.

InstallDC=(domain name)

This key is used only when installing a domain controller. It specifies the domain to which the server should be added.

InstallInternetServer=(IIS Parameters)

Though Microsoft's Internet Information Server is installed by default on Typical installations of Windows NT Server, this key is needed in an Answer file to specify that IIS is automatically installed and configured using the section this key defines.

[(IIS Parameters)]

This section is used to define and configure the various elements of the IIS installation.

InstallINETSTP=

Responses:

- 0. Do not install Internet services.
- 1 (default). Install Internet services.

InstallADMIN=

Responses:
- 0. Do not install the Internet Service Manager.
- 1. Install the Internet Service Manager.

InstallFTP=

Responses:
- 0. Do not install the FTP service.
- 1. Install the FTP service.

FTPRoot=(ftp root directory)

This key specifies the directory on the server, which serves as the root of the FTP service.

InstallWWW=

Responses:
- 0. Do not install the WWW service.
- 1. Install the WWW service.

WWWRoot=(www root directory)

This key specifies the directory on the server which serves as the root of the WWW service.

InstallGOPHER=

Responses:
- 0. Do not install the Gopher service.
- 1. Install the Gopher service.

GopherRoot=(gopher root directory)

This key specifies the directory on the server that serves as the root of the Gopher service.

InstallDir=(internet services install directory)

This key specifies the directory on the server where the Internet services are installed.

InstallW3SAMP=

Responses:

- 0. Install the sample WWW files to the Web server.
- 1. Do not install the sample WWW files.

InstallHTMLA=

Responses:

- 0. Install the Web-based Internet Service Manager.
- 1. Do not install the Web-based Internet Service Manager.

GuestAccountName=(name)

This key allows the installer to predefine the username of the Internet Guest account that is used by individuals to access the Internet-related services available under IIS.

GuestAccountPassword=(password string)

This option allows the installer to predefine the password of the Internet Guest account that is used by individuals to access the Internet-related services available under IIS. If a password is not defined, the installation process automatically generates a unique password for the account.

Following is an example of an Answer file that could be used to install NT Server. This particular script is designed to install a BDC onto an existing NT domain using TCP/IP only, configure IIS with WWW and FTP services, install the WINS service, and set the server licensing for 100 concurrent connections:

```
[Unattended]
OemPreinstall = yes
OemSkipEULA = yes
NoWaitAfterTextMode = 1
NoWaitAfterGUIMode = 1
FileSystem = LeaveAlone
ExtendOEMPartition = 0
ConfirmHardware = yes
NtUpgrade = no
Win31Upgrade = no
TargetPath = WINNT
OverwriteOemFilesOnUpgrade = yes
[OEM_Ads]
Banner = "NTDeployment's Installation of*Windows NT Server"

Background = setup.bmp
```

Chapter 3: Creating Answer Files 77

```
[GuiUnattended]
OemSkipWelcome = 1
OEMBlankAdminPassword = 1
TimeZone = "(GMT-05:00) Eastern Time (US & Canada)"
AdvServerType=LANSECNT

[UserData]
FullName = "Server Owner"
OrgName = "Organization Name"
ComputerName = Server Name
ProductId = "00000-oem-0000000-00000"

[LicenseFilePrintData]
AutoMode=PERSERVER
AutoUsers=100

[Display]
ConfigureAtLogon = 0
BitsPerPel = 8
XResolution = 640
YResolution = 480
VRefresh = 60
AutoConfirm = 1

[Network]
DetectAdapters = ""
CreateComputerAccount = Administrator, password
InstallDC = NTDOMAIN
InstallProtocols = ProtocolsSection
InstallServices = ServicesSection
InstallInternetServer = IISParamSection

[IISParamSection]
InstallINETSTP = 1
InstallADMIN = 1
InstallFTP = 1
FTPRoot = C:\Internet\FTPRoot
InstallWWW=1
WWWRoot = C:\Internet\WWWRoot
InstallGOPHER = 0
InstallDir = C:\Internet\Inetsrv
InstallW3SAMP = 0
InstallHTMLA = 1
GuestAccountName = IISGuest
GuestAccountPassword = Password

[ProtocolsSection]
TC = TCParamSection

[TCParamSection]
DHCP = no
IPAddress = 189.132.25.240
Subnet = 255.255.255.0
```

```
Gateway = 189.132.25.1
DNSServer = 189.132.25.46, 189.132.25.47, 189.132.25.211
WINSPrimary = 189.132.25.239
WINSSecondary = 189.132.25.238
DNSName = NTDOMAIN.COM

[ServicesSection]
NETMON = NETMONParamSection
SAP = SAPParamSection
TCPRINT = TCPPrintSection
WINS = WINSParamSection

[NETMONParamSection]

[SAPParamSection]

[TCPPrintSection]

[WINSParamSection]
```

Troubleshooting Answer Files

Many of the errors occurring during an unattended installation that are directly related to the Answer file can be attributed to misspelling a key or value, or improper syntax.

This tendency is even more likely when you are using a UDF in conjunction with an Answer file. When a UDF is being used in the installation to replace values present in the Answer file with customized data, ensure that the corresponding section headings are present in the Answer file as well. Thoroughly checking the spelling and context of each entry prior to deployment ensures an error-free installation. Normal behavior for an Answer file or UDF with faulty data is to halt and await user intervention on the item that requires attention or, when applicable, to use the default setting.

It is equally important to check completed installations to ensure that they were completed using the specified parameters of your startup switches, Answer file, and UDF. If you are attempting to completely automate the installation process and it halts, you might find the solution to your problem in Table 3.1, which lists some of the more common errors that are directly related to the Answer files, startup switches, and UDF settings.

Chapter 3: Creating Answer Files   79

Table 3.1   Common Errors found in Startup Switches, Answer Files, and UDFs

Problem	Solution
The installation halts at the welcome screen.	Ensure that the `OemSkipWelcome=` key is set to 1.
The installation halts with End-User License Agreement (EULA) screen.	Ensure that the key `OEMSkipEULA=` is set to yes.
The installation halts after text mode.	Check to ensure that the key `NoWaitAfterTextMode=` is set to 1.
The installation halts after text mode, even if the correct key is in the Answer file. The installation displays the message: `Pre-installation completed successfully—press any key to shut down and reboot the system.`	This reaction is due to the following keys appearing in the `[Unattended]` section of the Answer file: `ExtendOemPartition=1 NoWaitAfterTextMode=1` This was an option designed to enable PC manufacturers to halt their unattended installations after text mode in order to ship out to customers. The fix can be found at this Microsoft FTP site: `Ftp://ftp.microsoft.com/bussys/winnt/winnt-public/fixes/usa/NT40/Hotfixes-postsp2/setupdd-fix`. Extract the file to the DSP directory containing the NT installation files and then add the following lines to the Answer file under the `[Unattended]` section. Copy this file to the I386 folder from which you run Setup and then make sure the following lines exist as they appear below in the `[Unattended]` section of the Unattend.txt file: `ExtendOemPartition=1 nowaitNowaitaftertextmode=1`
The installation halts after GUI mode.	Check to ensure that the key `NoWaitAfterGUIMode=` is set to 1.
The installation halts in GUI mode, awaiting display adapter confirmation.	Check to ensure that the key `ConfigureAtLogon=` under `[Display]` is set to 1, that the key `AutoConfirm=` is set to 1, and that the Adapter settings of `BitsPerPel`, `Xresolution`, `Yresolution`, and `Vrefresh` are set correctly for your current adapter and monitor.

continues

Table 3.1 Continued

Problem	Solution
The installation halts in GUI mode during the setup of networking.	Ensure that the key `Attended` under `[Network]` is set to no. If `DetectAdapters=` is set to `""`, try specifying the correct network adapter. Check to ensure that the installed protocols and services are properly referenced.

The installation halts with the error message `The IPAddress key has an invalid IP address. Please correct the problem after the property sheet is displayed.`	This is a known bug in NT 4.0. It appears when a zero appears in either the first or second octet of a static IP address specified in the Answer file. `TCPIPParameters]`
	`DHCP = NO`
	`IPAddress = 128.143.0.22`
	`Subnet = 255.255.255.0`

Chapter 4

Customizing the Installation of NT

This chapter covers:

- What a Uniqueness Database file is and how to use it effectively
- Windows NT installation startup parameters
- Installing OEM-supplied network and video adapter drivers
- Modifying OEM-supplied installation files to make them unattended-aware
- Adding and removing NT's optional accessories
- Adding and removing NT's additional applications
- Adding and removing Windows NT services

After reading this chapter, you should be able to do the following:

- Create Uniqueness Database files for multiple simultaneous installations of NT
- Understand how to use NT's setup parameters
- Install manufacturer-supplied installation files and devices during an unattended deployment
- Modify a driver installation file to make it unattended-aware
- Add or remove any of NT's various accessories, applications, and services

In many deployments of Windows NT Workstation, administrators are devising unique methods of distributing the operating system to the desktop. Some are using bootable disks that contain custom scripts to access the installation, while others are using server login scripts to initiate the setup process. Each method used is suited to the variables involved, or required by the deployment equation, or is based on the knowledge and experience of the administrator.

Deciding on a method of distribution and access can have a significant impact on the deployment process. Careful consideration should go into designing a bullet-proof method of access, identification, and installation to ensure the most efficient form of deployment.

Uniqueness Database Files

Uniqueness Database files, known as *UDFs*, are used in conjunction with Answer files to further customize multiple simultaneous installations of Windows NT Workstation. When the information contained within a UDF is identical to the information contained within an Answer file, the information contained within the UDF is used. If the information present in a UDF regarding additional parameters, services, or settings for a particular ID is not in the Answer file, it is added to the installation set.

If the information contained within a UDF regarding a particular ID is left blank, the default for that parameter is used, overriding a specific setting for the same parameter in the Answer file. If a parameter is left blank and no default exists for that parameter, the installation halts and prompts the user for the necessary information. If an invalid ID is referenced in the [UniqueIDs] section of the UDF, the installation halts and prompts the user for a valid UDF.

UDFs are referenced as one of the WinNT or WinNT32 startup parameters for the installation with the switch /UDF:<unique ID referenced in the UDF>, <database file name>. An example that might be easier to understand is /UDF:JOE, C:\INSTALL\UNIQUE.UDB, where JOE would be the key within the file UNIQUE.UDB that the installation would search for and use to customize and configure that particular workstation.

Though the concept of UDFs is referred to as a UDF, the file extension on the database file itself is .UDB.

Creating a .UDB File

The .UDB file can contain customizing information regarding any part of the installation process defined in the Answer file *except* these sections:

[UNATTENDED]   [OEMBootFiles]

[MassStorageDrivers]   [OEM_Ads]

[KeyboardDrivers]   [Display]

[PointingDeviceDrivers] [Modem]

Chapter 4: Customizing the Installation of NT 83

But what about information contained within a UDF? Any information under these section headers in an Answer file may be specified in a UDF.

```
[UserData]

[GuiUnattended]

[Network]

[ProtocolsSection]

[ServicesSection]
```

Here is an example of how a UDF can be used in a mixed client and network environment. Windows NT Workstation is to be installed on four separate computers for users who have entirely separate specialized needs. They are Diane, Joe, and Mike. Diane is the head of marketing and requires access to the newly created NT domain as well as the legacy NetWare server "Netware_1." Because the initial Answer file only contains network selections for routing IP, additional protocols and services need to be added to ensure her access to both networks. Joe is her student intern, so changes made to the installation regarding his workstation should be minimal. Mike is a salesman who handles the East Coast section of the company.

You'll be installing NT on all of these machines simultaneously, so our standard Answer file won't work on all of them. A single Answer file used without a UDF attempts to use the same machine ID contained in the line `ComputerName =` for each installation. If the installation engine detects an existing system on the network with the same workstation name, it halts the installation and awaits user intervention.

In order to automate all three, we'll use a .UDB file containing the machine and user-specific settings for each of the users, overriding any matching data contained in the Answer file.

Contents of a Sample .UDB File

This section describes the individual IDs that are referenced in the startup sequence and the corresponding sections within the .UDB to check for specialized instructions.

```
[UniqueIDs]

DIANE = UserData, GuiUnattended, Network,
ProtocolsList, SelectedServicesList, InstallCSNW
JOE = UserData
MIKE = UserData, Network

[DIANE:UserData]
Full Name = "Diane Marks"
Computer Name = "DIANEM"
ProductID = "123-1234567"
```

84 Part I: Basic Configuration of an Unattended Installation

```
[DIANE:GuiUnattended]
TimeZone = "(GMT-06:00) Central Time (US & Canada)"

[DIANE:Network]
JoinDomain = "SRC_Corp"

[DIANE:ProtocolsList]
NWLINKIPX = NKLINKIPXParams

[DIANE:SelectedServicesList]
NWWKSTA = Install CSNW

[DIANE:InstallCSNW]
!DefaultLocation = Netware_1
!DefaultScriptOption = 1

[JOE:UserData]
Full Name = "Joe Daniels"
Computer Name = "JOED"
ProductID = "321-7654321"

[MIKE:UserData]
Full Name = "Mike Agaki"
Computer Name = "MIKEA"
ProductID = "132-1237654"

[MIKE:Network]
JoinDomain = "SRC_Corp"
```

By inserting multiple, user-specific data into a single file, UDFs can be especially helpful when you want to deploy multiple copies of NT that are customized to each user. Let's take a closer look at the structure of a .UDB file and see how each portion of the file plays into the installation process:

```
[UniqueID]
```

This header is required, as it lets the installation engine know that the following specified keys contained are used to define the additional customization settings for each installation.

```
UNIQUEID1 =

Options:
[UserData], [GuiUnattended], [Network], [ProtocolsSection], [ServicesSection]

[UNIQUEID1:UserData]

[UNIQUEID1:GuiUnattended]

[UNIQUEID1:Network]

[UNIQUEID1:ProtocolsSection]

[UNIQUEID1:ServicesSection]
```

Within each of the section headings, the UNIQUEID: is provided to let the installation process know that the referenced section is intended to replace the corresponding section header contained within the UNATTEND.TXT file. Should a section heading exist in a UDF without a UNIQUEID: identifier, that section header and its referenced keys and values are used in place of the corresponding information within the UNATTEND.TXT file.

> *Tip*
>
> *Section headers contained within a UDF that are intended to replace settings contained within an Answer file must be syntactically identical. If the section header for a specified network adapter's parameter is `[MyNetCardParams]`, then the same section header must appear in the UDF, preceded by the unique ID and a colon: `[UniqueID:MyNetCardParams]`. If a key beneath a section heading references an additional custom key, it must be referenced using the same syntax of `[UNIQUEID: Referenced Item]`.*

> *Tip*
>
> *If a section header appears alone in a UDF and is not preceded by a unique identifier, then the contents of that section heading are applied to every installation that uses that .UDB, replacing the same heading contained within the Answer file. This can be helpful if you just want to make an installation change for that particular installation round and not modify the original Answer file.*

Case Study: Fulbright & Jaworski, L.L.P.

The IT staff at Fulbright & Jaworski are proceeding with an NT workstation rollout of 1,800 desktop systems located in seven offices. This deployment is the spearhead that other network administrators for Fulbright & Jaworski will be watching and using in their own sections within the company. This deployment method uses an elaborate system of scripts and batch files to install and configure each workstation—including the scripting of an unattended-aware network adapter installation file—tailored to the needs of the individual workstation or its user. Custom Answer files are used to install and configure the appropriate NetWare client information so the designated workstation is logging into the correct NetWare server. Additional workstation-specific information is provided by a Uniqueness Database file, or UDF, used to supply unique information when running simultaneous installations of Windows NT.

Working on a night and day schedule, the designated desktop systems are given a hardware upgrade by the night staff. These upgrades are, in turn, converted to the Windows NT operating system during the day while the user is attending scheduled upgrade training. The entire process converts 12 desktop systems a day, producing at its completion both a customized NT workstation and a newly trained user.

Installation Startup Parameters for Windows NT

The first three chapters of this book covered the basic components required to create an unattended installation of Windows NT. With the material covered to this point, an administrator or consultant could deploy a very basic shell of the operating system to any number of target systems in any given network environment with the use of an Answer file. But there is still much that can be done to further customize the operating system itself during an automated deployment. This chapter covers how to further customize installations of NT Workstation to include options for launching NT's Setup program, running simultaneous installations of NT, customizing the optional components that are shipped with the operating system, and modifying OEM-supplied adapter files for the unattended installation process.

The following list contains startup parameters for the executable WINNT.EXE or WINNT32.EXE. If you are unfamiliar with the differences between these two install options, the first choice, WINNT.EXE, is for new installations of NT, and it includes installations on machines already housing Windows 3.x and 95 installs. WINNT32.EXE is for upgrading existing versions of Windows NT only.

That said, let's review the available startup parameters:

Startup Switch	Definition
/B	Causes the installation to copy the boot files directly to the hard drive, bypassing the need for NT's bootable floppies (requires that the /s be used to identify the necessary installation files).
/E:command	Specifies a program or command to be executed at the end of the GUI phase of the installation.
/I:Inf file	Specifies the filename (no path) of the setup information file. The default is DOSNET.INF.

Chapter 4: Customizing the Installation of NT 87

Startup Switch	Definition
/L	Creates a log file of the installation called $WINNT.LOG. It logs any errors the installation encounters while copying files to the temporary directory.
/OX	Creates the boot floppies for the CD-ROM installation. Useful if the floppies ever become missing or corrupt.
/R:*directory name*	Creates a directory on the target system with the corresponding name.
/RX:*directory name*	Names a directory to be copied to the target system during the installation.
/S:*path to installation files*	Identifies the full path to NT's installation files; this can be either a Uniform Naming Convention (UNC) or a mapped drive path. (The default is the current directory.)
/T:*drive letter*	Specifies a drive to store NT's temporary setup files.
/U:*Answer file*	Specifies the Answer file to be used with the installation (requires that the /s be used to identify the necessary installation files).
/UDF: ID, *<database file name>*	Specifies the ID to be referenced within the .UDB file from which customized data is retrieved and applied to the installation in progress.
/W	Used only with the WINNT.EXE option. Used for beginning the installation process from within Windows 3.x or Windows 95. Note that the /B option is disabled in this mode.
/X	Causes the installation to bypass the creation of the NT boot floppies.

When both UDFs and Windows NT's native startup parameters are used in conjunction with a scripted Answer file, multiple custom configurations of the operating system can be deployed at the same time. These startup parameters can also be placed in a simple batch file—further allowing for automation of the installation process—to include running them as part of a login script or schedule service.

88 Part I: Basic Configuration of an Unattended Installation

> *Tip*
>
> *WINNT.EXE is a 16-bit application and can take advantage of DOS's HIMEM.SYS, EMM386.EXE, and SMARTDRV.EXE to enhance the amount of available memory and enable disk caching to increase installation performance during the first text setup portion of the installation. These memory managers can be used from a bootable disk or a login script.*

Next is a simple script used to automatically connect to an NT share after booting with the MS-DOS Client. After boot, it begins a scripted installation of Windows NT, with the additional command-line parameters that will not create boot floppies or require them during the setup process.

```
net use i: \\ntservername\sharename /yes
i:\i386\winnt /b /u:i:\i386\unattend.txt /s:i:\i386 /x
```

For server-based distribution share points (DSPs), access can be acquired in most cases using a bootable disk or, in the case of an upgrade, an existing network connection.

Next is an example batch file that can be used to insert a selected machine name into the installation script without having to type out the entire command set.

```
@ECHO OFF
@ECHO TYPE "INSTALL" and the Machine Name you want installed
IF "%1"=="" GOTO :INSTALL
:INSTALL
I:\I386\WINNT /UDF:%1,I:\I386\IDENTITY.UDB /U:I:\I386\UNATTEND.TXT /B /X
GOTO :END

:END
EXIT
```

When using this batch file and typing **INSTALL MIKE**, the name MIKE is inserted into the installation options with the %1 variable, where it is used to reference the unique settings for MIKE in the UDF INDENTITY.UDB. Make certain that the name referenced when using this batch file is present in the .UDB file. If not, the installation either uses the defaults present within the UNATTEND.TXT or fails altogether.

> *Troubleshooting Tip*
>
> *When using the %1 variable in this manner, the unique ID referenced after install is case sensitive, and may not be passed correctly to the UDF should the name appear in capital letters in the UDF but be typed on the command line in lower case. Ensure that, when referencing the unique ID, the same case is used.*

Chapter 4: Customizing the Installation of NT 89

Next is an example of an installation startup script. This example uses different UNATTEND.TXT and .UDB files to identify the target workstations to the installation. It illustrates the installation of six new NT systems in a company where three computers are located in the finance department, two are in marketing, and the last two are owned by the vice president of the company and his executive secretary.

```
@rem INSTALL.BAT

@echo off
@echo type "INSTALL" and the machine name you are installing to
@echo example: INSTALL MACHINE26 (ALL CAPS)
If "%1"=="MACHINE26" goto MACHINE26
If "%1"=="MACHINE27" goto MACHINE27
If "%1"=="MACHINE28" goto MACHINE28
If "%1"=="MACHINE29" goto MACHINE29
If "%1"=="MACHINE30" goto MACHINE30
If "%1"=="MACHINE31" goto MACHINE31
If "%1"=="MACHINE32" goto MACHINE32
If "%1"=="" goto NOTGOOD

:NOTGOOD
@echo You have entered an invalid machine name, try again.

:MACHINE26
I:\APPSNT\I386\WINNT /B /UDF:MACHINE26, I:\APPSNT\I386\IDENTITY.UDB
/U:I:\APPSNT\I386\ FINANCE.TXT /S:I:\APPSNT\I386 /X
goto CONTINUE

:MACHINE27
I:\APPSNT\I386\WINNT /B /UDF:MACHINE27, I:\APPSNT\I386\IDENTITY.UDB
/U:I:\APPSNT\I386\ FINANCE.TXT /S:I:\APPSNT\I386 /X
goto CONTINUE

:MACHINE28
I:\APPSNT\I386\WINNT /B /UDF:MACHINE28, I:\APPSNT\I386\IDENTITY.UDB
/U:I:\APPSNT\I386\ FINANCE.TXT /S:I:\APPSNT\I386 /X
goto CONTINUE

:MACHINE29
I:\APPSNT\I386\WINNT /B /UDF:MACHINE29, I:\APPSNT\I386\IDENTITY.UDB
/U:I:\APPSNT\I386\ MARKET.TXT /S:I:\APPSNT\I386 /X
goto CONTINUE

:MACHINE30
I:\APPSNT\I386\WINNT /B /UDF:MACHINE30, I:\APPSNT\I386\IDENTITY.UDB
/U:I:\APPSNT\I386\ MARKET.TXT /S:I:\APPSNT\I386 /X
goto CONTINUE

:MACHINE31
I:\APPSNT\I386\WINNT /B /UDF:MACHINE31,A:\SECRET.UDB /U:A:\VP.TXT
/S:I:\APPSNT\I386 /X
goto CONTINUE
```

```
:MACHINE32
I:\APPSNT\I386\WINNT /B /UDF:MACHINE32,A:\SECRET.UDB /U:A:\VP.TXT
/S:I:\APPSNT\I386 /X
goto CONTINUE

@rem END
```

The first three entries are all referencing installation options in the finance department and use the unattended file FINANCE.TXT along with the UDF IDENTITY.UDB. The next two systems use the same .UDB file but reference a separate unattended file, MARKET.TXT.

The last two systems use the unattended file VP.TXT and UDF, SECRET.UDB, which are pulled from a floppy rather than stored on the DSP. This illustrates how different UNATTEND.TXT and .UDB files can be called to install entirely different configurations of NT using the same installation file set on a single DSP.

Adding OEM-Supplied Network Adapter Drivers

When creating customized automated installations of NT, it may become desirable or even necessary to script the installation to install simultaneous instances of the operating system while providing unique information for each copy of NT, such as use pre-selected or OEM-supplied adapter files in during the installation. This may be especially true if the hardware included within your target systems has been newly added to Microsoft's Hardware Compatibility List (HCL). This usually means that the drivers necessary to use a specific piece of hardware may not be present on the retail CD and therefore must be scripted into the installation process using the driver files supplied by the manufacturer.

Before installing an updated OEM-supplied driver for a network adapter, it should first be determined whether or not a retail driver exists within the driver libraries found on the retail CD. Tables 4.1 and 4.2 show the location and type of network adapter files that ship with the Windows NT distribution CD-ROM.

Table 4.1. Network Adapter Files Located in the \I386 Directory

Network Option Name	Literal String	INF File
ELNKMC	3Com 3C523 Etherlink/MC Adapter	oemnadem.inf
ELNKII	3Com Etherlink II Adapter (also II/16 and II/16 TP)	oemnade2.inf

Chapter 4: Customizing the Installation of NT

Network Option Name	Literal String	INF File
ELNK3EISA	3Com Etherlink III EISA Adapter	oemnadee.inf
ELNK3ISA509	3Com Etherlink III ISA/PCMCIA Adapter	oemnade3.inf
ELNK3MCA	3Com Etherlink III MCA Adapter	oemnaden.inf
ELNK16	3Com Etherlink16/ EtherLink16 TP Adapter	oemnade1.inf
AM1500T	Advanced Micro Devices AM2100/ AM1500T Adapter	oemnadam.inf
AMDPCI	AMD PCNET Family Ethernet Adapter	oemnadap.inf
MAPLE	COMPAQ 32-Bit DualSpeed Token-Ring Controller	oemnadnf.inf
NETFLX	COMPAQ NetFlex/ NetFlex-2 ENET-TR Controller	oemnadnf.inf
BONSAI	COMPAQ NetFlex-2 DualPort ENET Controller	oemnadnf.inf
RODAN	COMPAQ NetFlex-2 DualPort TR Controller	oemnadnf.inf
DURANGO	COMPAQ NetFlex-2 TR Controller	oemnadnf.inf
LT200	COPS/DayStar Digital LocalTalk Adapter	oemnadlt.inf
LT200MC	COPS/DayStar Digital LocalTalk Adaptes (MCA)	oemnadlm.inf
DE425	DEC DE425 EtherWORKS Turbo EISA Adapter	oemnaddt.inf
DE434	DEC DE434 EtherWORKS Turbo PCI TP Adapter	oemnaddt.inf
DE435	DEC DE435 EtherWORKS Turbo PCI Adapter	oemnaddt.inf
DE450	DEC DE450 EtherWORKS Turbo PCI Adapter	oemnaddt.inf
DE500	DEC DE500 Fast Ethernet PCI Adapter	oemnaddt.inf

continues

Table 4.1. Continued

Network Option Name	Literal String	INF File
DEC100	DEC EtherWORKS LC Adapter	oemnadd1.inf
DECETHERWORKS-TURBO	DEC EtherWORKS Turbo Adapter	oemnadd2.inf
DEC422	DEC EtherWORKS Turbo EISA Adapter	oemnadd4.inf
DEC101	DEC EtherWORKS Turbo/LC Adapter	oemnadd1.inf
DEC300	DEC FDDIcontroller/EISA	oemnadd3.inf
DEFPA	DEC FDDIcontroller/PCI	oemnaddf.inf
MULTIA	DEC multia's Ethernet Controller	oemnaddt.inf
DC21040	DEC PCI Ethernet DECchip 21040	oemnaddt.inf
DC21041	DEC PCI Ethernet DECchip 21041	oemnaddt.inf
DC21140	DEC PCI Fast Ethernet DECchip 21140	oemnaddt.inf
DC21142	DEC PCI Fast Ethernet DECchip 21142	oemnaddt.inf
DECSTAT	DEC Turbo Channel Ethernet Adapter	oemnadde.inf
DATAFIREST	Digi DataFire— ISA1S/T Adapter	oemnaddi.inf
DATAFIREU	Digi DataFire—ISA1U Adapter	oemnaddi.inf
DATAFIRE4ST	Digi DataFire—ISA4S/T Adapter	oemnaddi.inf
PCIMACISA	Digi PCIMAC—ISA Adapter	oemnaddi.inf
PCIMACMC	Digi PCIMAC—MC Adapter	oemnaddi.inf
PCIMAC4	Digi PCIMAC/4 Adapter	oemnaddi.inf
NE2000IBMCOMPAT	IBM Ethernet PCMCIA and Compatible Adapter	oemnadni.inf
IBMTOK	IBM Token Ring (ISA/PCMCIA) Adapter	oemnadtk.inf
IBMTOKMC	IBM Token Ring 4/16 Adapter /A	oemnadtm.inf

Chapter 4: Customizing the Installation of NT 93

Network Option Name	Literal String	INF File
IBMTOKA	IBM Token Ring Adapter /A	oemnadtm.inf
IBMTOK2ISA	IBM Token-Ring Network 16/4 ISA Adapter II	oemnadt2.inf
EE16	Intel Ether Express 16 LAN Adapter	oemnadin.inf
EE16MC	Intel Ether Express MCA Adapter	oemnadim.inf
IEEPRO	Intel EtherExpress PRO Ethernet Adapter	oemnadep.inf
MSMDGMPSM16	Madge Smart 16 Ringnode	oemnadma.inf
MSMDGMPATP	Madge Smart 16/4 AT Plus Ringnode	oemnadma.inf
MSMDGMPISA	Madge Smart 16/4 AT Ringnode	oemnadma.inf
MSMDGMPEISA	Madge Smart 16/4 EISA Ringnode	oemnadma.inf
MSMDGMPISACP	Madge Smart 16/4 ISA Client Plus Ringnode	oemnadma.inf
MSMDGMPPNP	Madge Smart 16/4 ISA Client PnP Ringnode	oemnadma.inf
MSMDGMPISAC	Madge Smart 16/4 ISA Client Ringnode	oemnadma.inf
MSMDGMPMCA	Madge Smart 16/4 MC Ringnode	oemnadma.inf
MSMDGMPMC32	Madge Smart 16/4 MC32 Ringnode	oemnadma.inf
MSMDGMPPC	Madge Smart 16/4 PC Ringnode	oemnadma.inf
MSMDGMPPCI	Madge Smart 16/4 PCI Ringnode	oemnadma.inf
MSMDGMPPCIBM	Madge Smart 16/4 PCI Ringnode (BM)	oemnadma.inf
MSMDGMPPCMCIA	Madge Smart 16/4 PCMCIA Ringnode	oemnadma.inf
MICRODYNEPCMCIA	Microdyne NE4000 PCMCIA Adapter	oemnadni.inf
LOOP	MS Loopback Adapter	oemnadlb.inf
NE2000MCA	NE/2 and Compatible MC Adapter	oemnadnm.inf

continues

94   Part I: Basic Configuration of an Unattended Installation

Table 4.1.   Continued

Network Option Name	Literal String	INF File
NPEISA	Network Peripherals FDDI EISA	oemnadnp.inf
NPMCA	Network Peripherals FDDI MCA	oemnadfd.inf
NE1000	Novell NE1000 Adapter	oemnadn1.inf
NE2000	Novell NE2000 Compatible Adapter	oemnadn2.inf
NE2000SOCKETEA	Novell NE2000 Socket EA Adapter	oemnadn2.inf
NE3200	Novell NE3200 EISA Adapter	oemnadne.inf
NE4000PCMCIA	Novell NE4000 PCMCIA Adapter	oemnadni.inf
AM1500T1	Novell/Anthem NE1500T Adapter	oemnadam.inf
AM1500T2	Novell/Anthem NE2100 Adapter	oemnadam.inf
P189X	ProNET-4/16 p189X NIC	oemnadpm.inf
P1390	Proteon p139X Adapter	oemnadp3.inf
P1990	Proteon p199X Adapter	oemnadp9.inf
WD8003EA	SMC (WD) 8003E /A	oemnadwm.inf
WD8003WA	SMC (WD) 8003W /A	oemnadwm.inf
WD8013EPA	SMC (WD) 8013EP /A	oemnadwm.inf
WD8013WPA	SMC (WD) 8013WP /A	oemnadwm.inf
SMCISA	SMC (WD) EtherCard	oemnadwd.inf
UBPC	Ungermann-Bass Ethernet NIUpc Adapter	oemnadub.inf
UBPCEOTP	Ungermann-Bass Ethernet NIUpc/EOTP Adapter	oemnadub.inf
UBPS	Ungermann-Bass Ethernet NIUps Adapter	oemnadum.inf

Table 4.2.   Network Adapter File Located in the \DRVLIB.NIC Subdirectory

Option Name	Literal String
3C508	3Com 3C508 ISA 16-bit Ethernet Adapter
ELINK527	3Com 3C527 Etherlink/MC 32 Adapter
3C592	3Com EtherLink III EISA Bus-Master Adapter (3C592)
3C590	3Com EtherLink III PCI Bus-Master Adapter (3C590)
3C597	3Com Fast EtherLink EISA 10/100Base-T Adapter (3C597)

Option Name	Literal String
3C595	3Com Fast EtherLink PCI 10/100Base-T Adapter (3C595)
3C905	3Com Fast EtherLink XL Adapter (3C905)
FLNK	3Com FDDILink EISA LAN Adapter
TLNK3EISA	3Com TokenLink III ISA Adapter in EISA mode (3C619B)
ACCNT	Accton EN166x MPX2 PnP Ethernet Adapter
ACCTONEN2216	Accton EN2216 Ethernet PCMCIA Adapter
ALANE0	Adaptec ATM LAN Emulation Adapter
AT1700	Allied Telesyn AT1700 Ethernet Adapter
AT1700	Allied Telesyn AT1720 Ethernet Adapter
A2560PCI	Allied Telesyn AT-2560 Series PCI/100 Ethernet Adapter
ANDTOK	Andrew ISA IIA Token Ring Adapter
E21XX	Cabletron E21XX Ethernet Adapter
E22XX	Cabletron E22XX Ethernet Adapter
F30XX	Cabletron F30XX FDDI Adapter
F70XX	Cabletron F70XX FDDI Adapter
T20XX	Cabletron T20XX Token-Ring Adapter
EMPCI	Cogent eMASTER+ PCI Adapter
CPQNDIS	Compaq Ethernet LAN Card
NetFlex3	Compaq NetFlex-3 Controller
$enet	Compex ENET16 P/PNP Ethernet Adapter
IRMAtrac	DCA IRMAtrac Token-Ring Adapter
DigiSyncFR	Digi SyncPort Frame Relay Adapter
DigiSyncX25	Digi SyncPort X.25 Adapter
DLINKDE220	D-Link DE-220 ISA Ethernet Adapter
DLINKDE650	D-Link DE-650 Ethernet PCMCIA Adapter
Diehl_DIVA	Eicon DIVA ISDN ISA Adapter
Diehl_DIVAPCM	Eicon DIVA PCMCIA ISDN Adapter
Diehl_DIVAPRO	Eicon DIVA PRO ISDN Adapter with Advanced DSP
Diehl_S2M	Eicon Primary Rate ISDN Adapter
Diehl_QUADRO	Eicon QUADRO ISDN Adapter
Diehl_SCOM	Eicon SCOM ISDN Adapter
Diehl_WAN	Eicon Virtual WAN-Miniport ISDN Interface
ECCARDS	Eicon WAN Adapters
HPTXPCI	HP 10/100TX PCI Ethernet Adapter
HP27245	HP 27245A PC LAN Adapter/8 TP

continues

Table 4.2. Continued

Option Name	Literal String
HPMCA	HP 27246A MC LAN Adapter/16 TP
HP27247A	HP 27247A PC LAN Adapter/16 TP
HP27247B	HP 27247B PC LAN Adapter/16 TP Plus
HP27250	HP 27250 PC LAN Adapter/8 TL
HP27252A	HP 27252A PC LAN Adapter/16 TL Plus
J2573A	HP DeskDirect (J2573A) 10/100 ISA LAN Adapter
J2577A	HP DeskDirect (J2577A) 10/100 EISA LAN Adapter
J2585A	HP DeskDirect (J2585A) 10/100 PCI LAN Adapter
J2585B	HP DeskDirect (J2585B) 10/100 PCI LAN Adapter
J2970A	HP DeskDirect (J2970A) 10BaseT/2 PCI LAN Adapter
J2973A	HP DeskDirect (J2973A) 10BaseT PCI LAN Adapter
IBMFEPCI	IBM 100/10 PCI Ethernet Adapter
IBMTOK4	IBM Auto 16/4 Token-Ring ISA Adapter
STREAMER	IBM Auto LANStreamer PCI Adapter
IBMISAETHER	IBM ISA Ethernet Adapter
IBMENIIN	IBM LAN Adapter/A for Ethernet
QUADENET	IBM PeerMaster Server Adapter
STREAMER	IBM Streamer Family Adapters
ETH16I	ICL EtherTeam16i Adapter
ETH32	ICL EtherTeam32 Adapter
E100BPCI	Intel 82557-based 10/100 Ethernet PCI Adapter
E10PCI	Intel EtherExpress PRO/10 PCI LAN Adapter
EPRONT	Intel EtherExpress PRO/10+ ISA Adapter
E10PPCI	Intel EtherExpress PRO/10+ PCI Adapter
E100BEXP	Intel EtherExpress PRO/100B PCI Adapter
FL32	Intel Flash32 EISA LAN Adapter
TKXP16	Intel TokenExpress 16/4 Adapter
TKXP32	Intel TokenExpress Server Adapter
LINKSYSE16	LinkSys Ether16 LAN Card
LINKSYSEC2T	LinkSys EthernetCard PCMCIA
LEC	Madge ATM LAN Emulation Client
BLUTOK	Madge Blue+ Token Ring Adapter
CC10BT	Megahertz CC10BT/2 Ethernet PCMCIA Adapter
XJEM3288	Megahertz XJEM3288 Ethernet+Modem PCMCIA Adapter
NE100PCI	Microdyne NE10/100 PCI Adapter
MGSL	MicroGate SyncLink Internet Adapter

Chapter 4: Customizing the Installation of NT   97

Option Name	Literal String
NSCNE4100	National Semiconductor InfoMover NE4100
NCRTOK	NCR StarLAN 16/4 Token-Ring Adapter
NPAT2	Network Peripherals FDDI—AT2
NPAT3	Network Peripherals FDDI—AT3
NCPF	Network Peripherals NuCard PCI FDDI
NiwRAS	Niwot Networks NiwRAS Adapter
GOCARD	Olicom Ethernet GoCard
OCE2XM	Olicom Ethernet ISA/IV Adapter
O100PCI	Olicom Ethernet PCI 10/100 Adapter
OCE4XMP10	Olicom Ethernet PCI/II 10 Adapter
OCE4XMP100	Olicom Ethernet PCI/II 10/100 Adapter
GOCARDMF	Olicom GoCard ET/Modem 288
PCMCIA	Olicom GoCard TR 16/4
COMBO	Olicom GoCard TR/Modem 144
OCTK16	Olicom Token Ring 16/4 Adapter
OCTK32	Olicom Token Ring Server Adapter
OTCJODNT	Ositech Jack of Diamonds Trumpcard
ES3210	Racal Interlan ES3210 EISA Ethernet Adapter
NI6510	Racal InterLan XLerator/EB/NI6510 Adapters
RTL8029	Realtek RTL8029 PCI Adapter
RnsFDDI	RNS 2200 PCI FDDI LAN Controller
SMC8216	SMC 8216 EtherCard Elite16 Ultra
SMC8416	SMC 8416 EtherEZ
SMC8432	SMC 8432 EtherPower PCI Ethernet Adapter
SMC9232	SMC 9232 Fast Ethernet Adapter
SMC9332	SMC 9332 EtherPower10/100 PCI Fast Ethernet Adapter
SMC8232	SMC EISA EtherCard Elite32 Ultra Adapter
ACLSER	Star Gate ACL/Avanstar Family Adapter
SKTOKNT	SysKonnect SK-NET 4/16+ Token Ring Adapter
SKFENT	SysKonnect SK-NET EISA FDDI Adapter
SKFPNT	SysKonnect SK-NET FDDI PCI Adapter
SKETHNT	SysKonnect SK-NET G16 Ethernet Adapters
SKETHNT	SysKonnect SK-NET G32+ Ethernet Adapters
SKFINT	SysKonnect SK-NET ISA FDDI Adapter
SKFMNT	SysKonnect SK-NET MCA FDDI Adapter
SKTOKNT_PCI	SysKonnect SK-NET Token Ring PCI Adapter

continues

Table 4.2. Continued

Option Name	Literal String
SKTOKNT	SysKonnect SK-NET TR4/16+ Token Ring Adapter
TC$4045e	Thomas-Conrad TC4045 Token Ring Adapter
TC$4046e	Thomas-Conrad TC4046 Token Ring Adapter
AL56	U.S. Robotics Allegra 56 Frame Relay
ALT1	U.S. Robotics Allegra T1 Frame Relay
USRBRI	U.S. Robotics Sportster ISDN Adapter
WAVELAN_ISA	WaveLAN ISA Bus Adapter
WAVELAN_MCA	WaveLAN MCA Bus Adapter
CENDIS3	Xircom CreditCard Ethernet
CE2XPS	Xircom CreditCard Ethernet IIps
CEM28XPS	Xircom CreditCard Ethernet+Modem 28.8
CM2NDIS3	Xircom CreditCard Ethernet+Modem II
CTNDNT	Xircom CreditCard Token Ring
XCSPE2	Xircom Pocket Ethernet II
XCSPE3	Xircom Pocket Ethernet III

If a driver for a specific network adapter currently exists within NT's driver libraries, it can be installed using the options available under the [Network] section of an UNATTEND.TXT or .UDB file using either the InstallAdapters= or Detect Adapters= option.

```
InstallAdapters= CompaqNetcard

[CompaqNetcard]
NETFLX=NetFlexParams

[NetFlexParams]
Tranceiver=0
BusType=1
BusNumber=0
```

It is important to note that if you are going to be relying on NT's native detection and installation of the appropriate driver during an unattended installation, the \DRVLIB.NIC subdirectory may be required on your DSP, should the corresponding driver be stored there.

Determining which adapter parameters to use during an unattended installation can be done by manually installing the desired network adapter onto a test NT system and then checking the system's Registry for the necessary information to place in the UNATTEND.TXT file under the netcard's parameters. After the card is installed, open the system Registry and locate the key ServiceName under HKEY_LOCAL_MACHINE\SOFTWARE\Microsoft\ Windows NT\ CurrentVersion\NetworkCards\1 (see Figure 4.1).

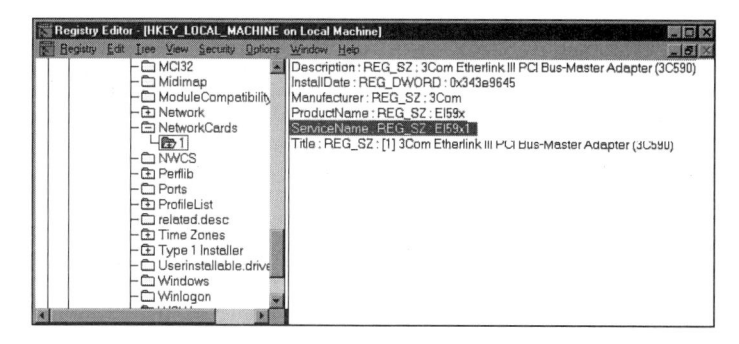

Chapter 4: Customizing the Installation of NT 99

Figure 4.1. *Registry information for* Netcards\1.

This key provides the installer with the name of the network adapter driver that has been installed under the Services section of the Registry. Figure 4.1 shows the system Registry information for an NT workstation using a 3COM EtherLink III 3C590 Bus Mastering PCI network adapter.

Next, go to HKEY_LOCAL_MACHINE\SYSTEM\CurrentControlSet\ Services\(Network Adapter Service Name)\Parameters (see Figure 4.2).

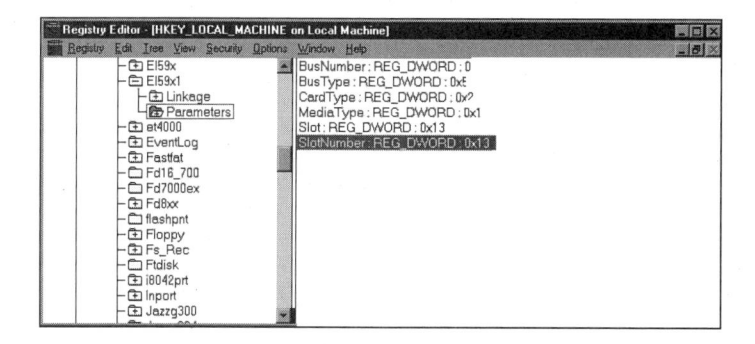

Figure 4.2. *Network interface card parameters.*

Each of the values present in the preceding screen can be placed under the [Netcard Parameters] section of the UNATTEND.TXT file, with the hex values translated into decimal values when moved to the Answer file. Next are the values and strings taken from the Netcard key of the Registry (from Figure 4.2):

```
BusNumber: REG_DWORD: 0
BusType: REG_DWORD: 0x5
CardType: REG_DWORD: 0x2
MediaType: REG_DWORD: 0x1
Slot: REG_DWORD: 0x13
SlotNumber: REG_DWORD: 0x13
```

This translates into the Answer file as follows:

```
[AdaptersList]
3C590 = 3C590Params

[3C590Params]
BusNumber=0
BusType=5
CardType=2
MediaType=1
Slot=19
SlotNumber=19
```

Notice how the parameters appear in both areas: hexadecimal in the Registry and decimal in the Answer file.

Tip

If you are having trouble converting numbers in the Registry from hex to decimal format, open the Registry using REGEDT32 and locate the specified entry that appears in hexadecimal format. Double-click on the entry and it appears in the DWORD Editor (see Figure 4.3). Select the Decimal option button, and the entry appears in decimal format (see Figure 4.4). The decimal entry can be used in the UNATTEND.TXT file for that adapter setting, which is converted back to hex during the unattended process.

Troubleshooting Tip

Be sure that you do not save the entry back to the Registry in decimal format by clicking the Cancel button after you are finished.

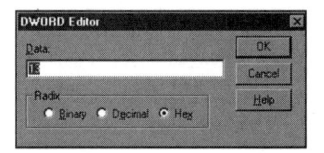

Figure 4.3. *Hexadecimal value entry in the DWORD Editor.*

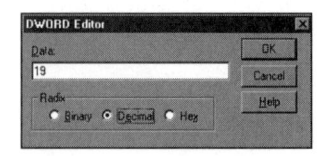

Figure 4.4. *Decimal value entry in the DWORD Editor.*

Chapter 4: Customizing the Installation of NT   101

If you open the 3C590 OEMSETUP.INF file and search for the adapter name under the [InstallOption] section header, you can verify some of the settings found in the Registry against what may be in the installation .INF.

```
; PCI (3c595, 3c590)
;
set BusTypeNum = 5
set BusMaster = "YES"
set Bus = "PCI"
ifstr(i) $(Option) == "3C595"
    set CardType = 0
else
    set CardType = 2
endif
endif
;;
;; If we used the OS to detect the card, then we already know bus
;;and slot information.
;;
ifint $(NTDetected) == $(TRUE)
    set BusNumber = $(DetectedBusNum)
    set SlotNum = $(DetectedSlotNum)
    set BusInterfaceType = $(BusTypeNum)
;
; Note: we need to record SlotNumber too so that we can use the
; "IsNetCardAlreadyInstalled" routine_
```

Because the .INF contains certain SET parameters below the detected card type 3c590, certain keys are set automatically as the card is installed and are therefore not necessarily required in the UNATTEND.TXT file. Also, the additional parameter of BusMaster= can be added to determine whether or not the card is permitted to function as a bus-mastering card. The final adapter parameters in the UNATTEND.TXT file may look like this:

```
[AdaptersList]
3C590 = 3C590Params

[3C590Params]
BusNumber=0
CardType=2
Slot=15
BusMaster=No
```

Bus-mastering has been disabled in this installation, rather than using the .INF default of Yes.

Replacing Device Drivers from the NT CD-ROM with Those from the Manufacturer

If an adapter file currently exists in the retail CD-ROM drive, the corresponding driver from the manufacturer can, in some instances, be used to replace that driver, taking its place on the DSP.

It is important to note that care should be used when replacing drivers from the retail CD-ROM with those from the manufacturer because updated OEM drivers may include some additional functionality and could require additional configuration during their installation. Careful comparison of the .INF used to install both the retail CD-ROM drivers and those from the manufacturer will best assure a trouble-free installation.

This can be done using any standard text editor, checking the .INFs for differences. In many cases, the driver itself can be replaced, leaving the retail CD-ROM installation .INF in place to install the updated driver. To do this, it must first be determined if the driver is located in the \i386 directory or the \DRVLIB.NIC subdirectory. If the corresponding file is located in the \i386 directory, locate the compressed version of the retail CD-supplied driver and delete or rename it; then copy the newer driver to the same directory.

If the .INF file needs to be replaced, you must first rename the OEM-supplied .INF, normally named OEMSETUP.INF, to match the name of the retail CD-ROM version's .INF file for the corresponding driver. Use Table 4.1 to locate the appropriate filename. Next, delete or rename the retail CD-ROM version of the .INF used to install the particular adapter. There is no need to compress the newly copied-over .INF or network adapter driver file. The installation is able to properly identify them in their uncompressed state and copy them both to the target system during the unattended process.

If the driver being replaced is one which exists in the \DRVLIB.NIC subdirectory, simply open the subdirectory under the \DRVLIB.NIC directory that is named for the adapter and replace the driver file. The .INF file used to install the driver should probably not be replaced, unless the newest .INF file provides some additional functionality that is not present in the retail CD-ROM version. An example of this might be replacing a driver that is currently not unattended-aware with one that is. (For more information on unattended-aware installation files, see the section "Scripting a Network Adapter .INF to be 'Unattended-Aware'" later in this chapter.)

For example, to replace the retail CD-ROM driver for 3COM's Etherlink III (3C509), do the following:

Chapter 4: Customizing the Installation of NT 103

1. Check Tables 4.1 and 4.2 for the location of the driver and its .INF.
2. Because it is located in the \i386 directory, locate the file elnk3.sy_ and rename it **elnk3.old**.
3. Copy the OEM-supplied file elnk3.sys to the \i386 directory.
4. Run the automated setup, testing for a proper installation of the new driver.

These steps should enable you to replace drivers currently available on the Windows NT Retail CD-ROM with OEM-supplied ones. But what about adding network adapter drivers for network interface cards that are not currently on the Windows NT Retail CD-ROM?

Installing OEM-supplied drivers can be accomplished in a number of different ways, depending on what suits your installation requirements. They can be installed using either an UNATTEND.TXT or .UDB file. The next example is a section of an UNATTEND.TXT used to install an OEM network adapter.

```
[Network]
InstallAdapters=[OEMAdapter]

[OEMAdapter]
OEMName=OEMParams, c:\Oemdrv

[OEMParams]
Tranceiver=0
InterruptNumber=5
IoBaseAddress=768
BusType=1
BusNumber=0
```

In this example, the adapter is referenced in the UNATTEND.TXT file. The location of the adapter driver files has been specified in the key OEMName= as c:\Oemdrv. This directory is one which can be created by using the \OEM\C\ directory under the DSP by creating an additional directory \Oemdrv and placing the adapter installation files there. This makes the drivers accessible, should they need to be reinstalled at some later point.

In most cases, the preceding method should prove effective. For those of you familiar with NT 3.51, the solution used to add drivers to the installation can still be used with NT 4.0 as an alternative.

The next example looks at installing 3COM's 3C59X network adapter driver using this optional method:

1. From the CD-ROM, copy the contents the directory \drvlib.nic\3c59x found on your Retail CD-ROM to your DSP.

2. Copy two files over, the OEMSETUP.INF and the EL59X.SYS files. Rename the OEMSETUP.INF to **OEMNAD*xx*.INF** (where *xx* is a unique character sequence not in use).

3. An unattended installation uses the DOSNET.INF file to identify those files which need to be copied during the first portion of the setup to the temporary directories C:\$WIN_NT$.~LS and C:\$WIN_NT$.~BT. Thus, it must be edited to include the newly copied over files as well. With Notepad, edit the file DOSNET.INF.

4. Add the following lines below the [FILES] section of DOSNET.INF:

   ```
   d1,oemnadxx.inf
   d1,el59x.sys
   ```

5. Open the file TXTSETUP.SIF found on your DSP and add the following lines under [SourceDisksFiles]. Ensure that they are added as they appear here.

   ```
   el59x.sys    = 1,,,,,,,,4,1
   oemnadxx.inf = 1,,,,,,,,2,0,0
   ```

   (As was stated earlier in the book, the file TXTSETUP.SIF is used to determine which files are copied over to target system during text mode setup.)

6. Open the file OEMNADZZ.INF in a text editor. This file is used to determine the files required to install network adapters under NT. You are first required to remove the read-only attributes from the file and extract it before moving to edit it. Use the version of EXPAND.EXE found on the Windows NT Retail CD-ROM to access the following:

`attrib -r oemnadzz.in_`	Removes the Read-Only attribute from the file.
`expand oemnadzz.in_ oemnadzz.inf`	Expands the file into the current directory.
`del` or `ren oemnadzz.in_`	Deletes [del] or renames [ren] the original compressed file.

7. Locate the file OEMNADZZ.INF found in the subdirectory of your DSP (which contains the installation files for NT) and open it in a text editor. Comment with the use of a semicolon the following lines in the following sections of the file:

   ```
   [PCIOptions]
   ;3C590

   [PCIFilename]
   ```

```
;drvlib.nic\3C59X\OEMSETUP.INF
;drvlib.nic\3C59X\OEMSETUP.INF

[EISAFilename]

;drvlib.nic\3C59X\OEMSETUP.INF
;drvlib.nic\3C59X\OEMSETUP.INF
```

This change causes the installation not to use the 3C59X drivers located in the DRVLIB.NIC on the DSP but to instead use the specified adapter files copied onto the DSP earlier. Save the changes to this file and ensure that it is placed with the installation files on your DSP.

8. Add the necessary lines regarding the configuration of the network adapter to the UNATTEND.TXT file:

```
[AdaptersList]
3C590 = 3C590Params

[3C590Params]
BusMaster=No
Bus=PCI
Slot=8
BusNo=0
```

This final example is a legacy option for administrators familiar with NT 3.51, but it can serve as an excellent example of the internal workings of the files involved in the process of installing network adapters. It is useful in that it shows how the DOSNET.INF and OEMNADZZ.INF may be modified to look for new drivers in a location other than the standard locations, and without having to modify the UNATTEND.TXT file.

Scripting a Network Adapter .INF to be "Unattended-Aware"

During an unattended installation of Windows NT, the Setup program may halt during the GUI phase of networking, prompting the installer for information regarding the adapter's configuration. This usually occurs because the .INF file used to install the drivers for the network adapter is not *unattended-aware*; that is, it is not designed to check the UNATTEND.TXT file for information regarding the configuration of the network adapter without prompting for user intervention.

Tables 4.3 and 4.4 highlight which adapters included with the Windows NT retail CD-ROM are already "unattended-aware" and require no modification.

Table 4.3. *"Unattended-Aware" Network Adapter Files in the \i386 Directory*

Network Option Name	Literal String	INF File
ELNKII	3Com Etherlink II Adapter (also II/16 and II/16 TP)	oemnade2.inf
ELNK3ISA509	3Com Etherlink III ISA/PCMCIA Adapter	oemnade3.inf
ELNK16	3Com Etherlink16/EtherLink16 TP Adapter	oemnade1.inf
AM1500T	Advanced Micro Devices AM2100/AM1500T Adapter	Oemnadam.inf
LT200	COPS/DayStar Digital LocalTalk Adapter	oemnadlt.inf
DEC100	DEC EtherWORKS LC Adapter	Oemnadd1.inf
DECETHERWORKSTURBO	DEC EtherWORKS Turbo Adapter	Oemnadd2.inf
DEC101	DEC EtherWORKS Turbo/LC Adapter	Oemnadd1.inf
DEFPA	DEC FDDIcontroller/PCI	Oemnaddf.inf
DECSTAT	DEC Turbo Channel Ethernet Adapter	Oemnadde.inf
NE2000IBMCOMPAT	IBM Ethernet PCMCIA and Compatible Adapter	Oemnadni.inf
IBMTOK	IBM Token Ring (ISA/PCMCIA) Adapter	Oemnadtk.inf
IBMTOKMC	IBM Token Ring 4/16 Adapter /A	oemnadtm.inf
IBMTOKA	IBM Token Ring Adapter /A	oemnadtm.inf
IBMTOK2ISA	IBM Token-Ring Network 16/4 ISA Adapter II	oemnadt2.inf
EE16	Intel Ether Express 16 LAN Adapter	oemnadin.inf
EE16MC	Intel Ether Express MCA Adapter	oemnadim.inf
IEEPRO	Intel EtherExpress PRO Ethernet Adapter	oemnadep.inf
MSMDGMPSM16	Madge Smart 16 Ringnode	oemnadma.inf
MSMDGMPATP	Madge Smart 16/4 AT Plus Ringnode	oemnadma.inf
MSMDGMPISA	Madge Smart 16/4 AT Ringnode	oemnadma.inf

Network Option Name	Literal String	INF File
MSMDGMPEISA	Madge Smart 16/4 EISA Ringnode	oemnadma.inf
MSMDGMPISACP	Madge Smart 16/4 ISA Client Plus Ringnode	oemnadma.inf
MSMDGMPPNP	Madge Smart 16/4 ISA Client PnP Ringnode	oemnadma.inf
MSMDGMPISAC	Madge Smart 16/4 ISA Client Ringnode	oemnadma.inf
MSMDGMPMCA	Madge Smart 16/4 MC Ringnode	oemnadma.inf
MSMDGMPMC32	Madge Smart 16/4 MC32 Ringnode	oemnadma.inf
MSMDGMPPC	Madge Smart 16/4 PC Ringnode	oemnadma.inf
MSMDGMPPCI	Madge Smart 16/4 PCI Ringnode	oemnadma.inf
MSMDGMPPCIBM	Madge Smart 16/4 PCI Ringnode (BM)	oemnadma.inf
MSMDGMPPCMCIA	Madge Smart 16/4 PCMCIA Ringnode	oemnadma.inf
MICRODYNEPCMCIA	Microdyne NE4000 PCMCIA Adapter	oemnadni.inf
LOOP	MS Loopback Adapter	oemnadlb.inf
NE2000MCA	NE/2 and Compatible MC Adapter	oemnadnm.inf
NE1000	Novell NE1000 Adapter	oemnadn1.inf
NE2000	Novell NE2000 Compatible Adapter	oemnadn2.inf
NE2000SOCKETEA	Novell NE2000 Socket EA Adapter	oemnadn2.inf
NE4000PCMCIA	Novell NE4000 PCMCIA Adapter	oemnadni.inf
AM1500T1	Novell/Anthem NE1500T Adapter	oemnadam.inf
AM1500T2	Novell/Anthem NE2100 Adapter	oemnadam.inf
P189X	ProNET-4/16 p189X NIC	oemnadpm.inf
P1390	Proteon p139X Adapter	oemnadp3.inf
P1990	Proteon p199X Adapter	oemnadp9.inf

continues

Table 4.3. Continued

Network Option Name	Literal String	INF File
SMCISA	SMC (WD) EtherCard	oemnadwd.inf
UBPC	Ungermann-Bass Ethernet NIUpc Adapter	oemnadub.inf
UBPCEOTP	Ungermann-Bass Ethernet NIUpc/EOTP Adapter	oemnadub.inf

Table 4.4. "Unattended-Aware" Network Adapter Files in the \DRVLIB.NIC Directory

Option Name	Literal String
3C592	3Com EtherLink III EISA Bus-Master Adapter (3C592)
3C590	3Com EtherLink III PCI Bus-Master Adapter (3C590)
3C597	3Com Fast EtherLink EISA 10/100Base-T Adapter (3C597)
3C595	3Com Fast EtherLink PCI 10/100Base-T Adapter (3C595)
3C905	3Com Fast EtherLink XL Adapter (3C905)
ACCNT	Accton EN166x MPX2 PnP Ethernet Adapter
ACCTONEN2216	Accton EN2216 Ethernet PCMCIA Adapter
ALANE0	Adaptec ATM LAN Emulation Adapter
DLINKDE220	D-Link DE-220 ISA Ethernet Adapter
DLINKDE650	D-Link DE-650 Ethernet PCMCIA Adapter
IBMTOK4	IBM Auto 16/4 Token-Ring ISA Adapter
IBMISAETHER	IBM ISA Ethernet Adapter
E100BPCI	Intel 82557-based 10/100 Ethernet PCI Adapter
E10PPCI	Intel EtherExpress PRO/10+ PCI Adapter
E100BEXP	Intel EtherExpress PRO/100B PCI Adapter
LINKSYSE16	LinkSys Ether16 LAN Card
LINKSYSEC2T	LinkSys EthernetCard PCMCIA
LEC	Madge ATM LAN Emulation Client
BLUTOK	Madge Blue+ Token Ring Adapter
XJEM3288	Megahertz XJEM3288 Ethernet+Modem PCMCIA Adapter
NSCNE4100	National Semiconductor InfoMover NE4100
OCE4XMP10	Olicom Ethernet PCI/II 10 Adapter
OCE4XMP100	Olicom Ethernet PCI/II 10/100 Adapter
PCMCIA	Olicom GoCard TR 16/4
COMBO	Olicom GoCard TR/Modem 144
OCTK16	Olicom Token Ring 16/4 Adapter

Chapter 4: Customizing the Installation of NT 109

If the network adapter you are currently using is not in either of these two tables, then the adapter installation files that have shipped with the NT CD-ROM are not currently usable without modification during an unattended installation.

The next thing to check is the manufacturer's Web or FTP site to see if the latest release of the driver has been updated to be "unattended-aware." If there are no unattended updates available, then the process of modifying the existing installation .INF must be done in order to script it into the unattended process.

To determine whether or not the OEM-supplied installation .INF file is unattended-aware, open the .INF file, usually named OEMSETUP.INF, in a standard text editor and search for the string STF_GUI_UNATTENDED. The editor should turn up several instances of the string; look for a line that contains code similar to the following:

```
ifstr $(!STF_GUI_UNATTENDED) == "YES"
            Debug-Output "$(InfFile) $(Option): Running in GUI unattended
mode"
            ifstr(i) $(!AutoNetInterfaceType) != ""
                set BusInterfaceType = $(!AutoNetInterfaceType)
            else
                set BusInterfaceType = 5
            endif
            ifstr(i) $(!AutoNetBusNumber) != ""
                set BusNumber = $(!AutoNetBusNumber)
            else
                set BusNumber = 0
            endif
```

If this code is present, then the installation .INF file is unattended-aware; the STF_GUI_UNATTENDED symbol tells the networking portion of the installation that it will be running in unattended mode. If it is not present, then the sections of the .INF file that call a user interface dialog option, (that causes dialog boxes or windows to pop up) known as *POPS*, during the installation process must be suppressed. The sections requiring user intervention must also be modified to instead call up the UTILITY.INF file. The UTILITY.INF file is used by Windows NT to assist in the installation of network-related parameters during the installation process. POPS code within the installation .INF usually looks like this:

```
adapteroptions = +
    Debug-Output "$(InfFile) $(Option): Adapteroptions"
    set from = adapteroptions
    read-syms FileDependentDlg$(!STF_LANGUAGE)
    SetHelpFile $(!STF_WINDOWSSYSPATH)"\"$(OptionHelpFile) $(MinHelpId)
$(MaxHelpId) $(Help$(Option)Id)

;begin POPS dialog

    ui start "InputDlg"
```

In order to bypass pop-up screens created by this code, the following section of additional code must be inserted into the installation .INF file directly after the line `adapteroptions = +`, so the code entered looks something like the following:

```
adapteroptions = +
  set from = adapteroptions
    ifstr(i) $(!STF_GUI_UNATTENDED) == "YES"
        ifstr(i) $(!AutoNetInterfaceType) != ""
        set BusInterfaceType = $(!AutoNetInterfaceType)
        else
        set BusInterfaceType = 1
        endif
        ifstr(i) $(!AutoNetBusNumber) != ""
        set BusNumber = $(!AutoNetBusNumber)
        else
        set BusNumber = 0
        endif
            goto skipoptions
    endif
```

> **Warning**
>
> *The `goto skipoptions` line refers to a subroutine which may or may not exist in the .INF file. The `skipoptions` subroutine must be used to bypass any GUI pop-ups that may occur during the automated netcard installation. If the `skipoptions` key does not exist, then examine the code under the `adapteroptions` string and search for the `goto` routine, which might have been replaced with the `skipoptions` subroutine. With this code in place, the `STF_GUI_UNATTENDED` symbol is used by NT's network installation process to reference the `STF_UNATTENDED_SECTION` symbol. This done, the setup process now knows what is necessary for the UTILITY.INF to use to reference the netcard Registry parameters that are present in the UNATTEND.TXT file.*

Next, search the installation .INF for the value, `Set NewValueList`; it should look something like this:

```
Set NewValueList = {+
      {type,     $(NoTitle), $(!REG_VT_SZ),       $(NetRuleSoftwareType)},+
      {use,      $(NoTitle), $(!REG_VT_SZ),       $(NetRuleSoftwareUse)}, +
      {bindform, $(NoTitle), $(!REG_VT_SZ),
$(NetRuleSoftwareBindForm)}, +
      {class,    $(NoTitle), $(!REG_VT_MULTI_SZ), $(NetRuleSoftwareClass)}, +
      {bindable, $(NoTitle), $(!REG_VT_MULTI_SZ),
$(NetRuleSoftwareBindable)}, +
      {InfOption, $(NoTitle), $(!REG_VT_SZ),      $(EnetOption)}+
      }
   Shell $(UtilityInf), AddValueList, $(Key_SoftwareNetRules), $(NewValueList)
```

Below the `Shell $(UtilityINF)...` line, add the following code:

Chapter 4: Customizing the Installation of NT 111

```
ifstr(i) $(!STF_GUI_UNATTENDED) == "YES"
    Shell $(UtilityInf), AddDefaultNetCardParameters,$(KeyParameters)
endif
```

This section of code is designed to prompt the UTILITY.INF file to obtain the necessary Registry parameters from the UNATTEND.TXT file, in turn passing that information on to the installation process for updating the target system Registry.

Finally, check the Registry parameters for the network interface card you are attempting to automate by looking on a system that currently has the card installed. All of the Registry parameters for the card should be `REG_DWORD` values, with the exception of the `IoBaseAddress` key, which is a `REG_SZ` value. If any of the parameters present in the Registry are not `REG_DWORD`, you may be required to perform additional configuration changes to the .INF file used to install the card. If the installation .INF is not using `REG_DWORD` values, then the .INF requires further modification to use that value type. This is usually under the `Set NewValueList` section but may exist elsewhere in the .INF and require further script changes:

```
Set NewValueList = {+
            {BusType,$(NoTitle),$(!REG_VT_DWORD),$(BusInterfaceType)},+
            {CardType,$(NoTitle),$(!REG_VT_DWORD),$(CardType)},+
            {MediaType,$(NoTitle),$(!REG_VT_DWORD),1},+
            }.
```

Summary of the Process

When attempting to make an OEM-supplied .INF file unattended-aware, follow these steps:

1. Check the Registry parameters for the netcard you are attempting to automate on a system that currently has it installed. Note that the Registry parameters are all `REG_DWORD` values, except for the `IoBaseAddress` key, which is a `REG_SZ` value. If the installation .INF is not using `REG_DWORD` values, then the .INF requires further modification to use that value type, which is usually under the `Set NewValueList` section but may exist elsewhere in the .INF and require further script changes:

    ```
    Set NewValueList = {+
                {BusType,$(NoTitle),$(!REG_VT_DWORD),$(BusInterfaceType)},+
                {CardType,$(NoTitle),$(!REG_VT_DWORD),$(CardType)},+
                {MediaType,$(NoTitle),$(!REG_VT_DWORD),1},+
                }.
    ```

2. Next, test your newly modified .INF in an unattended installation, noting any errors which may occur. Record them and re-check your .INF for errors or required changes.

112 Part I: Basic Configuration of an Unattended Installation

3. Finally, if the .INF correctly installs the adapter, check the new installation's Registry and compare it against that of a manual installation, ensuring that they share the automated install and possess the correct entries.

> ### Troubleshooting Tip
>
> Sometimes the error message The current netcard parameters are not verifiably correct and may result in usage problems or system failure. Use them anyway? *appears during the unattended installation of a network adapter. This is usually because the specified settings are different from those that the installation has detected. This message can also appear even though the data presented is correct.*
>
> *First, make sure that the adapter settings you have chosen are correct by running the installation on a test system and ensuring that no errors regarding the netcard parameters appear in the event log. If the adapter settings function, you can bypass the display of this pop-up window and the subsequent pause in the installation by editing the .INF further. Search for the key* WARNING *within the installation .INF. Next, add the following code:*
>
> ```
> Set from = adapteroptions
>     Set to = skipoptions
>     Shell $(UtilityInf),RegistryErrorString,VERIFY_WARNING
>     ifint $($ShellCode) != $(!SHELL_CODE_OK)
>     goto ShellCodeError
>     endif
>     set Error = $($R0)
>
>     ;Remove the Goto Warning line
>     ;Goto Warning
>
>     ;Add the Goto SkipOptions line
>     Goto SkipOptions
>
>     skipoptions = +
>         ifint $(OldVersionExisted)==$(TRUE)
> ```
>
> *This causes the installation to go directly to the* skipoptions *subroutine, bypassing the* WARNING *display. The actual* WARNING *text can be modified by opening the UTILITY.INF and searching for the text* VERIFY_WARNING. *The preceding text can be modified to display different text, should you want to alter it.*

Installing Specialized Video Adapters

During an unattended installation, Windows NT attempts to autodetect the correct display adapter type, but because of its limited detection options, it may not properly identify your adapter. It may instead replace your adapter with the standard VGA adapter type in 640×480 at 16 colors unless specified otherwise in the UNATTEND.TXT file.

When customizing your installation, it may be desirable or even necessary to specify the correct driver for your display adapter because many of the OEM manufacturers have new or recently updated drivers for NT. As with the network adapter setup in the previous section, the drivers must be specified in the UNATTEND.TXT file and referenced properly in an installation file type that the installation process can recognize, called the TXTSETUP.OEM. This is used to appropriately update the target system's driver and Registry information. The following is an example of the contents of a TXTSETUP.OEM used to install the Matrox Millenium video adapter:

```
TXTSETUP.OEM

[Disks]
d1 = "OEM Video Disk",\OEMVideo.tag,\

[Defaults]
DISPLAY = MGA64

[DISPLAY]
MGA64 = Matrox Millenium 64 - OEM"

[Files.display.mga64]
driver = d1,mga64.sys,mga64
dll = d1,mga64.dll

[Config.mga64]
value=device0,InstalledDisplayDrivers,REG_MULTI_SZ,mga64
value=device0,VgaCompatible,REG_DWORD,0
```

> **Tip**
>
> *If you want to use this file to install other video adapter drivers, it is easy to do so. The preceding example uses Matrox drivers, but in most cases you can replace instances of* MGA64 *in each section with your specific display adapter name. Under* [Files.display.(display adapter name)], *replace the appropriate sections with the necessary drivers from the manufacturer.*

After this file has been created, it should be copied to the OEM\TEXTMODE subdirectory on the DSP. There, it is copied along with the adapter files to the target system and referenced in the UNATTEND.TXT:

```
[Unattended]
OemPreinstall = yes

[DisplayDrivers]
"Matrox Millenium - OEM" = OEM

[Display]
BitsPerPel  = 16
XResolution = 1024
YResolution = 768
VRefresh    = 70
AutoConfirm = 1

[OemBootFiles]
MGA64.SYS
MGA64.DLL
TXTSETUP.OEM
```

The line `OemPreinstall = yes` causes the automated setup process to include the additional files and installation instructions located in the `$OEM$` subdirectory of the DSP during the deployment. The sections `[DisplayDrivers]` and `[Display]` inform the installation of the correct driver type and settings to use during setup, and the `[OemBootFiles]` section lets the installation know which files to use to correctly install and configure the adapter.

When checking the parameters for use in the UNATTEND.TXT file, you may want to check the Registry for an existing NT workstation currently using the same display adapter and for the correct parameters to use. Should you choose to insert custom settings, do the following:

1. Open HKEY_LOCAL_MACHINE\HARDWARE\DEVICEMAP\VIDEO; in the right-hand screen under the value `Device0` should appear the Registry entry for the display adapter.

2. Locate the entry from `Device0` in REGEDT32, which should appear as follows:

    HKEY_LOCAL_MACHINE\SYSTEM\CurrentControlSet \Services*(Display Adapter Service Name)*\Device0

3. In the right-hand window, the default settings for the display adapter card appear in hexadecimal format. Double-click on the entry and it opens in the DWORD Editor. You can then select the Hex option button to see what the entry is in decimal format and record it for use in your UNATTEND.TXT file.

4. Be sure to click Cancel when exiting so that you do not save the entry back to the Registry in decimal format.

More on Use of the TXTSETUP.OEM File and Writing Custom Installation Files

The TXTSETUP.OEM file is not used solely to install video adapter files; it is used to install any number of specialized drivers during the text mode portion of the installation process. This can include computer types (HALs), display adapters, keyboards drivers, mouse drivers, CD-ROM drivers, and SCSI drivers.

The format of a TXTSETUP.OEM file is the section name, [section], followed by the key and value(s):

```
[Section]
key = value1,value2,...
```

Comments can be placed in the TXTSETUP.OEM for informative purposes using either the pound sign (#) or a semicolon (;) at the beginning of each line:

```
#comment1
```

or

```
;comment2
```

Entries which contain commas, embedded spaces, or hashes need to be enclosed with double quotation marks (""entry"")

These sections are required to appear in a TXTSETUP.OEM in order for it to function properly:

The Disks section	[Disks]
The Defaults section	[Defaults]
The Components section	[Component]
The Files.component.ID section	[Files.component.ID]
The Config.KeyName section	[Config.KeyName]

The [Disks] Section

The [Disks] section is used to identify all of the information setup it requires to install the specified device.

```
[Disks]
d1 = device description, identifier filename, location of file
d2 = device description, identifier filename, location of file

d1, d2, d3,…
```

Each entry—d1, d2—is used to identify the corresponding disk used to install the device. The output

    device description

identifies the device to be installed. This is the "friendly" name that appears should the installer need to be prompted for the installation disk or correct file location. In the output

    identifier filename

filename is used to inform the installation that the correct disk installation set is being used to install the device. It's also referred to as the "marker" file. The output

    location of file

identifies the directory that contains the installation files. Do not use driver letters but do include directory identifiers. The \ specifies the root of where the marker file was located, which is the \$OEM$\TEXTMODE subdirectory on the DSP. A file cannot exist in a subdirectory of the \$OEM$\ TEXTMODE, such as \DISK1, which can translate into \$OEM$\TEXTMODE \DISK1. The setup fails with an error code of 18.

    [Disks]
    d1 = "Cirrus Logic 542x Linear Installation Diskette", \disk1, \

The [Defaults] Section

The [Defaults] section identifies the device category (SCSI, display, and so on) and the specific ID (OEMSCSI, clinear, and so on) used to install the specific device. For the output

    [Defaults]
    Component=ID

Component identifies the class of device being installed. They are computer (HAL), CD-ROM, display, keyboard, mouse, or SCSI device.

ID identifies the unique name of the component being installed. This unique name is used later in the [Components] section to identify the options available for a specified device. Next is an example:

    [Defaults]
    display = clinear

The [Component] Section

The [Component] section is used to define the installation options available for a specified device. The [Component] type being installed is used within the brackets, so if the component key in the [Defaults] section is DISPLAY, then the [Components] section header is [DISPLAY]:

```
[Component]
ID=Device Description
ID
```

Taken from the [Defaults] value bearing the same name, ID defines the unique string that identifies the installation option for the specified device.

Device Description is the description of the component being installed; for example:

```
[Display]
clinear = "Cirrus Logic 542x Linear"
```

The [Files.component.ID] Section

The [Files.component.ID] section is used to identify which files are copied and installed, should the device option be chosen. Separate sections must be present if more than one option should exist for any given device. So if two options should exist for a Display component, then two [Files.component.ID] section headings should exist for each.

```
[Files.component.ID]
filetype = file location, filename [keyname]
filetype
```

This key specifies the filetype that is used during the installation. The summary of available filetypes is contained in Table 4.5.

Table 4.5. Filetype Descriptions

Filetype	Description
driver	Can be used for all components. The file specified with this key is copied to %systemroot%\system32\drivers.
port	Used in the installation of keyboard mouse, or SCSI devices. This key is used to mark a difference between port and class drivers but is equivalent to the driver type.
class	Used when installing keyboard and mouse devices. Can be used to replace an existing driver. The file specified with this key is copied to %systemroot%\system32\drivers.

continues

118   Part I: Basic Configuration of an Unattended Installation

Table 4.5.   Continued

Filetype	Description
dll	Can be used for all components. Can be useful during the GDI portion of a display component installation. The file specified with this key is copied to %systemroot%\system32\.
hal	Used only to install a computer component. The file specified with this key is copied to %systemroot%\system32\hal.dll (80386/ 80486) or \os\winnt\hal.dll (ARC path).
inf	Can be used for all components. Defines the installation .INF that should be copied for use should a reinstallation become necessary. The file specified with this key is copied to %systemroot%\system32\.
detect	Used only to install a computer component (80386/ 80486). When used, it overwrites the existing hardware identifier (NTDETECT.COM) found in the root of C:\.

file location identifies the location of the file referenced, using the information regarding the component located in the [Disks] section at the beginning of the TXTSETUP.OEM file.

Filename is the name of the actual file used, minus any directory information. The file location key identifies the location of the filename specified.

The [KeyName] Section

[KeyName] is used to identify the section header containing Registry additions that need to be made after the file for a specified component is installed. This is usually used when using class, driver, or port filetypes. When specified, it is used in the section heading of [Config.KeyName].

```
[Files.Display.clinear]
dll = d1, framebuf.dll
driver = d1, clinear.sys, clinear
inf = d1, oemsetup.inf
```

The [Config.KeyName] Section

The [Config.KeyName] section is present when the KeyName option is present in the [Files.component.ID] section in the string identifying a class, port or driver filetype. This section is used to specify additions to the HKLM\SYSTEM\CurrentControlSet\Services portion of the Registry necessary for the specified filetype/component to function.

```
[Config.KeyName]
    value = subkey_name, value_name, value_type, value…
```

`value` identifies the Registry value that is automatically entered for the specified `KeyName`.

`subkey_name` specifies the subkey of HKLM\SYSTEM\CurrentControlSet\Services where the entry should be made. If the key is not present, it is created automatically. If an empty string is made using double quotations (`""`), then the addition is made under the HKLM\SYSTEM\CurrentControlSet\Services\KeyName.

`value_name` defines the value's name to be set within the key.

`value_type` identifies the data type of the entry, either REG_BINARY, REG_DWORD, REG_EXPAND_SZ, REG_MULTI_SZ, or REG_SZ.

`Value` identifies the actual entry to be made, and it is governed by the `value_type` by which it is defined. Should the `value_type` be `REG_DWORD`, the entry may be different than if it were `REG_SZ` because these entries have different requirements when used in the Registry.

More on Value Types and Corresponding Value Entries

In Table 4.6, the Registry data types determine what types of string entries are permissible and how they are interpreted by the operating system.

Table 4.6. Registry Data Type Entry Options

Data Type	Entry Options
REG_BINARY	One value is permitted. It must be a string of hexadecimal digits; each pair is interpreted as a byte value.
REG_DWORD	One value is permitted. It must be a string of 1–8 hexadecimal digits.
REG_EXPAND_SZ	One value is permitted. It is defined as the zero-terminated string to be stored.
REG_MULTI_SZ	More than one value is permitted. Each entry is interpreted as a component of the MULTISZ.
REG_SZ	One value is permitted. It is defined as the zero-terminated string to be stored.

```
[Config.clinear]
    value = Device0, DefaultSettings.BitsPerPel, REG_DWORD, 8
    value = Device0, DefaultSettings.Interlaced, REG_DWORD, 0
    value = Device0, DefaultSettings.VRefresh, REG_DWORD, 3c
```

120   Part I: Basic Configuration of an Unattended Installation

```
value = Device0, DefaultSettings.XResolution, REG_DWORD, 280
value = Device0, DefaultSettings.YResolution, REG_DWORD, 1e0
value = Device0, InstalledDisplayDrivers, REG_MULTI_SZ, framebuf
value = Device0, VgaCompatible, REG_DWORD, 1
```

So the final example, when placed together, looks like this:

```
[Disks]
d1 = "Cirrus Logic 542x Linear Installation Diskette", \disk1, \

[Defaults]
display = clinear

[Display]
clinear = "Cirrus Logic 542x Linear"

[Files.Display.clinear]
dll = d1, framebuf.dll
driver = d1, clinear.sys, clinear
inf = d1, oemsetup.inf

[Config.clinear]
value = Device0, DefaultSettings.BitsPerPel, REG_DWORD, 8
value = Device0, DefaultSettings.Interlaced, REG_DWORD, 0
value = Device0, DefaultSettings.VRefresh, REG_DWORD, 3c
value = Device0, DefaultSettings.XResolution, REG_DWORD, 280
value = Device0, DefaultSettings.YResolution, REG_DWORD, 1e0
value = Device0, InstalledDisplayDrivers, REG_MULTI_SZ, framebuf
value = Device0, VgaCompatible, REG_DWORD, 1
```

Adding and Removing NT's Accessories

Automated deployments of Windows NT run, by default, a "typical" installation type for the operating system. This type of installation may not be suitable for all types of deployments of Windows NT. A typical setup may include or exclude certain applications, accessories, and basic environment variables from which an administrator may want to choose when building a custom installation.

Modifying which accessories are installed again involves modifying their corresponding installation .INF files. They are as follows:

ACCESSOR.INF	MULTIMED.INF
COMMUNIC.INF	OPTIONAL.INF
GAMES.INF	PINBALL.INF
IMAGEVUE.INF	WORDPAD.INF
MMOPT.INF	

Chapter 4: Customizing the Installation of NT   121

Each of these files contains the necessary information for installing NT's available accessories and can be modified by altering the numerical that represents its particular installation type. The different types and their values are as follows:

- 0. Manual installation only (must be selected in order to be installed).
- 10. Typical or custom (installed by default in an automated installation as well as during a custom installation).
- 14. Typical, portable or custom (installed by default, as well as during custom and portable installations).

Table 4.7 offers a full listing of each accessory and its installation type.

Table 4.7. NT Accessories' Installation Type

.INF File Name	Accessories Controller	Default Installation Type
ACCESSOR.INF	Calculator	10 – Typical or Custom
	Character Map	10 – Typical or Custom
	Clipboard Viewer	14 – Typical, Portable or Custom
	Clock	
	Desktop Wallpaper	14 – Typical, Portable or Custom
	Document Templates	
	Mouse Pointers	0 – Manual Only
	Object Package	10 – Typical or Custom
	MS Paint	0 – Manual Only
	Quick View	14 – Typical, Portable or Custom
	Screen Savers Open GL	
	Standard Screen Savers	10 – Typical or Custom
		10 – Typical or Custom
		10 – Typical or Custom
		10 – Typical or Custom
COMMUNIC.INF	MS Chat	14 – Typical, Portable or Custom
	Phone Dialer	
	Hyper Terminal	14 – Typical, Portable or Custom
		14 – Typical, Portable or Custom
GAMES.INF	Freecell	0 – Manual Only
	Mine Sweeper	0 – Manual Only
	Solitaire	0 – Manual Only
IMAGEVUE.INF	Wang Imaging	10 – Typical or Custom
MMOPT.INF	Media Options	10 – Typical or Custom
	Musica Sounds	0 – Manual Only
	Jungle Sounds	0 – Manual Only

continues

Table 4.7. Continued

.INF File Name	Accessories Controller	Default Installation Type
	RobotZ Sounds	0 – Manual Only
	Utopia Sounds	0 – Manual Only
MULTIMED.INF	CD Player	14 – Typical, Portable or Custom
	Media Player	14 – Typical, Portable or Custom
	Sound Recorder	14 – Typical, Portable or Custom
	Volume Control	14 – Typical, Portable or Custom
OPTIONAL.INF	Accessibility Options	14 – Typical, Portable or Custom
PINBALL.INF	Space Cadet Table	0 – Manual Only
WORDPAD.INF	WordPad	10 – Typical or Custom

If you want to alter the existing scheme to suit your installation needs, you need to first expand the corresponding .INF file containing the setup options you want to alter. This must be done using the EXPAND.EXE found on the NT Retail CD-ROM under the \i386 subdirectory. Next is an example of how to expand the file for editing:

```
EXPAND IMAGEVUE.IN_ IMAGEVUE.INF
REN IMAGEVUE.IN_ IMAGEVUE.OLD
```

This example expands the file, IMAGEVUE.INF, in the same directory. The compressed file must be renamed so that it is not used in place of the modified IMAGEVUE.INF.

After the file has been expanded, open the file in any standard text editor and locate the section of the file related to the accessory you want to modify. The following example shows the Wang Imaging tool:

```
[ImageVue]
CopyFiles       = ImageVueCopyFiles, ImageVueCopyFiles_HELP, mfcdllsx.files,
SharedCopyFiles, ImageOcxs, SampleFiles
Delfiles        = ImageVue.Win.Del, OldFiles
AddReg          = ImageVueReg, ImageVue.install.reg, mfcdllsx.register
OptionDesc      = %IMAGEVUEOPT_DESC%
Tip             = %IMAGEVUEOPT_TIP%
Parent          = AccessTop
UpdateInis      = ImageVueInis

; This line controls the Installation type for the accessory
InstallType     = 10 ;Typical, Custom.
```

Chapter 4: Customizing the Installation of NT   123

```
IconIndex     = 65  ;Windows Logo mini-icon for dialogs.
Uninstall     = ImageVue_remove
Upgrade       = ImageVueUpgrade
```

Altering the `InstallType` key to `0` omits the accessory from the installation; leaving it as is ensures that it is installed.

Removing Unnecessary Applications

As with NT's accessories, there are certain applications and services that NT installs by default during an unattended installation that an administrator may want to remove or configure. These are the Briefcase utility, the NT welcome screen, MS Exchange and Explorer, and the default Screen Saver settings.

The Briefcase

The file with SYNCAPP.EXE controls NT's Briefcase utility. In order to remove this file from the installation process, it must first be edited out of two installation files—TXTSETUP.SIF and LAYOUT.INF. The first file, TXTSETUP.SIF, controls which files are copied from the DSP to the target system and placed in NT's two staging installation directories, \$WINNT$.~BT and \$WINNT$.~LS. The file LAYOUT.INF controls where files stored in the NT's staging directories are copied to their final location on the target system. Editing both of these files ensures that the SYNCAPP.EXE file is not be copied over to the target system or added to the list of files copied into the \WINNT\SYSTEM32? subdirectory.

Locate the file TXTSETUP.SIF in the directory on your DSP containing NT's installation files. Open the file in a standard text editor and search the file for the entry SYNCAPP.EXE under the `[SourceDiskFiles]` section. Place a semi-colon (;) in front of the entry for the file as follows:

```
[SourceDiskFiles]
...
supp_ed.cnt    = 1,,,,,,,_x,21,0,0
supp_ed.hlp    = 1,,,,,,,_x,21,0,0
switch.inf    = 1,,,,,,,7,3,0
;syncapp.exe   = 1,,,,,,,2,0,0
synceng.dll    = 1,,,,,,,2,0,0
syncui.dll    = 1,,,,,,,2,0,0
sysdm.hlp     = 1,,,,,,,21,0,0
...
```

> *Tip*
>
> *Make copies of each file before you modify them for your custom installation. Should you encounter difficulties with an improperly modified file, you can always return to the original.*

Close and save the file, then locate the file LAYOUT.INF in the same directory. Open it in a test editor and search for the entry SYNCAPP.EXE under the [SourceDisksFiles] section; then place a semicolon in front of it.

```
[SourcediskFiles]
...
supp_ed.cnt  = 1,,1024,,,,_x,21,0,0
supp_ed.hlp  = 1,,30208,,,,_x,21,0,0
switch.inf   = 1,,6656,,,,,7,3,0
;syncapp.exe = 1,,28672,,,,,2,0,0
synceng.dll  = 1,,58880,,,,,2,0,0
syncui.dll   = 1,,154112,,,,,2,0,0
sysdm.hlp    = 1,,44544,,,,,21,0,0
...
```

This ensures that the Briefcase utility is not copied over during the unattended process.

The Welcome Screen

After installation is complete and the first reboot and subsequent logins of new accounts to a Windows NT system have taken place, the NT Welcome screen and tips are displayed, unless they are disabled manually when the option presents itself after the second login of a new account. The capability to disable this screen is done through editing two files—the TXTSETUP.SIF and DOSNET.INF files. The TXTSETUP.SIF file is used to create the correct directory structures on the target system. It is also used to identify the files to be copied over to the directories for referencing on the target system during the text mode portion of the installation. The DOSNET.INF identifies the files that are copied to the target system to be used by the installation during the MS-DOS portion of setup.

Open the DOSNET.INF file and search for the file WELCOME.EXE under the [FloppyFiles.1] section, placing a semicolon (;) in front of the entry.

```
[FloppyFiles.1]
...
d1,wdl.trm
d1,weitekp9.dll
d1,weitekp9.sys
;d1,welcome.exe
d1,wfwnet.drv
d1,win.com
d1,win.ini
...
```

Next, open the file TXTSETUP.SIF in a standard text editor and search for the same entry, WELCOME.EXE, under the [SourceDisksFiles] section, placing a semicolon (;) in front of it.

```
[SourceDiskFiles]
...
wd1.trm       = 1,,,,,,,2,1,0
weitekp9.dll  = 1,,,,,,,2,1
weitekp9.sys  = 1,,,,,,_x,4,1
;welcome.exe  = 1,,,,,,,1,0,0
wfwnet.drv    = 1,,,,,,,2,1,0
win.com       = 1,,,,,,,2,1,0
win.ini       = 1,,,,,,,1,2
...
```

This prevents the Welcome screen executable, WELCOME.EXE, from being copied over to the target station and appearing after new accounts log on to the system.

A second method of disabling the Welcome screen during an unattended installation, using a registry edit, is covered in the Registry Editing section contained in Chapter 5, "Installing Additional Applications."

Disabling the Installation of MS Exchange and Explorer

Both Microsoft Exchange and Internet Explorer can be removed from automated installations of Windows NT as follows:

1. Expand the file SYSSETUP.INF located in the directory containing NT's setup files.

2. Rename the compressed file SYSSETUP.IN_ to SYSSETUP.OLD.

3. Open the expanded file in any standard text editor and search for the section `[BaseWinOptionInfs]`.

4. To disable the installation of Exchange, place a semicolon (;) in front of the `MSMAIL.INF` entry.

    ```
    [BaseWinOptionsInfs]
    accessor.inf
    communic.inf
    games.inf
    imagevue.inf
    mmopt.inf
    ;msmail.inf (disables the installation of Exchange)
    multimed.inf
    optional.inf
    pinball.inf
    wordpad.inf
    ```

5. Close and save the file back to the directory containing NT's installation files.

To disable the installation of MS Internet Explorer, open SYSSETUP.INF. Follow the same steps for accessing the file used to disable Exchange, and search for the section [Infs.Always]. Place a semicolon (;) in front of the entry iexplore.inf,DefaultInstall.

```
[Infs.Always]
;iexplore.inf,DefaultInstall
```

After making the change, save and close the file back to the directory containing NT's installation files.

Troubleshooting UDBs, Startup Parameters, Specialized Adapter Errors, and Custom Scripts

In most instances, thoroughly checking—and more importantly, recording—the additions, changes, or subtractions you make to the files contained in your custom installation assists you in tracking down problematic installation options that have gone awry. During the testing phase of an automated deployment, try not to make multiple changes to files simultaneously because this can make the diagnosis much more difficult to determine should errors occur. As with an Answer file, if an incorrect entry is detected or a missing parameter is determined, the installation usually halts and prompts the user for action. Some of the more cryptic messages are listed in Table 4.8.

Table 4.8. Troubleshooting Installation Startup Errors

Problem	Solution
The installation halts with the error `One or more minor errors occurred installing Windows NT. The errors will not prevent Windows NT from running.` It then prompts if you'd like to look at the log file.	You can check the log file right away or wait until after Windows NT restarts; then check the Setup log file located at %SystemRoot%\setuplog.txt.
`Warning: Setup was unable to invoke external program <drive>:\<directory>\<program> because of the following error: CreateProcess returned error 3.`	The external program specified with /E: switch in the startup parameters using WINNT or WINNT32 was invalid. Check the parameters again and ensure that they point to the proper driver letter and directory for the additional program.

Chapter 4: Customizing the Installation of NT 127

Problem	Solution
The installation halts, prompting the user for the location of NT's installation files.	The startup switch `/S:` contains the incorrect path to NT's setup files.
`File caused a unexpected error (0) at the line 1213 in d:\nt\private\ntos\boot\setup\ oemdisk.c. Press any key to continue.`	The variable component has not been correctly defined in the TXTSETUP.OEM file for the section `[Files.component.ID]`. Recheck the entry to ensure that the entry appears as `filetype = file location, filename [keyname]` where `filetype` is not the device description but the `filetype` option, that is, driver, dll, inf, hal, and so on.
`File \$WIN_NT$.~BT\$OEM$ \TEXTMODE\DISK1\<filename> could not be loaded. The error is 18. Setup cannot code continue. Press any key to exit.`	The installation cannot use subdirectories of the TEXTMODE directory on the DSP. The installation files must be in the root of the TEXTMODE directory.
Incorrect syntax:	Correct syntax:
`[Disks]`	`[Disks]`
`d1 = "Device Description", \disk1,\DISK1`	`d1 = "Device Description", \disk1, \`

Part **II**

Advanced Configuration of an Unattended Installation

5 Installing Additional Applications

6 Securing Desktop Environments

7 System Policies and User Profiles

8 Maintaining the Environment

Chapter 5

Installing Additional Applications

This chapter covers:

- Using the CMDLINES.TXT file
- Adding applications to the installation
- Using system Registry tools, REGEDIT.EXE
- Creating install packages with SYSDIFF.EXE
- Working with silent installations and service packs
- Installing and configuring printers

After reading this chapter, you should be able to do the following:

- Install applications and printers during an unattended installation
- Install service packs and Hotfixes
- Apply Registry edits during an unattended installation
- Create custom install packages using SYSDIFF.EXE

The CMDLINES.TXT File and How it Works

You might recall in Chapter 3, "Creating Answer Files," the importance of the key OEMPreinstall=Yes when applying customized settings in an UNATTEND.TXT file. This key is not only responsible for enabling custom parameters within the UNATTEND.TXT file, but also for informing the installation engine that there are additional defined parameters that must be processed during the installation. These additional commands are stored in the

CMDLINES.TXT file, which should be created in the root of your Distribution Share Point's (DSP) OEM directory.

> **Author's Note**
>
> *The CMDLINES.TXT can only be placed in the root of the OEM subdirectory of your DSP. It cannot be placed in another location.*

Like all files used in an unattended installation, the CMDLINES.TXT file is a standard text file, and it can be edited using any text editor. Following is an example of the contents and structure of a CMDLINES.TXT file:

```
[Commands]
".\executable_file [switch] [option] [file] "
".\command_file [switch] [option] [file] "
".\batch_file [switch] [option] [file] "
```

In the preceding example, you can see how .BAT, .COM, and .EXE files can be referenced in the CMDLINES.TXT. A command file can be executed by a simple reference or by a switched reference. It can also be used to process another file. The commands and their additional parameters must appear in quotes or they are not processed. And it is assumed that these commands and parameters have been stored in the OEM subdirectory along with the CMDLINES.TXT file itself, as they appear in the example. This trait is evidenced by the .\ preceding each file.

Should the referenced command file be stored elsewhere, the path should be mapped using the OEM as the root (see Figure 5.1).

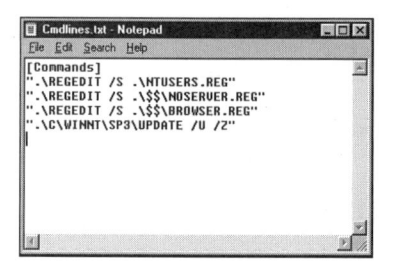

Figure 5.1. *Sample CMDLINES.TXT file contents.*

In this figure, the Registry editing tool, REGEDIT.EXE, is used to silently install .REG files using the /s switch. One of the .REG files, NTUSERS.REG, is stored in the root of the \$OEM$. The second and third instances of REGEDIT are used to install the .REG files NOSERVER.REG and BROWSER.REG, which are stored in the \$OEM$\$$ directory.

Chapter 5: Installing Additional Applications 133

The final command processed in the CMDLINES.TXT file is the Service Pack 3 installation executable, UPDATE.EXE, which is stored in the \OEM\C\ WINNT\SP3 subdirectory. In this way, the service pack is installed during the GUI phase of the installation as well as being copied over to the target workstation and stored in the directory C:\WINNT\SP3 for later use should the service pack require reinstallation.

The commands stored in the CMDLINES.TXT are started in the order in which they appear in the file. At the completion of the GUI portion of the setup process, but before the final reboot, the installation engine checks for the existence of the CMDLINES.TXT file. If present, the install processes the commands contained within it.

This order of operations is important. The installation has not completed the final reboot and logon sequence, so finalizing the desktop and the settings for the Start menu and program files and installing applications using the CMDLINES.TXT may not be appropriate. This is due to the fact that the application's setup process cannot update the Start menu with the appropriate Program group for the application during the GUI phase of the installation.

In some instances, the installation of an application may not finish because certain portions of the OS may not available for update at that time. Therefore, it might be appropriate to reserve the use of the CMDLINES.TXT file for system updates, the application of Registry files, and, when used, the System Difference tool options applied with SYSDIFF.EXE. Only through testing the direct referencing of an application's setup in the CMDLINES.TXT can it be determined whether or not the application can be installed with this method.

If through testing you find that an application installs successfully when directly referenced in the CMDLINES.TXT, the Start menu can be updated with the application's Program group using the \OEM\C (or another system drive letter). Follow these steps:

1. Create the directory <Drive Letter>\<%SystemRoot%>\Profiles \Defaul~1\Startm~1\Programs in the \OEM subdirectory of the DSP.

2. Copy the Program group you want to install onto the target system into the \Programs subdirectory.

3. Update or create the file $$RENAME.TXT in the \$OEM$\<Drive Letter> so that the 8.3 filenames can be converted correctly to their appropriate long filenames, as in the following example:

   ```
   [\WINNT\PROFILES\DEFAUL~1]
   Startm~1 = ""Start Menu""

   [\WINNT\PROFILES\]
   Defaul~1 = ""Default User""
   ```

If you want to install the Program group in the All Users section of the target system's Start menu, then follow the preceding steps, modifying the directories created on the DSP to reflect the following path:

```
<Drive Letter>\<%SystemRoot%>\Profiles\ Alluse~1\ Startm~1\Programs
\<Application Program Group Folder>
```

Next, add the following lines to the $$RENAME.TXT file of the <Drive Letter> subdirectory as follows:

```
[\WINNT\PROFILES\Alluse~1]
Startm~1 = ""Start Menu""
[\WINNT\PROFILES\]
Alluse~1 = ""All Users""
```

This method can also be used to add the program icon to the target system's desktop. Simply create these additional subdirectories on the DSP. For default users, apply the following output:

```
<Drive Letter>\<%SystemRoot%>\Profiles \Defaul~1\Desktop
```

For All Users:

```
<Drive Letter>\<%SystemRoot%>\Profiles \Alluse~1\Desktop
```

Be sure to update the $$RENAME.TXT file if necessary.

> **Tip**
>
> *This method of adding elements to a user's profile or desktop environment can also be used to update or configure a user's APPLICATION DATA, FAVORITES, PERSONAL, and SEND TO directories and menu options during the installation. It may also be used to copy a custom NTUSER.DAT file during the unattended installation. For more on customizing the NTUSER.DAT file, see the "Creating Custom User Profiles" section in Chapter 6.*

Case Study: University of Canterbury Library, New Zealand

The library at the University of Canterbury currently has 180 PCs running OS/2 as its desktop OS, along with a library information management system called *Horizon*, which is operated by Ameritech Library Services. The University of Canterbury library will be upgrading its current installations of OS/2 to Windows NT. This migration has been spurred by Ameritech's recent move to port its Horizon Server system to the Windows NT Operating System by the first part of 1998. Currently, only the Public Access Client for the Horizon information management software is available for NT.

In addition to the new Horizon client/server software, some of the library PCs will be required to support installations of MS Office. The PCs will require Registry modifications and program icons to customize the desktop environments as well. Currently, the Horizon Windows User Interface (or WUI) client is not scriptable for a silent installation, so the computer technician at Canterbury's library is testing the WUI NT Client to see if it can be installed using SYSDIFF.

We may be seeing more examples of cases like the University of Canterbury library in the near future. As software developers begin to take advantage of NT's 32-bit operating system, offering expanded capabilities with their products, organizations seeking to enhance their services or gain a competitive edge in the market will also be looking to migrate to Windows NT. The University of Canterbury's library client migration was a necessity because Horizon's developers chose Windows NT as the new platform for their product.

As more and more applications are developed specifically for Windows NT, administrators of NT systems may be looking to deliver a more complete desktop environment to their clients during the unattended installation process, which may include customized applications or software. For many administrators, the installation of the OS is only part, possibly one-third, of the entire installation process.

The additional requirement of deploying applications, installing service packs, and adding customized settings and printers during an unattended installation of Windows NT has been the chief source of many of the problems surrounding the unattended process. How can it be done? This chapter provides some examples on how these things might be accomplished.

Adding Applications to the Installation

As mentioned earlier in this chapter, directly referencing an application's setup executable using the CMDLINES.TXT file is not advisable, but an application's installation can be accessed indirectly using the CMDLINES.TXT file, using a .REG file.

.REG Files

Following is an example of a .REG file:

```
[Commands]
".\REGEDIT /S .\LOGON.REG"
".\REGEDIT /S .\MSOFFICE.REG"
```

In the previous example, REGEDIT.EXE is referenced in order to install two Registry updates, LOGON.REG and MSOFFICE.REG.

LOGON.REG

The first .REG file, LOGON.REG, is used to autologon to the system after the final installation reboot, bypassing the login prompt.

This may be a desirable option for a number of reasons. Automatically processing a logon can allow for the installation of any additional applications. It can also allow system customizations that may require an interactive session but not a manual login to continue. Figure 5.2 shows the contents of the file LOGON.REG.

```
REGEDIT4
[HKEY_LOCAL_MACHINE\SOFTWARE\Microsoft\Windows NT\CurrentVersion\Winlogon]
"AutoAdminLogon" = "1"
"DefaultUserName" = "Administrator"
"DefaultPassword" = ""
"DefaultDomain" = ""MyDomainName"
```

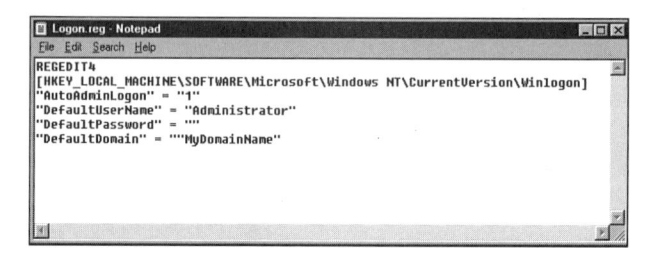

Figure 5.2. *LOGON.REG.*

> **Troubleshooting Tip**
>
> *Be sure to reference the subkeys correctly. If you do not, the .REG file fails to work. Pay special attention to the existence of spaces in the* KeyName *path. Unintentional omission creates new keys rather than updating the correct existing keys.*

Notice that the .REG file contains the key and value of "DefaultPassword" = "". This option is used because the key and value OEMBlankAdminPassword = 1 is being used in the UNATTEND.TXT file for this installation, which causes the setup to leave the administrator's password on the target system blank. Now we are using that blank password to script an automatic login to the system. Use of this option automatically logs on to the local system with the administrator's account, allowing for full access to the target system should any additional installation parameters be specified.

> **Author's Note**
>
> *The administrator's password remains blank until it is changed. If left blank, the autologon process only occurs once for the very first logon sequence and then disables itself.*

MSOFFICE.REG

The next file, MSOFFICE.REG, contains a reference to a system Registry command known as a RUNONCE statement, which processes an external command one time after a system reboot. This particular type of Registry update is extremely useful for installing applications or system updates remotely. Following are the contents of MSOFFICE.REG:

```
REGEDIT4

[HKEY_LOCAL_MACHINE\SOFTWARE\Microsoft\Windows\CurrentVersion\RunOnce]
"RunThis" = "C:\\Temp\\Msoffice.bat"
```

Here the Registry is updated so that after the first logon, the batch file MSOFFICE.BAT is run, starting a silent installation of MS Office 97. Notice that the file being referenced is contained in the string that points to the file on the local drive system.

The RUNONCE statement is processed after the final reboot, so the installation files that were originally copied to the system and stored in the temporary install directories have already been removed. Because of this, the .BAT file needs to be copied to a local drive so that it is available after the first logon. Using the OEM\<Drive Letter> subdirectory, you can copy the appropriate file(s) necessary to process this command to the target system.

In the preceding example, the subdirectory \OEM\C\TEMP was created on the DSP and the file MSOFFICE.BAT was copied to it. From there, MSOFFICE.BAT was copied to the target system's C:\TEMP directory.

MSOFFICE.BAT

Next, take a look at the contents of the MSOFFICE.BAT file:

```
NET USE Z: \\SERVERNAME\SHARE
Z:\MSOFFICE.97\SETUP.EXE /B 1 /C "<MS Office Product ID" /QT
```

The first line processes a NET USE command, which maps the drive Z: to the server and share containing the MS Office installation files. If a login to the specific share is necessary, the username and password can be supplied in the .BAT file as follows:

```
NET USE Z: \\SERVERNAME\SHARE /USER:USERNAME PASSWORD
```

Author's Note

Supplying usernames and passwords in clear text may not be desirable. If this method is used to attach to the required server/share, steps should be taken to ensure that the files contained in the C:\TEMP or selected directory are either secured or deleted upon completion of the automated installation.

The second line begins the MS Office installation using its *silent* installation options. Applications that are capable of installation without requiring user intervention are silent installs. Here the Office installation, which is setting up a Typical installation of MS Office, is denoted by the /B 1 switch. The /C option allows for the specification of the product ID (so that the installation does not halt and request that it be manually entered). The final switch, /QT, suppresses all of MS Office's setup screens and backdrops.

> *Tip*
>
> *More information on the available options for installation can be found in the NETWRK8.TXT file with the Office CD, on pages 1048–50 in the "Microsoft Office 97 Resource Kit," or on Microsoft's Web site at http://www.microsoft.com/office/.*

Moving Installation Files

An option to installing MS Office from the network after the first logon is to move the required MS Office installation files to the target system during the first part of the installation and then to reference the local installation file set in the MSOFFICE.BAT. To do this, create a subdirectory under the \$OEM$\ <Drive Letter> on the DSP, such as \$OEM$\C\MSOFFICE.97. Copy the MS Office installation files to the subdirectory and then edit the MSOFFICE.BAT file so that it looks something like this:

```
C:\MSOFFICE.97\SETUP.EXE /B 1 /C "<MS Office Product ID>" /QT
```

Deleting Temporary Installation Files

If you want to delete the temporary installation files contained in the directory C:\MSOFFICE.97, add the following line into the .BAT file:

```
COPY C:\MSOFFICE.97\DELTREE.BAT C:\WINNT\PROFILES\ALLUSE~1\
STARTM~1\PROGRAMS\STARTUP\
C:\MSOFFICE.97\SETUP.EXE /B 1 /C "<MS Office Product ID>" /QT
```

This first line copies the file DELTREE.BAT from the directory C:\MSOFFICE.97 to the Startup group of All Users.

> *Tip*
>
> *Ensure that the file DELTREE.BAT is copied to the \OEM\C\ MSOFFICE.97 DSP subdirectory after it is created.*

The next line processes the installation. After MS Office completes its installation process, the OS reboots. This initiates the file DELTREE.BAT, which can be edited to look something like the following:

```
CD\
C:\
DELTREE /Y C:\MSOFFICE.97
DEL F:\WINNT\PROFILES\ALLUSE~1\STARTM~1\PROGRAMS\ STARTUP\DELTREE.BAT
EXIT
```

This file deletes the temporary installation directory of C:\MSOFFICE.97 and all of its subdirectories. Upon completion, it removes itself from the Startup group.

This process, which is used to install MS Office during an unattended installation, can be used to install applications with the capability of a silent setup option.

IntranetWare Client 32

This next example involves customizing an installation of Windows NT for NetWare environments through the installation of Novell's IntranetWare Client 32. This is an excellent add-on client service application for Windows NT. It provides additional functionality when using NT Workstation under NetWare networks, replacing Microsoft's limited Client Service for NetWare (CSNW).

The Client32 is available for free from Novell's Web site at **http://www.novell.com/novellsw/platform.html**. After the files necessary for installation are downloaded and extracted, the help files can be accessed for additional information regarding the Client itself.

Novell has provided three different ways of automating the installation of the IntranetWare Client 32:

- The installation parameters for the Client 32 can be added into the UNATTEND.TXT under the [Services] section, replacing the need for the Microsoft Client for NetWare.

- It can be installed in a silent mode using the Client's setup program SETUPNW.EXE with /U:<Novell Answer File> using a RUNONCE .REG file to reference the installation in a batch file (much like the MS Office install).

- The last installation method is to use the Automatic Client Upgrade (ACU) option in the system login script of the logon server.

It is up to the deploying administrators to determine which of the three available options best suits their installation needs.

Automating the Client32 Installation Using UNATTEND.TXT

Of the three options available, the most appealing is to script the installation into the UNATTEND.TXT file, but there are some problems with this method of installing the IntranetWare Client.

First, the use of uniqueness database files (UDFs) is not supported with the IntranetWare Client as it is with Microsoft's Client Service for NetWare. This means that when you are installing the IntranetWare Client in an UNATTEND.TXT file, user-specific network information, such as preferred server, cannot be set with the use of a UDF. In order for the option of setting different network information to be available, unique UNATTEND.TXT files must be created for each configuration option set (See the "Installation Startup Parameters for Windows NT" section in Chapter 2 on how to reference different UNATTEND.TXT files when starting the installation process).

Second, when the installation of the IntranetWare Client is scripted into the UNATTEND.TXT file and is used in conjunction with SYSDIFF .IMG packages, the .IMG fails to update the system properly. This failure occurs because certain Registry keys are intentionally omitted from the SYSDIFF process, including those regarding network client software. Therefore, the first method of installing the Client might be reserved for installations of Windows NT that are not using UDFs or System Difference packages.

To install the IntranetWare Client during the unattended installation process (by adding it to the UNATTEND.TXT), locate the custom UNATTEND.TXT file in the installation file set for the IntranetWare Client under the \I386\NLS\ENGLISH subdirectory. After opening it in a standard text editor, locate the following section:

```
;   Novell Modified Section

;   These sections of the UNATTEND.TXT file are the ones that the Novell
;   IntranetWare Client 4.10 Installation either modifies for its own use or are
;   included in the UNATTEND.TXT file that ships with the Novell IntranetWare
;   Client 4.10 Installation.
```

From this section of the custom UNATTEND.TXT file forward is what must be copied into your UNATTEND.TXT and then modified to reflect the specific settings for your deployment. Of special note is the IntranetWare Client entry under the [ServicesList] section. Following is an excerpt from the Novell-supplied UNATTEND.TXT file:

```
[Network]
InstallServices=ServicesList

[ServicesList]
NWFS = NovellNetWareClientParameters, \$OEM$\NET\NTCLIENT\I386
```

Notice how the reference to the NWFS contains the additional string \OEM\NET\NTCLIENT\I386. This reference points the installation engine to the appropriate DSP subdirectory for installing the service.

Chapter 5: Installing Additional Applications   141

> **Tip**
>
> *Additional configuration information can be set in the UNATTEND.TXT. For more information on this method of installing the IntranetWare Client, check the Novell Web site for document #2917084, "Integrated NT 4.0 and NW Client Installation."*

Automating the Client32 Installation Using SETUPNW.EXE /U

The second option, using the SETUPNW.EXE /U option, can be used in an installation much like that used to install MS Office in an earlier example. A .REG file can be referenced in the CMDLINES.TXT that calls a batch file containing the installation string required to start the IntranetWare Client installation. Following is an example .REG file, NETWARE.REG, that can be used to reference the file NOVELL.BAT:

```
REGEDIT4
[HKEY_LOCAL_MACHINE\SOFTWARE\Microsoft\Windows\CurrentVersion\
RunOnce]
"RunThis" = "C:\\TEMP\\NOVELL.BAT"
```

> **Tip**
>
> *Just as with the MS Office installation, the file NOVELL.BAT must be copied to a subdirectory on the DSP called \OEM\C\TEMP so that it can be copied to the target system during the automated installation process.*

Following is an example of the batch file NOVELL.BAT:

```
C:\NTCLIENT\I386\SETUPNW.EXE /U:C:\NTCLIENT\I386\NOVELL.TXT
```

This file references the Client 32 installation files that have been copied to the target system during the unattended setup from the \OEM\C\NTCLIENT\ I386 subdirectory. The /U: switch is used to reference the .TXT file containing the answers necessary to automate the installation of the client. This particular file, NOVELL.TXT, is the modified UNATTEND.TXT file found in the \NLS\ENGLISH subdirectory of the Client 32 installation.

It is important to note that the concept of an UNATTEND.TXT file with regards to Microsoft's NT installation is expanded in the context of the Client 32 installation. An UNATTEND.TXT can be used to automate a Windows NT installation, and the custom UNATTEND.TXT contained in the Client 32 installation file set can be used as the Answer file for use with SETUPNW.EXE.

> **Tip**
>
> *For more on this method of installing the client, check the Novell Web site for document #2929495, "Unattended IntranetWare NT Client Install."*

Automating the Client 32 Installation Using the Automatic Client Upgrade

The third method of installing the IntranetWare Client is through the use of Novell's Automatic Client Upgrade (ACU) option. As was mentioned earlier, this method of installing the client is initiated by an NT Workstation logging into a NetWare server. In order for this to be possible, the MS Client Service for NetWare must first be installed (with the processing of login scripts enabled) during the unattended installation to make it possible to connect to a NetWare server. Following is an excerpt from an UNATTEND.TXT file:

```
[ProtocolsSection]
NWLNKIPX = NWLNKIPXParamSection

[NWLNKIPXParamSection]

[ServicesSection]
NWWKSTA = NWWKSTAParamSection
[NWWKSTAParamSection]
!DefaultLocation = Netware_Server_Name
!DefaultScriptOptions = 3
```

(This only represents a portion of a complete Answer file.)

To enable the ACU option, open the system login script and add the following lines:

```
IF OS IS LESS THAN "WINNT" THEN BEGIN
    BREAK OFF
    MAP Z: = SYS:PUBLIC\
#Z:\INSTALL\NTCLIENT\SETUPNW.EXE /ACU /U:
WRITE "This PC will be upgraded to Novell's IntranetWare Client,"
Z:\INSTALL\NTCLIENT\UNATTEND.TXT
ENDIF
```

In the preceding output, the installation files for the Client have been copied to the SYS:PUBLIC\INSTALL\NTCLIENT directory. In order for the Client installation to be completely hands off, the following settings of these options within the Novell-supplied UNATTEND.TXT must be altered:

```
[SetupNWInstallOptions]
!DisplayInitialScreen = No ;(The default is set to Yes)
!AskReboot = No ;(The Default is set to Yes)

[NovellNetWareClientParameters]
!AcceptLicenseAgreement = Yes ;(The default is set to No)
```

> *Tip*
>
> *Ensure that the login ID being used to access the NetWare server possesses at least Read and File Scan in the directory containing the Client's installation files.*

Chapter 5: Installing Additional Applications   143

The IntranetWare Client's installation engine checks the Major and Minor internal version numbers of the current NetWare client, so it does not continually attempt to upgrade the system if it detects that the current client possesses the same version number.

> *Tip*
>
> *For more on automating the installation and using the ACU option, check the Novell Web site for document #2929497, "ACU IntranetWare Client using UNATTEND.TXT."*

Automating the Client 32 Installation Using SETUPAPI.DLL

The final example for application installation is the use of Windows NT's SETUPAPI.DLL to install applications using Windows 95–style .INF files. SETUPAPI.DLL is used by NT's System Difference tool, SYSDIFF.EXE, but it can be referenced from within the CMDLINES.TXT file.

SETUPAPI32.DLL is a dynamic link library (DLL), not an executable file, so it must be used in conjunction with NT's RUNDLL32.EXE in order to properly process a referenced installation .INF file. Following is an example of the proper syntax for the use of the SETUPAPI.DLL in a CMDLINES.TXT file:

```
[Commands]
"RUNDLL32 SETUPAPI.DLL,InstallHinfSection <Section Name> <Reboot Mode>
<INF Filename>"
```

The first section of the string `"RUNDLL32 SETUPAPI.DLL InstallHinfSection` does not change. The `<Section Name>` points to the appropriate install section header contained within the referenced `<INF Filename>`. The `Reboot Mode` refers to the numerical parameters the SETUPAPI.DLL responds to, and it tells it which reboot option is necessary for the install type referenced. Table 5.1 shows the reboot modes and their definitions.

Table 5.1.   Reboot Mode Definitions

Reboot Mode	Definition
0 or 128	SETUPAPI.DLL does not reboot the system, nor does it prompt the user for a reboot.
1 or 129	SETUPAPI.DLL always reboots the system without prompting the user, regardless of whether the system requires it or not.
2 or 130	SETUPAPI.DLL always prompts the user for a reboot, showing the message `Reboot Machine, Yes/No`. It does not check to see if the system requires a reboot.
3 or 131	If SETUPAPI.DLL determines that a reboot is required, it does so without prompting the user.
4 or 132	If SETUPAPI.DLL determines that a reboot is required, it prompts the user, showing the message `Reboot Machine, Yes/No`.

The reboot codes may or may not be required when processing the installation of an application, but they may be necessary when installing a new service, which might require a reboot to start.

Figure 5.3 shows an example of the SETUPAPI.DLL used in the CMDLINES.TXT.

```
[Commands]
"RUNDLL32 SETUPAPI.DLL,InstallHinfSection DefaultInstall 128 .\Hplj4.inf"
```

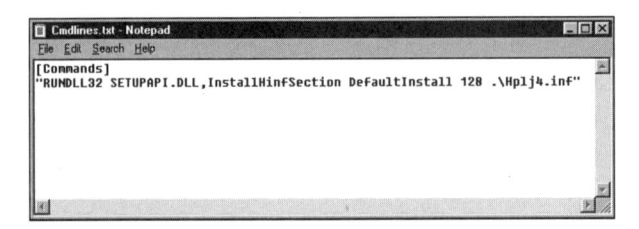

Figure 5.3. *Use of the SETUPAPI.DLL in the CMDLINES.TXT.*

The figure shows a SYSDIFF.INF file that has been slightly modified. An HP LaserJet 4 is being installed. The string is pointing to the [DefaultInstall] section in the HPLJ4.INF file, and SETUPAPI.DLL has been set to not reboot (code 128).

This particular type of installation method exists as an optional method of applying Registry edits. You might recall the MSOFFICE.REG file we used earlier in the chapter, which was used to copy the MSOFFICE.BAT file to the target system's Registry:

```
MSOFFICE.REG

REGEDIT4
[HKEY_LOCAL_MACHINE\SOFTWARE\Microsoft\Windows\CurrentVersion\
RunOnce]
"RunThis" = "C:\\Temp\\Msoffice.bat"
```

Following is the same Registry addition, as it might look as an .INF-style file:

```
MSOFFICE.INF

[Version]
Signature = "$Windows NT$"

[MyAdditions]
AddReg = AddReg

[AddReg]
HKLM,"SOFTWARE\Microsoft\Windows\CurrentVersion\RunOnce",
"RunThis",,"C:\Temp\Msoffice.bat"
```

The preceding file might be referenced in the CMDLINES.TXT as follows:

```
[Commands]
"RUNDLL32 SETUPAPI.DLL,InstallHinfSection MyAdditions 128 .\
Msoffice.inf"
```

Notice that the reboot code is set to 128. This is because the .INF is being installed through the CMDLINES.TXT and does not require a reboot. This set of commands is processed at the end of the GUI portion of the OS installation, so a reboot is not required. This means that the system is already set to reboot itself automatically upon completion of the commands contained within the CMDLINES.TXT file.

> *Tip*
>
> *It is important to test custom or modified .INF files before deploying NT to ensure that the application or change that has been installed functions properly and has no adverse effects on the OS.*
>
> *When using this method of installing additional applications or functionality to Windows NT during the unattended process, it is also critical to ensure that the changes do not require user intervention, thereby negating the concept of an unattended process.*

Using SYSDIFF

When you are faced with automating the installation of applications during an unattended installation, another issue is those applications, services, or functions whose installation process does not use a silent or unattended installation method. For this Microsoft has created the *System Difference tool*, or *SYSDIFF.EXE*.

SYSDIFF.EXE is an extremely useful utility for importing applications that do not have silent or unattended installation options, customized settings, or environment variables belonging to multiple systems.

> *Tip*
>
> *Microsoft recommends relying on an installation's capability to process a silent installation, only using this tool when it is necessary. The SYSDIFF.EXE and SYSDIFF.INF files can be found on the Windows NT Retail CD-ROM in the \SUPPORT\DEPTOOLS\I386 or \SUPPORT\OPK\I386 (or other processor type) subdirectory.*

SYSDIFF can be used to import applications that require manual or attended installations, as well as desktop, printer, and environment settings. This capability makes SYSDIFF extremely valuable, but it does possess some limitations:

- SYSDIFF does not import NTFS permissions, nor does it import security settings to the Registry or User and Groups.

- Generally, SYSDIFF should not be used to install device drivers, services, or network-related software because the portions of the Registry that govern the operation of these elements are dynamic and may rely upon the current interactive session, or they are intentionally excluded from SYSDIFF's operation. Only after thoroughly testing an application's capability to be installed correctly using SYSDIFF can you determine whether or not it can be distributed in this fashion.

SYSDIFF works by taking a "snapshot" of a system, recording Registry and file system contents and settings in an image, or .IMG, file. This snapshot is used later to compare the system contents after an application is manually installed or an environment variable is changed. The snapshot is created using the following command:

```
SYSDIFF.EXE /SNAP /LOG:C:\TEMP\SNAPSHOT.LOG C:\TEMP\SNAPSHOT.IMG
```

The command structure of the string is something like the following:

```
SYSDIFF.EXE /SNAP /LOG:<Log File> <Snap Image File>
```

The switch /SNAP tells SYSDIFF to take a "snapshot" of the system. The optional /LOG switch is used to create a log file of the snapshot process. The file SNAPSHOT.IMG names the .IMG file that will contain the snapshot information. The filenames and locations of both the log and image files can be anything you want, which creates the option of generating multiple difference images and logs that can be used in an unattended installation.

After the snapshot of the system has been taken, you can go ahead and make whatever changes you'd like to incorporate into your other systems, such as adding printers, applications, and so forth (as described previously). When you are ready to create your installation .IMG file, type this command using SYSDIFF:

```
SYSDIFF.EXE/DIFF/LOG:C:\TEMP\DIFFERNCE.LOG C:\TEMP\SNAPSHOT.IMG
C:\TEMP\DIFFRNCE.IMG
```

The command structure of this string looks like this:

```
SYSDIFF.EXE /DIFF /LOG:<Log File> <Snap Image File>
<Diff Image File>
```

This string takes another snapshot of your system and compares it with the first snapshot you took, SNAPSHOT.IMG. Another .IMG file, DIFFRNCE.IMG, is created, containing all of the differences that exist between the two images.

This is a point which eludes some users of SYSDIFF. A snapshot can be taken at any time, and from the time the initial snapshot is taken to the time the difference file is created, only the changes that have occurred to the operating system are recorded in the difference .IMG.

After the difference file is created, it can be applied to multiple installations of Windows NT, removing the necessity for the manual implementation of the desired changes. The difference file can then be applied using one of two options, as noted in the following sections.

Direct Application of .IMG Files

The first option is to simply apply the .IMG directly to the target systems. This can be done by copying the compiled difference image file (in our example, DIFFRNCE.IMG) to the root of the OEM subdirectory of the DSP and adding the following string to the CMDLINES.TXT file:

```
[Commands]
".\SYSDIFF.EXE /APPLY /M .\DIFFRNCE.IMG"
```

Troubleshooting Tip

In order for SYSDIFF to be accessible for use in the CMDLINES.TXT file during an unattended installation, copy the SYSDIFF.EXE and .INF to the root of the \\OEM subdirectory of the DSP.

The /M switch (mandatory) applies the package to the default user profile on the target system so that all new profiles created on the system contain the new settings. If this switch is missing from an /APPLY statement in the CMDLINES.TXT file, the package only updates the administrator's profile with the desired settings, and new users receive NT's default profile instead of the custom one.

Tip

Creating difference image files that contain multiple or large application installations coupled with environment variable changes may either fail or not wholly import the updates correctly. This method of applying difference files should be reserved for small packages that have been tested thoroughly.

For larger installation packages using SYSDIFF, use the /INF option, which is explained in more detail in the following section.

Expanding .IMG Files with /INF

The second method of applying a SYSDIFF package to target systems during an unattended installation is to create the difference file using the steps in the previous section and then to use the /INF switch, as shown in the following output:

```
SYSDIFF /INF C:\TEMP\DIFFRNCE.IMG Z:\DSP\I386\
```

When you are using the preceding example, the /INF expands the difference image file, DIFFRNCE.IMG, into the DSP Z:\DSP\I386, which is a mapped network drive. As the image file is extracted, several events occur:

> *Tip*
>
> *When you are applying a SYSDIFF image file, ensure that the system root of the systems being installed to is the same as that of the system the image was made on. Otherwise, the application of the image to the target system fails.*

1. The OEM subdirectory is created, or if it already exists, is updated to contain the appropriate subdirectories and files from the difference image file.

2. The CMDLINES.TXT is updated with the appropriate SETUPAPI.DLL command string, which is similar to the following:

   ```
   [Commands]
   "RUNDLL32 SETUPAPI.DLL,InstallHinfSection DefaultInstall
   128 .\diff.inf"
   ```

3. It creates the file DIFF.INF and copies it to the root of the OEM subdirectory. This file contains all of the necessary Registry and .INI settings taken from the difference image file, which is created in a Windows 95–style .INF.

4. If necessary, the CMDLINES.TXT creates or updates the $$RENAME.TXT file in order to convert the files from the 8.3 naming convention to their proper long filenames when they are transferred to the target system.

The beauty of using this method of installing difference packages instead of using the first method is that it permits you to add, modify, or remove certain portions of the installation package. You can do this by either editing the DIFF.INF or adding/subtracting files and directories from the DSP directory structure created by the /INF option. This particular type of installation method also reduces the amount of network bandwidth being utilized during the installation process because multiple smaller files are being copied over to the target system rather than one large image file.

SYSDIFF Error Codes

As was mentioned earlier in this section, you may encounter difficulties when applying difference packages during an unattended installation. SYSDIFF error messages can be interpreted by typing NET HELPMSG <error code> at the DOS prompt.

Chapter 5: Installing Additional Applications 149

Oftentimes, though, the displayed message is either cryptic or not sufficient enough to give you any clues about the nature of the error. If this message does not help you resolve the error message, try re-running the SYSDIFF process with the `/LOG` switch and note where the installation stops or fails. This should give you some clue about what the SYSDIFF application was attempting at the time it stopped. If SYSDIFF fails during a `/SNAP` session, check the three open windows SYSDIFF is using for where the `/SNAP` session stopped.

Table 5.2 defines some of the more common error codes that may occur when using SYSDIFF.

Table 5.2. SYSDIFF Error Messages

Error Message	Meaning
`Diff Failed (error = 32)`	A file that SYSDIFF has tried to access is in use. Make sure that no programs are running during the `/SNAP` and `/DIFF` phases. If this fails, try re-running the session or recompiling the image.
`System Error 5`	The error message occurs when a SYSDIFF session attempts to access a restricted key(s) in the Registry that is associated with an installed application or service it is attempting to DIFF. Identify the program associated with the restricted key and remove it from the installation set.
`Error 112`	This is a standard Win32 error. It means that insufficient disk space exists to store the difference file during the comparison of the snapshot. Make sure that there is enough space for the DIFF file where you are storing it during the creation process.
`Diff Failed (error = 2)`	One of the command arguments in the SYSDIFF string is incorrect. Recheck the string for correct spelling and syntax.
`Installation Failed`	An error occurred while applying the difference image file. Open the DIFF.INF and check the Registry keys against what was actually applied to the target system. The missing key designates where the installation failed. Either apply the required key manually or re-create the difference file.

Troubleshooting Tip

Microsoft has identified a time-stamping issue with SYSDIFF in which the files copied to the target system during the application of a difference file do not retain their original timestamp.

To fix this problem, download the updated version of SYSDIFF.EXE from the Microsoft FTP server at ftp://ftp.microsoft.com/bussys/ winnt/winnt-public/fixes/usa/nt40/utilities/Sysdiff-fix/.

Tip

For more information on diagnosing SYSDIFF error messages, search for the following Knowledge Base articles on Microsoft's Web site: Q157576 "Troubleshooting Problems Using SYSDIFF.EXE Tool" and Q165533 "General SYSDIFF Troubleshooting Tips."

When diagnosing compiled difference image files, it can also be useful to use the /DUMP command switch to process a possibly corrupt image file. This switch "dumps" the contents of the image file into a readable file that can be used for diagnosis. Use the following string:

```
SYSDIFF.EXE /DUMP C:\TEMP\DIFFRNCE.IMG C:\TEMP\DUMP.DMP
```

Using REGEDIT.EXE

As you can see from the previous section, using the REGEDIT.EXE tool in the CMDLINES.TXT can be highly effective during the unattended installation process. The use of .REG files is not limited to processing external command files. They can also be used to modify how the OS functions, to figure out what kinds of services are enabled or disabled, and to enhance system security, to name a few.

Chapter 1, "Why NT Workstation?" mentioned that by default, Windows NT Workstation is installed with a few services and options that might not be desirable on your network, most notably the Server and Browser services, along with NT Workstation's default status as a backup master browser. All three of these functions can be disabled through the use of registry edits applied in the CMDLINES.TXT file.

You can disable the Browser and Backup Browser Status services by using the following two registry edits, BROWSER.REG and NOSRVLST.REG:

```
BROWSER.REG

REGEDIT4

HKEY_LOCAL_MACHINE\SYSTEM\CurrentControlSet\Services\Browser\
"Start" = DWORD: 00000004
```

Troubleshooting Tip

These registry edits must be used in conjunction with one another or a Service Event Failure *error message appears. Use of these two edits should be carefully considered. Often in large installations of NT it is desirable to intersperse backup master browsers among workstations, especially in instances in which groups may be across a router or a WAN link.*

You may also want to enable the option of maintaining the browse list on a workstation or two in these situations so that workstations are using a local browse master rather than crossing a router or WAN link for a resource list.

BROWSER.REG

This Registry edit disables the Browser service, setting the startup parameter for the service to `Disabled`.

```
NOSRVLST.REG

REGEDIT4

HKEY_LOCAL_MACHINE\SYSTEM\CurrentControlSet\Services\Browser\
Parameters\
"MaintainServerList" = "No"
```

By default, the setting for this key on NT workstations is `Auto`. This edit changes the setting to disable the workstation's status as a possible master browser.

NOSERVER.REG

The next edit, NOSERVER.REG, is used to disable the Server service on NT workstations. This may be desirable should you want to restrict users from directly sharing files and printers with one another. Ensure that the computer browser edit, BROWSER.REG, is used in conjunction with this edit or the service control monitor displays an error every time the system is rebooted.

```
NOSERVER.REG

HKEY_LOCAL_MACHINE\SYSTEM\CurrentControlSet\Services\LanmanServer\
"Start" = DWORD: 00000004
```

Both Device and System services can have their respective startup options altered using a .REG file in the CMDLINES.TXT, but caution should be taken before doing so. Not all Device or System services can be modified in this fashion because some of them either rely on or are relied upon by another service or process.

Testing .REG Files

The best way to determine whether the altering of a Device or System service can be accomplished without an adverse effect is to first test it on an existing NT workstation.

Before starting the test, make sure that you have a valid Emergency Repair Disk (ERD) to restore the Registry; you might encounter trouble after applying the Registry change or the Last Known Good Configuration option at system startup.

If the change produces the desired results after a system reboot, follow these steps:

1. Open the system's Registry using REGEDT32.EXE, the other, more comprehensive native Registry editing tool supplied with the operating system. This can be done by going to the Run line on the Start menu and typing **REGEDT32**.

2. After the REGEDT32 has opened, locate the following key path:

   HKEY_LOCAL_MACHINE\SYSTEM\CurrentControlSet\Services

   Under the Services key, you can find all of the Device and System services for the operating system.

3. Highlight the desired service and both the values and the corresponding strings for the service appear in the right-hand screen.

4. Locate the Start value and note the Hex string.

5. After you have determined the appropriate DWORD string for the Start value, you can apply it by placing it into a .REG file similar to the ones illustrated in Table 5.3.

Table 5.3 contains the startup parameters and their meanings.

Table 5.3. Registry Device and Software Service Startup Parameters

DWORD Value	Parameter
0x2	Automatic
0x3	Manual
0x4	Disabled
0	Boot*
0x1	System*

*These options apply to Device services only.

> *Troubleshooting Tip*
>
> It is extremely important to test the .REG file to ensure that it alters the Service startup parameter correctly. Try this out on your test workstation by ensuring or resetting the Service's default startup parameter and applying your .REG file. (This can be done within NT by simply double-clicking on the file.)
>
> After the system responds that the file has been registered with the system's Registry, open REGEDT32 and go to the appropriate key. Check the Start value and ensure that it has been changed to the desired value before rebooting the test system. If the test system reboots properly, you can use the custom .REG file in your deployment.

Service Pack Updates

Service packs are an essential part of deploying and maintaining Windows NT. Service packs represent a crucial improvement to the OS. They address a wide range of issues that are brought to their attention by the user community, including enhancing security, updating system files, and adding increased functionality.

This said, many deployments of NT may require that these updates be a regular part of the installation process. Service packs cannot be installed using SYSDIFF.EXE. But there are many ways in which the installation of a service pack can easily be scripted into an unattended installation of Windows NT, such as using the /E: option along with the WINNT.EXE setup command or installing it through a system login script.

Of the three service packs currently available, Service Pack 1 is a self-extracting archive, and Service Packs 2 and 3 can be extracted using the /x switch. After they are extracted, locate the file UPDATE.EXE, which is the file used to initiate service pack installation. Table 5.4 lists the command-line options for each service pack's UPDATE.EXE.

Table 5.4. Service Pack Command-line Switches

Service Pack Version	Available Switches	Definition
Service Pack 1*	/U	Unattended installation.
Service Pack 2	/U	Unattended installation.
	/C	Create uninstall directory.
	/Z	Do not restart (when used during the GUI phase of an unattended installation).

continues

Table 5.4. Continued

Service Pack Version	Available Switches	Definition
Service Pack 3	/F	Force open applications to close.
	/N	Do not create an uninstall directory.
	/U	Unattended installation.
	/Q	Quiet mode.
	/Y	Performs an uninstall of the service pack.
	/Z	Do not restart (when used during the GUI phase of an unattended installation).

* *Service Pack 1 must be installed using a* RUNONCE *statement placed in the system registry during the unattended process which references the installation .EXE. See Microsoft's Knowledge Base article Q168814 for more details.*

The first example shows how service packs can be installed by using a simple line in the CMDLINES.TXT file:

```
[Commands]
".\SP3\UPDATE /U /Z"
```

In this example, Service Pack 3 has been extracted to the \OEM\SP3\ subdirectory of the DSP. The service pack switch /U forces the service pack to install itself in unattended mode. The /Z switch causes the service pack to not require a reboot because installation of the service pack during the GUI phase of an unattended installation does not require reboot.

A service pack update can also be installed through the use of the WINNT.EXE or WINNT32.EXE command-line switch /E: in the installation startup parameters. Ensure that the service pack installation files are accessible during the initial portion of the installation.

Finally, a service pack installation can be scripted using an installation method much like the one used for the installation of MS Office. The service pack installation string can be placed in a batch file and referenced with a RUNONCE statement in a .REG file, which is applied in the CMDLINES.TXT using REGEDIT.EXE.

Applying Hotfixes

Hotfixes are usually used to represent solutions to immediate, specific problems that are uncovered in the OS and must be addressed directly. Most Hotfixes are incorporated in the next release of a service pack to ensure that the update reaches the larger user community. Thus, the application of Hotfixes for service packs prior to Service Pack 3 should normally not be necessary.

Thankfully, Microsoft has included additional functionality within Service Pack 3's UPDATE.EXE to process Hotfixes if they are extracted into a subdirectory of the service pack installation files called HOTFIX. In this way, a Hotfix is updated along with the service pack during an unattended installation of Windows NT. Note, however, that this extraction creates a prompt for user intervention. A solution is to extract the contents of a Hotfix (using the /X switch) into the OEM subdirectory of the Distribution Share Point and reference the HOTFIX.EXE with a -M switch (for unattended mode) within the CMDLINES.TXT.

Installing and Configuring Printers

One of the most important aspects of creating an unattended installation is the ability to add printers to workstations during the setup process. The simplest way to accomplish this task is through the use of a *SYSDIFF image file*. This can be done by taking a snapshot of an NT workstation, installing the appropriate printer, and then creating a difference file. The difference file can be extracted to the DSP with the /INF option and installed with an addition to the CMDLINES.TXT file:

```
[Commands]
"RUNDLL32 SETUPAPI.DLL,InstallHinfSection DefaultInstall 128 .\diff.inf"
```

Following is an example DIFF.INF containing only the installation and configuration of a Hewlett-Packard LaserJet 4 printer.

```
DIFF.INF

; Dump of sysdiff package e:\temp\diff.img
; File created with sysdiff version 40006
; Sysroot: F:\WINNT
; Usrroot: F:\WINNT\Profiles\Administrator
; Usrroot: F:\WINNT\Profiles\ADMINI~1
; TotalDiffCount: 11

[Version]
Signature = "$Windows NT$"

[DefaultInstall]
AddReg = AddReg
DelReg = DelReg
UpdateInis = UpdateInis

[AddReg]
HKLM,"SYSTEM\CurrentControlSet\Control\Print\Printers\HP LaserJet 4","Attributes",65537,2048
HKLM,"SYSTEM\CurrentControlSet\Control\Print\Printers\HP LaserJet 4","ChangeID",65537,695080
HKLM,"SYSTEM\CurrentControlSet\Control\Print\Printers\HP LaserJet 4","Datatype",0,"RAW"
HKLM,"SYSTEM\CurrentControlSet\Control\Print\Printers\HP LaserJet 4","Default DevMode",196609,\
```

156 Part II: Advanced Configuration of an Unattended Installation

```
48,00,50,00,20,00,4c,00,61,00,73,00,65,00,72,00,4a,00,65,00,74,00,20,00,34,\
00,00,00,00,00,00,00,00,00,00,00,00,00,00,00,00,00,00,00,00,00,00,00,00,\
00,00,00,00,00,00,00,00,00,00,00,00,00,00,01,04,01,03,dc,00,70,00,03,63,01,\
00,01,00,01,00,00,00,00,00,00,01,00,0f,00,58,02,02,00,01,00,58,02,02,00,\
00,00,4c,00,65,00,74,00,74,00,65,00,72,00,00,00,00,00,00,00,00,00,00,00,\
00,00,00,00,00,00,00,00,00,00,00,00,00,00,00,00,00,00,00,00,00,00,00,00,\
00,00,00,00,00,00,00,00,00,00,00,00,00,00,00,00,00,00,00,00,00,00,00,00,\
00,00,00,00,00,00,00,00,00,00,00,00,00,00,00,00,00,00,00,00,00,00,00,00,\
00,00,00,00,00,00,00,00,00,00,00,00,00,00,00,00,00,00,00,00,20,00,ff,ff,ff,\
ff,25,03,00,00,00,00,00,00,ff,ff,ff,ff,ff,ff,ff,ff,00,00,02,00,04,00,11,00,\
ff,ff,00,00,ff,ff,00,00,01,00,ff,ff,01,00,01,00,00,00,ff,ff,01,00,02,00,ff,\
ff,ff,ff,ff,ff,ff,ff,ff,ff,ff,ff,ff,ff,ff,ff,ff,ff,ff,ff,ff,ff,ff,ff,ff,\
ff,ff,ff,ff,00,00,00,00,18,00,00,00,00,00,10,27,10,27,10,27,00,00,10,27,00,\
00,00,00,00,00,00,00
HKLM,"SYSTEM\CurrentControlSet\Control\Print\Printers\HP LaserJet 4","Default
Priority",65537,0
HKLM,"SYSTEM\CurrentControlSet\Control\Print\Printers\HP LaserJet
4","Description",0,""
HKLM,"SYSTEM\CurrentControlSet\Control\Print\Printers\HP LaserJet
4","dnsTimeout",65537,15000
HKLM,"SYSTEM\CurrentControlSet\Control\Print\Printers\HP LaserJet
4","Location",0,""
HKLM,"SYSTEM\CurrentControlSet\Control\Print\Printers\HP LaserJet
4","Name",0,"HP LaserJet 4"
HKLM,"SYSTEM\CurrentControlSet\Control\Print\Printers\HP LaserJet
4","Parameters",0,""
HKLM,"SYSTEM\CurrentControlSet\Control\Print\Printers\HP LaserJet
4","Port",0,"LPT1:"
HKLM,"SYSTEM\CurrentControlSet\Control\Print\Printers\HP LaserJet 4","Print
Processor",0,"winprint"
HKLM,"SYSTEM\CurrentControlSet\Control\Print\Printers\HP LaserJet 4","Printer
Driver",0,"HP LaserJet 4"
HKLM,"SYSTEM\CurrentControlSet\Control\Print\Printers\HP LaserJet
4","Priority",65537,1
HKLM,"SYSTEM\CurrentControlSet\Control\Print\Printers\HP LaserJet
4","Security",196609,\
01,00,04,80,14,01,00,00,24,01,00,00,00,00,00,00,14,00,00,00,02,00,00,01,0a,\
00,00,00,00,0a,14,00,00,00,02,00,01,01,00,00,00,00,00,03,00,00,00,00,00,09,\
14,00,00,00,00,10,01,01,00,00,00,00,00,03,00,00,00,00,00,00,14,00,08,00,02,\
00,01,01,00,00,00,00,00,01,00,00,00,00,00,00,0a,14,00,00,00,00,20,01,01,00,00,\
00,00,00,01,00,00,00,00,00,00,00,18,00,0c,00,0f,00,01,02,00,00,00,00,00,05,20,\
00,00,00,20,02,00,00,00,0b,18,00,00,00,00,10,01,02,00,00,00,00,00,05,20,00,\
00,00,20,02,00,00,00,00,18,00,0c,00,0f,00,01,02,00,00,00,00,00,05,20,00,00,\
00,26,02,00,00,00,00,0b,18,00,00,00,00,10,01,02,00,00,00,00,00,05,20,00,00,00,\
26,02,00,00,00,00,18,00,0c,00,0f,00,01,02,00,00,00,00,00,05,20,00,00,00,25,\
02,00,00,00,0b,18,00,00,00,00,10,01,02,00,00,00,00,00,05,20,00,00,00,25,02,\
00,00,00,00,00,00,00,00,00,00,00,00,00,00,00,00,00,00,00,00,00,00,00,00,\
00,01,02,00,00,00,00,00,05,20,00,00,00,20,02,00,00,01,05,00,00,00,00,00,05,\
15,00,00,00,aa,02,32,00,1c,2e,3b,2b,51,2b,ba,14,01,02,00,00
HKLM,"SYSTEM\CurrentControlSet\Control\Print\Printers\HP LaserJet 4","Separator
File",0,""
HKLM,"SYSTEM\CurrentControlSet\Control\Print\Printers\HP LaserJet 4","Share
Name",0,""
```

Chapter 5: Installing Additional Applications 157

```
HKLM,"SYSTEM\CurrentControlSet\Control\Print\Printers\HP LaserJet
4","SpoolDirectory",0,""
HKLM,"SYSTEM\CurrentControlSet\Control\Print\Printers\HP LaserJet
4","StartTime",65537,0
HKLM,"SYSTEM\CurrentControlSet\Control\Print\Printers\HP LaserJet
4","Status",65537,128
HKLM,"SYSTEM\CurrentControlSet\Control\Print\Printers\HP LaserJet
4","TotalBytes",196609,\
    00,00,00,00,00,00,00,00
HKLM,"SYSTEM\CurrentControlSet\Control\Print\Printers\HP LaserJet
4","TotalJobs",65537,0
HKLM,"SYSTEM\CurrentControlSet\Control\Print\Printers\HP LaserJet
4","TotalPages",65537,0
HKLM,"SYSTEM\CurrentControlSet\Control\Print\Printers\HP LaserJet
4","txTimeout",65537,45000
HKLM,"SYSTEM\CurrentControlSet\Control\Print\Printers\HP LaserJet
4","UntilTime",65537,0
HKLM,"SYSTEM\CurrentControlSet\Control\Print\Printers\HP LaserJet
4\PrinterDriverData","Country",65537,1
HKLM,"SYSTEM\CurrentControlSet\Control\Print\Printers\HP LaserJet
4\PrinterDriverData","FontCart",65536,"0"
HKLM,"SYSTEM\CurrentControlSet\Control\Print\Printers\HP LaserJet
4\PrinterDriverData","FreeMem",196609,\
    00,08,00,00
HKLM,"SYSTEM\CurrentControlSet\Control\Print\Printers\HP LaserJet
4\PrinterDriverData","Model",0,"HP LaserJet 4"
HKLM,"SYSTEM\CurrentControlSet\Control\Print\Printers\HP LaserJet
4\PrinterDriverData","RasddFlags",196609,\
    00,00
HKLM,"SYSTEM\CurrentControlSet\Control\Print\Printers\HP LaserJet
4\PrinterDriverData","TrayFormTable",65536,"Auto Select","Letter","0","Upper
Paper tray","0","0","Manual Paper feed","0","0","Lower Paper
tray","0","0","Envelope Feeder","0","0","Large Capacity","0","0"
HKLM,"SYSTEM\CurrentControlSet\Control\Session
Manager","PendingFileRenameOperations",65536,"\??\F:\WINNT\System32\SET7.tmp","
!\??\F:\WINNT\System32\PJLMON.DLL"
HKCR,"CLSID\{645FF040-5081-101B-9F08-
00AA002F954E}\DefaultIcon","",0,"F:\WINNT\System32\shell32.dll,31"
HKCU,"Software\Microsoft\Windows\CurrentVersion\Explorer\StreamMRU","MRUList",0
,"axvjwbosptucfrqnmlkihged"
HKCU,"Software\Microsoft\Windows NT\CurrentVersion\Devices","HP LaserJet
4",0,"winspool,LPT1:"
HKCU,"Software\Microsoft\Windows NT\CurrentVersion\PrinterPorts","HP LaserJet
4",0,"winspool,LPT1:,15,45"
HKCU,"Software\Microsoft\Windows NT\CurrentVersion\Windows","Device",0,"HP
LaserJet 4,winspool,LPT1:"
[DelReg]
[UpdateInis]
"F:\WINNT\WIN.INI","Devices",,"HP LaserJet 4=winspool,LPT1:"
"F:\WINNT\WIN.INI","PrinterPorts",,"HP LaserJet 4=winspool,LPT1:,15,45"
"F:\WINNT\WIN.INI","Windows",,"Device=HP LaserJet 4,winspool,LPT1:"
```

As you can see, quite a bit can go into the installation process of just one printer.

If a printer is the only thing that you want to be installed using a difference file, or if the printer is part of a small group of options you want to import, simply apply the difference file without extracting it by using the /INF option. Copy the .IMG file containing the custom settings to the \OEM subdirectory of the DSP and then reference the file in the CMDLINES.TXT file as follows:

```
[Commands]
".\SYSDIFF /APPLY /M .\PRINTER.IMG"
```

Printers can also be installed using a tool from the Microsoft Zero Administration Kit, *CON2PRT.EXE*. This tool can be used to attach to available printer shares on NT servers or workstations. It can also be used in a standard batch file to automatically add printers to workstations during an unattended installation:

```
Usage: CON2PRT [Switches]
```

Switch	Function
/C	Used to connect a system to a printer share. /C \\SERVENAME\PRINTSHARE, for example.
/CD	Used to connect a system to a printer share and set it as the default printer. /C \\SERVERNAME\PRINTSHARE, for example.
/F	Deletes all existing printer connections. It must be the first switch specified if used in conjunction with other switches.
/H or /?	Displays currently attached print shares. It cannot be used in conjunction with other options.

Tip

Ensure that the appropriate printer drivers are available on the print server for the desired printer.

Chapter 6

Securing Desktop Environments

This chapter covers:
- NT's default security settings
- NT's vulnerability to intrusion
- NT's security options
- Setting NTFS permissions with CACLS.EXE
- Editing the Registry for security
- NT's User and Group permissions

After reading this chapter, you should be able to do the following:
- Understand the security concerns with NT's out-of-the box settings
- Be able to configure NT's Registry and file system security during an unattended installation
- Use NT's additional security features, such as User and Group permissions, to augment your network security

Windows NT Security Options

Windows NT provides administrators with a wealth of security options that can be used to provide a flexible, multilayered security model tailored to suit an administrator's needs.

Windows NT's security options that are configurable during the unattended process can be broken down into these categories:
- The use of NT's File System (NTFS) and the Access Control List (ACL)
- User and group rights

160   Part II: Advanced Configuration of an Unattended Installation

- User and Group Registry permissions
- System Policies and user profiles

Each of these security categories can be implemented and configured to a greater or lesser extent during the unattended installation process. These are covered throughout the next two chapters.

Case Study: Pinkerton Security Agency

The Pinkerton Security Agency recently decided to move toward a 32-bit desktop environment and chose NT as the logical solution. Because their user community handles various types of sensitive client data, but also requires access to the Internet, natural concern arose over the security of that information on systems vulnerable to intrusion. The deployment of Windows NT Workstation required enhancing NT's security to include modified NTFS permissions, Zero Administration Kit (ZAK) Policies and enhanced Registry security.

With the rapid development of businesses and organizations implementing network computing, security has grown to be a major concern for network administrators. This is especially true with the advent of increased interactivity between corporate networks and the Internet. With the Internet's increasing importance as a resource for information and events, implementing security with deployments of NT could be considered, in certain environments, an absolute necessity.

The NT deployment at Pinkerton is not unique. Network administrators in organizations of all types are turning to NT as an excellent choice for a secure desktop.

NT's Default Security Settings

Windows NT possesses a variety of different security features, all of which, when used in conjunction, can create an extremely secure desktop environment. But Windows NT does not, by default, configure itself to use these features. In fact, NT's standard installation leaves the operating system with only minimum security standards in place. These default settings can, if ignored, represent a real security threat to the integrity of the operating system, any installed applications, and locally stored, sensitive data.

Author's Note

This book does not follow in great detail the intricacies of NT security—only the methods by which it can be configured during an unattended installation of Windows NT. Taking the time to thoroughly familiarize yourself with NT's various security tools and how they work—and don't work—together will go a long way toward helping you develop a better sense of what kinds of security should be configured in your deployment of NT.

In addition to the Microsoft resource kits, Tom Sheldon's Windows NT Security Handbook *is an excellent introduction and reference to Windows NT's complex security model.*

The default settings that represent the greatest danger to the integrity of the operating system are as follows:

- The default permissions of NTFS volumes when they are used, particularly with regards to the group Everyone.
- Anonymous users' ability to browse objects and gain access to the system Registry.
- NT's out-of-the-box vulnerability to hacking (pre-service pack installations of NT).

Problems with the Everyone Group

Much of NT's vulnerability comes from the default settings that are applied to the operating system in an *out-of-the-box installation*—that is, an installation which accepts the defaults for the setup process. You might recall in Chapter 1, "Why NT Workstation?" how some of the major concerns with NT's post-installation settings left holes that could be exploited by less-than-reputable people. Many of these holes in NT's default security can be nullified by replacing a few simple settings, but some may require more involved solutions to protect the workstations.

NT's default security structure, as stated previously, can be taken advantage of by exploiting the default settings granted to the group Everyone. You may soon grow to dislike this group because it is the principal source of many security woes. Administrators who may not fully understand the security implications of the group Everyone discard any thought of altering the group's access. By default, the group Everyone possesses the following rights to NT systems:

- Permission to read certain portions of the system Registry remotely.
- Permission to remotely browse resources such as domain usernames and share names.
- Excessive rights to the local file system of an NT workstation, such as the \%SYSTEMROOT and \SYSTEM32 directories.
- Full Control access in newly created directories and, more importantly, network shares. (Granted by default).

It is also important to note that the group Everyone is literally all-inclusive, including every User account as well as the Guest, Internet, and Anonymous (Null) logon sessions.

You can begin to appreciate the possible trouble this group can cause in an environment in which security might be required. Careful review of your security policy as it relates to new NT workstations is a must during the testing phase of your deployment planning. A misstep or oversight could result in an inadvertent breach of security.

NT's Vulnerability to Intrusion

Not all of NT's security weaknesses are related to default settings within the Registry, Permission, or file system structure. Some of NT's vulnerability to attack has come from very clever and resourceful hackers who have learned how to exploit some of the more subtle weaknesses in NT's operating system.

As an example, one threat to an NT workstation's—and less remotely, an NT server's—security is the GetAdmin hack. Created by Konstantin Sobolev, this small executable (small enough to be placed on a floppy disk) exploits a problem in a low-level kernel routine that causes a global flag to be set, allowing calls to NtOpenProcessToken, regardless of the user's current permissions. In effect, it allows any user with an account (except "GUEST") to gain Administrator privileges to a local system from that system's console by subverting the local system security and granting Administrative privileges to the account specified. This means that users logging on to the local system with guest accounts can use this exploit to grant themselves administrator equivalency on the NT system.

You can see that a hostile or disgruntled person might exploit this hack to gain Administrative access to a workstation—or worse, a server—and use that access to some undesirable end.

Other hacks of an equally threatening nature exist. Denial of service attacks, IP floods, and SMB protocol downgrades are in existence or are in the works, all to the frustration of network administrators simply trying to make it through their day.

To combat these problems, Microsoft periodically releases *service packs* and *Hotfixes* as a defense against these exploits. These released updates to the operating system carry with them the necessary fixes that are designed to thwart attacks. But it is a constant battle and with each new exploit comes the need for a service pack or Hotfix update.

Currently, both Service Pack 3 and the GetAdmin Hotfix, in addition to a few registry edits, are required to protect systems from most NT-related assaults.

Therefore, it is highly recommended that you use Service Pack 3 and any security Hotfixes in your deployment if security is an issue in your network environment.

NTFS Permissions and the Group Everyone

One of the best ways to secure sensitive data or operating system files on an NT Workstation from intrusion or possible deletion is by using *NTFS volumes* with your deployments of NT. This enables an administrator to set specific permissions for both individual and group accounts to the file system.

Their use during an unattended installation is governed by editing the `FileSystem=` key in the UNATTEND.TXT file to include the value `ConvertNTFS`. A FAT file system under NT can also be made into an NTFS volume with the use of NT's native conversion tool, CONVERT.EXE, as in the following example:

```
CONVERT.EXE C: /FS:NTFS
```

But in order for NTFS volumes to be of use, they must be configured beyond the default settings, which are extremely lax and allow for nearly unlimited access to the file system by all users. Here again, we return to the group Everyone and its default presence in the file security framework.

The default settings governing the group Everyone are as follows:

- Full Control on any newly created directory under NTFS
- Full Control on any newly created share
- Change permission on the root of each logical NTFS drive
- Change permission in both the System32 and Win32App subdirectories of `%SystemRoot%`

Again, depending on your network security environment, this type of access may not present a problem. But in more secure environments, this type of access needs to be severely restricted.

NT's Default NTFS Permissions

Next, let's take a look at the rest of the default file system permissions that are present when an NTFS volume is created on an NT system. Table 6.1 shows a complete listing of NT's default NTFS permissions.

Table 6.1. Default NTFS Rights

File System	Group	Permission
Root of NTFS drive	Administrators, System, Creator/Owner	Full Control
	Everyone	Change
%SystemRoot%\System32	Administrators, System, Creator/Owner	Full Control
	Everyone	Change
%SystemRoot%\System32\config	Administrators, System, Creator/Owner	Full Control
	Everyone	List
%SystemRoot%\System32\drivers	Administrators, System, Creator/Owner	Full Control
	Everyone	Read
%SystemRoot%\System32\spool	Administrators, System, Creator/Owner	Full Control
	Everyone	Read
	Power users	Change
%SystemRoot%\System32\repl	Administrators, System, Creator/Owner	Full Control
	Everyone	Read
%SystemRoot%\System32\repl\import	Administrators, System, Creator/Owner	Full Control
	Everyone	Read
	Replicator	Change
	Network	No Access
\users	Administrators	Read, Write, Execute, and Delete
	Everyone	List
\users\default	Everyone	Read, Write, and Execute
	Creator/Owner	Full Control
\win32app	Administrators, System, Creator/Owner	Full Control
	Everyone	Change
\temp	Administrators, Creator/Owner	Read, Write, Execute and Delete
	Everyone	Read

As mentioned earlier, the group Everyone has change access in the root of each logical drive, which can cause trouble should the user intentionally or inadvertently delete files from the root of the volume where NT is installed.

The group Everyone also possesses change access in the \%SystemRoot%\ and \%SystemRoot%System32 subdirectories, which house most of NT's critical operating system files, such as dynamic link libraries and system support files. Access to certain subdirectories under the \%SystemRoot% are vital for key functions under NT, such as Print Spooling, access to fonts, and temporary storage space for programs such as Internet Explorer.

But the default access granted to the group Everyone presents an additional risk for potential deletion or modification and should be altered if you desire stricter local station security. In this next section, we'll see how these potential problems can be altered to suit your security needs during the unattended installation process.

Modifying File System Security During an Unattended Installation

The CACLS tool can be used during an unattended installation to reset the local file system security if an NTFS volume is used. This can be accomplished with the use of a RUNONCE statement in a .REG batch file referencing multiple statements of the CACLS tool. The file can also be referenced as a scheduled event using NT's AT command. See Chapter 8, "Maintaining the Environment," for more on use of the AT Scheduling tool.

Following is an example of a .REG file that might be used, which is called SECURITY.REG:

```
REGEDIT4

[HKEY_LOCAL_MACHINE\SOFTWARE\Microsoft\Windows\CurrentVersion\RunOnce]
"RunThis" = "c:\\batch\\cacls.bat"
```

It references a .BAT file that is housed in the \OEM\C\BATCH subdirectory on the Distribution Share Point (DSP) directory. This file can be copied to any directory you choose using the OEM subdirectory. Simply modify the SECURITY.REG file to reflect the new location.

The .REG file is itself referenced in the CMDLINES.TXT file

```
[Commands]
".\REGEDIT /S .\SECURITY.REG"
```

where the executable REGEDIT.EXE and the file SECURITY.REG are both stored in the OEM subdirectory on the DSP.

Setting File System Security During Deployment Using a .BAT File

> **Troubleshooting**
>
> It is extremely important to fully test any security-enhancing/altering function prior to a deployment. Heavy-handed changes performed in a global fashion can have disastrous consequences.
>
> Case in point—suppose a batch file that alters NTFS permissions during an installation is not thoroughly tested. During a series of wildcard changes (*.*), it effectively locks out users from the workstation because their ID has had its privileges revoked on files necessary to begin the logon process.
>
> I would strongly caution administrators on the restrained use of the NO ACCESS option during the automated process of setting the ACLs. . A lockout would result in more work diagnosing why the lockout occurred. A good resource for making changes to file system security during deployment is the MS ZAK Administrator's Guide.

As previously mentioned, the CACLS.EXE tool can be referenced in a batch file, enabling an administrator to reset ACLs or file system permissions during the unattended installation process. CACLS.EXE is, however, somewhat flawed in that it requires a response of Y or N from the user to reset certain permissions. The solution is also scriptable by using an echo y¦ preceding the change request. Ensure that no space exists between the y and the pipe symbol ¦. Next is an example:

```
echo y¦cacls.exe c:\boot.ini /g administrators:f system:f users:r
echo y¦cacls.exe c:\ntbootdd.sys /g administrators:f system:f users:r
echo y¦cacls.exe c:\ntdetect.com /g administrators:f system:f users:r
echo y¦cacls.exe c:\ntldr /g administrators:f system:f users:r
```

This particular set of changes can be used to reset file permissions on a target system, defining the security for the NT boot files located in the root of C:. The /G switch in the command-line statement is used to grant user IDs a specific permission, defined in the second portion of the statement. The :f is used to grant a user Full Permission to that particular file, and :r is for read-only.

CACLS.EXE

A full accounting of CACLS and its uses are as follows:

Usage: CACLS [options]

Option	Function
/t	Changes the rights of specified files in the current directory and subdirectories for the username(s) or group(s) specified.
/e	Add changes to ACL instead of overwriting previous ACLs.
/c	Continue changing ACLs even when there are errors.
/g username:right	Grant the username(s) or group(s) one of the following rights: R – read C – change F – full control
/r username	Revoke rights for the username(s) or group(s) specified.
/p username:right	Replace a right specified for the username(s) or group(s) specified. The optional values are: N – none R – read C – change F – full control
/d username	Denies access for the username(s) or group(s) specified.

> *Tip*
>
> *If you have access to the MS NT Server Resource Kit Version 4.9, Supplement II, the XCACLS.EXE tool provides an even greater measure of control over modifying NTFS permissions during an unattended installation of Windows NT. It even includes a* /Y *option, removing the necessity for the* ECHO Y¦ *statement when referencing it in a batch file.*

With this in mind, it is important for administrators to understand how the use of CACLS.EXE can affect rights management on local workstations. If misapplied, the specified switches that are used with a CACLS.EXE command can caused unintended restrictions or permissions for users and groups.

It is important to review the newly applied ACL settings during the testing phase of your deployment to ensure that the proper types of settings are in place. Also, note that when reviewing the ACL settings for files and directories, the CALCS.EXE tool can again be used. To examine the settings for a particular file or directory, use the following command from the DOS prompt.

    CACLS <DRIVE>:\<DIRECTORY>\<FILENAME>

The appropriate output will appear beneath it, highlighting the permissions for users and groups to the file or directory specified.

You may notice some additional information contained in the output when reviewing permission sets with the CACLS tool. These are (OI), (IO), or (CI), which appear after the user or group, but before the permission variable. These denote the Inheritance setting for the file or directory in question. They are as follows:

- Objects—Represent files.

- Containers—Represent directories.

- Object Inherit (OI)—Files created in the specified directory inherit the designated right.

- Container Inherit (CI)—Subdirectories created under the specified directory inherit the designated right.

- Inherit Only (IO)—Does not apply to the specified directory—only to existing subdirectories.

If you look at Table 6.1 again, you can begin to determine how NT's default permissions might be modified to best suit your deployment needs. Many of the directories and their contents can be made read-only to most users, thereby securing the operating system from harm.

However, it is important to note that while you are planning your security template, most of NT's accounts—regardless of whether they are users, administrators, or of a custom make—require specific types of access to certain files and directories of the operating system should they require the capability to log on to the system interactively.

These requisite exceptions are necessary for certain functions of NT to operate correctly. The minimum settings are as follows:

Change access to C:\TEMP (or specified temporary directory)

Change access to folder C:\WINNT (or %SystemRoot%) *

Change access to \%SystemRoot%\Temporary Internet Files

Change access to \%SystemRoot%\System32\Fonts

Change access to \%SystemRoot%\System32\Cookies

Change access to \%SystemRoot%\System32\Forms

Change access to \%SystemRoot%\System32\Help

Change access to \%SystemRoot%\System32\History

Change access to \%SystemRoot%\System32\Occache

Change access to \%SystemRoot%\System32\Profiles

Change access to \%SystemRoot%\System32\SendTo

Change access to \%SystemRoot%\System32\Ras

Change access to \%SystemRoot%\System32\Spool\Drivers

Change access to \%SystemRoot%\System32\Spool\Printers

To the Directory only, not to the directory contents.

Should additional applications be installed, further testing of these settings may be required because some programs may require greater access to \%SystemRoot% \System32 or some other directory.

Optionally, NT's startup files can be protected. Here's how:

1. Locate the files BOOT.INI, NTLDR, NTDETECT.COM in the root of the boot volume.

2. Grant Full Control to the administrator and system accounts (this can optionally be extended to include the AUTOEXEC.BAT and CONFIG.SYS files).

3. Grant Read access to the root of the boot partition for all other accounts.

Creating a CALCS.BAT File Using ZAK

Microsoft's recently released ZAK Administration Kit contains a sample batch script for their AppStation/Taskstation templates, using CACLS.EXE. Though it's an excellent example of securing an NT workstation, ZAK uses a somewhat cumbersome option, CACLS.EXE. CACLS.EXE requires a Y/N response to certain changes to the ACLs, so Microsoft devised a way of automating this requirement by adding a responding file, known as the *YESFILE*. The YESFILE contains only the letter Y. It is copied over to the target system during the setup process and then referenced in the CACLS.EXE batch file using a redirecting statement, as follows:

```
cacls.exe %SystemRoot%\system32\wowexec.exe /e /g everyone:r
<%SystemRoot%\zak\scripts\yesfile
```

The last section of the string, `<%SystemRoot%\zak\scripts\yesfile`, calls the YESFILE from the directory to which it was installed during setup.

This particular method can result in failure, should the file not be copied over during the installation process, be made inadvertently inaccessible by an earlier ACLs change, or have been deleted. To make the batch file self-sufficient, implement CACLS.EXE commands using `ECHO Y¦` preceding the `CACLS.EXE` command, as discussed earlier in this section. Taking the same example from the *ZAK Guide*, you will find that it looks like this:

```
Echo y¦ cacls.exe %SystemRoot%\system32\wowexec.exe /e /g everyone:r
```

170   Part II: Advanced Configuration of an Unattended Installation

With this in mind, let's take a look at some of the ZAK ACL settings and see if they can be improved using the previous table highlighting NT's exception directories.

In this modified example, Users—instead of the group Everyone—are given Read permission to all of the files and folders on the top level of the system drive. In fact, the group Everyone has been completely removed. This may or may not be desirable for your deployment because you may want to permit some access for members of the group Everyone.

Here, the permissions to only the files in the root of the volume containing Windows NT are reset.

```
pushd %SystemDrive%\
echo y¦ cacls.exe . /g administrators:f system:f users:r
echo y¦ cacls.exe * /c /g administrators:f system:f users:r
```

As mentioned earlier, users may not require Users access to NT's boot files, as well as to the AUTOEXEC.BAT and CONFIG.SYS files. Only the system administrators should have access to modify these files.

```
echo y¦ cacls.exe boot.ini /g administrators:f system:f
echo y¦ cacls.exe ntbootdd.sys /g administrators:f system:f
echo y¦ cacls.exe ntdetect.com /g administrators:f system:f
echo y¦ cacls.exe ntldr /g administrators:f system:f
echo y¦ cacls.exe autoexec.bat /g administrators:f system:f
echo y¦ cacls.exe config.sys /g administrators:f system:f
```

The file next resets the permissions for the Program Files directory and its subdirectories.

```
echo y¦ cacls.exe "Program Files" /c /t /g administrators:f system:f users:r
```

The Change permission allows the members of the User group to use the Hyperterminal, WordPad, and Windows Messaging programs.

```
echo y¦ cacls.exe "Program Files\Windows NT" /c /t /g administrators:f system:f users:c
```

Next, grant users the Change permission to the Temp directory, which many programs require access to. To restrict the deletion of this file by users, use the OEM\C\TEMP option on the DSP to copy over a blank file to C:\TEMP (or whatever drive letter is being used to store Windows NT).

Add an `attrib` statement to restrict deletion and hide the folder. You can then restrict users from seeing this folder by enabling them to view hidden files.

```
echo y¦ cacls.exe Temp /c /t /g users:c administrators:f system:f
```

As with the root of the `%SystemDrive%`, users are given read permission on the files contained within the \%SystemRoot% and Change access to the directory itself. This is because certain applications may require more than Read access to this folder in order to function.

```
cd %SystemRoot%
echo y¦ cacls.exe * /c /g administrators:f system:f users:r
echo y¦ cacls.exe . /g administrators:f system:f users:c
```

Here the permissions to subdirectories of the %SystemRoot% are applied, as follows:

```
echo y¦ cacls.exe config /t /c /g administrators:f system:f users:r
echo y¦ cacls.exe cursors /t /c /g administrators:f system:f users:r
echo y¦ cacls.exe help /t /c /g administrators:f system:f users:r
echo y¦ cacls.exe forms /t /c /g administrators:f system:f users:r
echo y¦ cacls.exe inf    /t /c /g administrators:f system:f users:r
echo y¦ cacls.exe java /t /c /g administrators:f system:f users:r
echo y¦ cacls.exe media /t /c /g administrators:f system:f users:r
echo y¦ cacls.exe ShellNew /t /c /g administrators:f system:f users:r
echo y¦ cacls.exe system /t /c /g administrators:f system:f users:r
echo y¦ cacls.exe system32 /t /c /g administrators:f system:f users:r
echo y¦ cacls.exe SendTo /t /c /g administrators:f system:f users:c
echo y¦ cacls.exe profiles /g administrators:f system:f users:c
```

This next section is optional because it may represent a problem for certain deployment options. In the *ZAK Guide*, this next series of CACLS options is used to deny access to all .COM, .CPL, .EXE, .HLP, .INF, and .TXT file types in the %SystemRoot%. Later, the permissions for only certain files using these file types are granted to Users.

```
echo y¦ cacls.exe *.inf /t /g administrators:f system:f
echo y¦ cacls.exe *.exe /t /g administrators:f system:f
echo y¦ cacls.exe *.hlp /t /g administrators:f system:f
echo y¦ cacls.exe *.txt /t /g administrators:f system:f
echo y¦ cacls.exe *.com /t /g administrators:f system:f
echo y¦ cacls.exe *.cpl /t /g administrators:f system:f
```

Next, folder permissions within %SystemRoot% are reset, allowing access to some while denying access to others. Again, Change access may be necessary on the directory in question for specific applications to function, but in many cases their contents can be secured with read-only permissions.

```
cd %SystemRoot%
echo y¦ cacls.exe system32 /e /g users:c
echo y¦ cacls.exe help /e /g users:c
echo y¦ cacls.exe forms /e /g users:c
echo y¦ cacls.exe cookies /t /c /g administrators:f system:f users:c
echo y¦ cacls.exe history /t /c /g administrators:f system:f users:c
echo y¦ cacls.exe occache /t /c /g administrators:f system:f users:c
echo y¦ cacls.exe repair /t /c /g administrators:f system:f
echo y¦ cacls.exe system32\viewers /t /c /e /g users:r
echo y¦ cacls.exe "Temporary Internet Files" /t /c /e /g administrators:f system:f users:c
```

Part II: Advanced Configuration of an Unattended Installation

In order to print, users require the Change permission here:

```
echo y¦ cacls.exe system32\spool\printers /t /c /e /g users:c
echo y¦ cacls.exe system32\spool\drivers /t /c /e /g users:c
```

Here, access is restored to certain files in the `%SystemRoot%`:

```
cd %SystemDrive%\
cacls.exe explorer.exe /t /e /g users:r
cacls.exe iexplore.exe /t /e /g users:r
cacls.exe userinit.exe /t /e /g users:r
cacls.exe nddeagnt.exe /t /e /g users:r
cacls.exe systray.exe /t /e /g users:r
cacls.exe runapp.exe /t /e /g users:r
cacls.exe net.exe /t /e /g users:r
cacls.exe net1.exe /t /e /g users:r
cacls.exe mapisvc.inf /t /e /g users:r
cacls.exe mapisp32.exe /t /e /g users:r
cacls.exe newprof.exe /t /e /g users:r
cacls.exe con2prt.exe /t /e /g users:r
cacls.exe fixprf.exe /t /e /g users:r
cacls.exe winhlp32.exe /t /e /g users:r
cacls.exe mspaint.exe /t /e /g users:r
cacls.exe mplay32.exe /t /e /g users:r
cacls.exe sndrec32.exe /t /e /g users:r
cacls.exe wordpad.exe /t /e /g users:r
cacls.exe packager.exe /t /e /g users:r
cacls.exe windows.hlp /t /e /g users:r
cacls.exe taskmgr.exe /t /e /g users:r
cacls.exe internat.exe /t /e /g users:r
cacls.exe cmd.exe /t /e /g users:r
```

These last files are reset to ensure users can run MS-DOS applications, but they can be restricted:

```
echo y¦ cacls.exe %SystemRoot%\system32\ntvdm.exe    /e /g users:r
echo y¦ cacls.exe %SystemRoot%\system32\wowexec.exe /e /g users:r
echo y¦ cacls.exe %SystemRoot%\system32\command.com /e /g users:r
```

This example can be modified to suit your own installation need; it only stands as an example of how CACLS.EXE may be used during an installation. It is important to note that security should represent the final change to occur during an installation because the resetting of file system security can inadvertently impede the correct installation and registering of software that may be installed during the unattended process. Thoroughly reviewing your security needs and testing the security portion of your installation ensures a smooth deployment.

User and Group Rights

As with NTFS permissions, it may become desirable to create user accounts during an unattended installation and modify the default rights that are granted to each of them. Creating User accounts during an unattended installation is easy enough; simply use a .REG file in the CMDLINES.TXT file to reference a batch file containing the NET statements you want to use.

Following is an example of the .REG file, ADDUSERS.REG:

```
REGEDIT4

[HKEY_LOCAL_MACHINE\SOFTWARE\Microsoft\Windows\CurrentVersion\RunOnce]
"RunThis" = "c:\\batch\\addusers.bat"
```

This file is referenced in the CMDLINES.TXT file in much the same way the SECURITY.REG file is used in an earlier example:

```
[commands]

".\REGEDIT /S ADDUSERS.REG"
```

The batch file itself, ADDUSERS.BAT, might look something like this:

```
NET LOCALGROUP "Finance" /ADD /COMMENT: "Finance Users"
NET USER DAVISPW /ADD /HOMEDIR: "C:\HOME\DAVISPW"
/EXPIRES:6/1/99 /FULLNAME: "Peter W. Davis" /COMMENT: "Peter Davis/Finance Group"
/PASSWORDREQ: YES"
NET LOCALGROUP "Finance" /ADD DAVISPW
```

In this example, a new local group is created, Finance. A new user is also created, Peter Davis, who has his home directory set up in C:\HOME\DAVISPW and is given an account expiration of June 1, 1999. The account DAVISPW is then added to the local group Finance.

Because most NET options do not require confirmation before making additions, the account is automatically created and, by default, is made a member of the Users group.

> *Tip*
>
> *A full accounting of the NET.EXE options is referenced in Appendix A of this book or can be found by simply opening a DOS window under NT and typing NET /? | MORE.*

Modifying Default User and Group Permissions

Before looking at how to modify User and Group permissions on target systems, let's first review the permissions that NT grants by default. Table 6.2 contains the default Group Rights on an NT workstation, including the advanced rights.

Table 6.2. Default User Rights

User Right	Default Group Rights on NT Workstation
Access this Computer from the Network (SeNetworkLogonRight). Allows a user to connect over the network to the computer.	Administrators, Everyone and Power Users
Act as part of the operating system (SeTcbPrivilege). Allows a process to perform as a secure, trusted part of the operating system. Some subsystems are granted this right.	(None)
Add Workstations to the Domain (SeMachineAccountPrivilege). Allows users to added workstations to a particular domain. This right is meaningful only on domain controllers.	(None)
Back up Files and Directories (SeBackupPrivilege). Allows a user to back up files and directories. This right supersedes file and directory permissions.	Administrators, Backup Operators, Server Operators (NT Server)
Bypass Traverse Checking (SeChangeNotifyPrivilege). Allows a user to change directories, access files, and subdirectories even if the user has no permission to access parent directories.	Everyone
Change the System Time (SeSystemTimePrivilege). Allows a user to set the time for the internal clock of the computer.	Administrators, Power Users
Create a Pagefile (SeCreatePagefilePrivilege). Allows the user to create new pagefiles for virtual memory swapping.	Administrators

User Right	Default Group Rights on NT Workstation
Create a Token Object (`SeCreateTokenPrivilege`). Allows a process to create access tokens. Only the local security authority can do this.	(None)
Create Permanent Shared Objects (`SeCreatePermanentPrivilege`). Allows user to create special permanent objects, such as \\Device, that are used within Windows NT.	(None)
Debug Programs (`SeDebugPrivilege`). Allows a user to debug various low-level objects, such as threads.	Administrators
Force Shutdown from a Remote System (`SeRemoteShutdownPrivilege`). Allows the user to shut down a Windows NT system remotely over a network.	Administrators, Power Users
Generate Security Audits (`SeAuditPrivilege`). Allows a process to generate security audit log entries.	(None)
Increase Quotas (`SeIncreaseQuotaPrivilege`). Nothing. This right has no effect in current versions of Windows NT.	(None)
Increase Scheduling Priority (`SeIncreaseBasePriorityPrivilege`). Allows a user to boost the execution priority of a process.	Administrators and Power Users
Load and Unload Device Drivers (`SeLoadDriverPrivilege`). Allows a user to install and remove device drivers.	Administrators
Lock Pages in Memory (`SeLockMemoryPrivilege`). Allows a user to lock pages in memory so that they cannot be paged out to a backing store, such as Pagefile.sys.	(None)
Log on as a Batch Job (`SeBatchLogonRight`). Nothing. This right has no effect in current versions of Windows NT.	(None)
Log on as a Service (`SeServiceLogonRight`). Allows a process to register with the system as a service.	(None)

continues

Table 6.2. Continued

User Right	Default Group Rights on NT Workstation
Log on Locally (`SeInteractiveLogonRight`). Allows a user to log on at the computer, from the computer's keyboard.	Administrators, Everyone, Guests, Power Users, Users, and Backup Operators
Manage Auditing and Security Log (`SeSecurityPrivilege`). Allows a user to specify what types of resource access (such as file access) are to be audited and to view and clear the security log. Note that this right does not allow a user to set system auditing policy using the Audit command in the Policy menu of User Manager. Also, members of the Administrators group always have the ability to view and clear the security log.	Administrators
Modify Firmware Environment Variables (`SeSystemEnvironmentPrivilege`). Allows a user to modify system environment variables stored in non-volatile RAM on systems that support this type of configuration.	Administrators
Profile Single Process (`SeProfSingleProcess`). Allows a user to perform profiling (performance sampling) on a process.	Administrators and Power Users
Profile System Performance (`SeSystemProfilePrivilege`). Allows a user to perform profiling (performance sampling) on the system.	Administrators
Read Unsolicited Input from a Terminal Device (`SeUnsolicitedInputPrivilege`).	(None)
Replace a process-level token (`SeAssignPrimaryTokenPrivilege`). Allows a user to modify a process's security access token. This is a powerful right used only by the system.	(None)
Restore files and directories (`SeRestorePrivilege`). Allows a user to restore backed-up files and directories. This right supersedes file and directory permissions.	Administrators, Backup Operators

User Right	Default Group Rights on NT Workstation
Shut down the system. (`SeShutdownPrivilege`). Allows a user to shut down Windows NT.	Administrators, Backup Operators, Power Users, and Users
Take ownership of files or other objects (`SeTakeOwnershipPrivilege`). Allows a user to take ownership of files, directories, printers, and other objects on the computer. This right supersedes permissions protecting objects.	Administrators

Of the permissions given by default, there are several user rights of which administrators of high-security installations should be aware and possibly audit. Of these, you might want to change the default permissions on three specific user rights. Table 6.3 highlights these recommended changes.

Table 6.3. Recommended Changes

User Right	Default Group Rights on NT Workstation	Recommended Change
Log on locally. Allows a user to log on at the computer, from the computer's keyboard.	Administrators, Everyone, Guests, Power Users, and Users.	Remove Everyone and Guests from having this right.
Shut down the system. Allows a user to shut down Windows NT.	Administrators, Everyone, Guests, Power Users, and Users.	Remove Everyone, Guests, and Users from having this right.
Access this computer from the network. Allows a user to connect over the network to the computer.	Administrators, Everyone and Power Users.	Administrators, Power Users, and Users.

NTRIGHTS.EXE

To modify these permissions, the tool NTRIGHTS.EXE can be used. This tool is part of Microsoft's Windows NT Server Resource Kit, Supplement II, which has by far the most useful tools available for the unattended installation process.

NTRIGHTS is used to change User and Group rights from the command line, and it can be scripted into a file, much like the CACLS tool. NTRIGHTS uses NT's identifiers for each right; so, to grant a user the right Access this Computer from the Network, the tool would need NT's identifier `SeNetworkLogonRight`.

Following is a sample string of how NTRIGHTS might be used:

```
NTRIGHTS +R SeNetworkLogonRight -U \\<MachineName>\Username
```

This would grant the user the right to log on to the specified system. NTRIGHTS also adds a specified right to the event log, permitting it to be monitored. Following are the options for NTRIGHTS:

Usage: `NTRIGHTS [+R/-R] Specified Right -U [User/Group] -M \\REMOTE_SYSTEM\User/Group -E`

Option	Function
+/- R	Grants/Revokes the defined right for the specified user.
-U	Defines the User/Group to receive the right.
-M	Used to assign the defined right for the specified user on a remote system.
-E	Records the change to the System Event log.

Securing the System Registry

Another default installation concern is the security of the system Registry and its vulnerability to possibly unwanted changes from both internal and remote sources. The default security settings for the Registry are again open to the Everyone group that possesses Full Control in certain areas. This may, in part, be due to the required permissions to the Registry that enable users to alter their environment settings and install or configure software.

This, however, may not be desirable in environments where security or the integrity of the operating system is a concern. In fact, even in the most minimum-security environments, some precautions should be taken to ensure that system registries and the data they contain are at least secured from outside browsing. This is especially true for networks with direct, unrestricted, or filtered access to the Internet.

> **Tip**
>
> *I would again recommend Tom Sheldon's* Windows NT Security Handbook *for NT administrators. This book will help you fully understand the process of securing NT.*
>
> *In addition to this book, Microsoft has released an excellent white paper called "Securing Windows NT Installation," which can be found at* http://www.microsoft.com/security. *In it, Tom Sheldon describes some of the more useful suggestions and registry edits—many of which you can see in this section.*

> **Tip**
>
> *Registry edits can be used in an unattended installation through the use of the CMDLINES.TXT file and REGEDIT.EXE, so Registry modifications presented here are in the format they would appear in if they were to be used in the* [commands] *section of the CMDLINES.TXT. This is referenced as*
>
> ```
> [commands]
> ".\REGEDIT /S .\YOURFILE.REG"
> ```
>
> *with the understanding that each edit would be copied to the root of the OEM subdirectory on the DSP and installed using a copy of REGEDIT.EXE copied to the OEM subdirectory.*

Protecting the Registry from External Tampering

Windows NT Workstation does not, by default, restrict remote access to the Registry. In order to protect it from external access, a key must be added to the Registry.

```
REGEDIT4

[HKEY_LOCAL_MACHINE\SYSTEM\CurrentControlSet\Control\SecurePipeServers\]
"Winreg"
```

This Registry edit exists in two parts. After the registry edit containing the WINREG key is placed on the target system, the security placed on the WINREG key determines which IDs possess remote access to the system's Registry. This means that the security for the key must be set, either by using REGEDT32.EXE to remotely access the system as administrator, or by using REGSEC.EXE during the unattended installation process. This removes the access the group Everyone may possess in the Registry of the target system.

Modifying Registry Permissions During an Unattended Installation

Microsoft's NT Server Resource Kit contains two useful utilities for modifying the system Registry:

- *REGSEC.EXE* automatically removes the entire group Everyone from the Registry and can be run during an unattended installation as a RUNONCE statement in a .REG file.

- *SECADD.EXE* can be used to remove the group Everyone from HKEY_LOCAL_MACHINE or to add the Read permission to a defined key for a specified user.

> *Tip*
>
> *Supplement II of the Microsoft NT Server Resource Kit contains an additional Registry tool, REG.EXE. This enables an administrator to import sections of a Registry that have been unloaded and stored in a file to a target system's Registry during the unattended installation process. For more on importing Registry files using the REG.EXE tool, see the Supplement II help file.*

Manually Securing the Registry from the Group Everyone

If you intend to manually secure the Registry from the group Everyone—that is, sitting at the local workstation or remotely editing the Registry using REGEDT32—modify the following keys, adding permissions that protect the Registry from any tampering from this group.

> *Author's Note*
>
> *The following edits represent only a few of the possible configuration options that can be configured through editing the Registry. As you can see, keeping track of these edits as they might be used in an unattended installation can fast become a daunting task. I would also caution users on the use of registry edits without proper testing. You can be certain that the edits you are making are at the least benign, at the most helpful, only through careful examination, testing, and implementation.*

Grant the group Everyone the following permissions on the following specified keys:

```
QueryValue

Enumerate Subkeys

Notify

Read Control

HKEY_LOCAL_MACHINE:
\Software
```

This change determines who can or cannot install software.

> *Troubleshooting*
>
> *Do not recurse this change into the subkeys of this tree because doing so may make any currently installed unusable.*

\Software\Microsoft\RPC (and its subkeys) locks the RPC services.

\Software\Microsoft\Windows NT\ CurrentVersion

Chapter 6: Securing Desktop Environments 181

\Software\Microsoft\Windows NT\ CurrentVersion\Profile List
\Software\Microsoft\Windows NT\ CurrentVersion\AeDebug
\Software\Microsoft\Windows NT\ CurrentVersion\Compatibility
\Software\Microsoft\Windows NT\ CurrentVersion\Drivers
\Software\Microsoft\Windows NT\ CurrentVersion\Embedding
\Software\Microsoft\Windows NT\ CurrentVersion\Fonts
\Software\Microsoft\Windows NT\ CurrentVersion\FontSubstitutes
\Software\Microsoft\Windows NT\ CurrentVersion\Font Drivers
\Software\Microsoft\Windows NT\ CurrentVersion\Font Mapper
\Software\Microsoft\Windows NT\ CurrentVersion\Font Cache
\Software\Microsoft\Windows NT\ CurrentVersion\GRE_Initialize
\Software\Microsoft\Windows NT\ CurrentVersion\MCI
\Software\Microsoft\Windows NT\ CurrentVersion\MCI Extensions
\Software\Microsoft\Windows NT\ CurrentVersion\PerfLib

Removing Read access for the group Everyone on this key denies remote users the right to see any performance data on the system. Consider granting Read access to the Interactive account so that only users logged on interactively can view and store performance data.

\Software\Microsoft\Windows NT\ CurrentVersion\Port (and all subkeys)
\Software\Microsoft\Windows NT\ CurrentVersion\Type1 Installer
\Software\Microsoft\Windows NT\ CurrentVersion\WOW (and all subkeys)
\Software\Microsoft\Windows NT\ CurrentVersion\Windows3.1 MigrationStatus (and all subkeys)
\System\CurrentControlSet\Services\LanmanServer\Shares
\System\CurrentControlSet\Services\UPS

If a UPS device is installed, security not only has to be placed on this key, but on any installed command file for the UPS device itself. Security for these files should reflect only the accounts that require access. Administrators and System should possess Full Control; all other user accounts' access should be tailored to suit your security needs:

\HKEY_CLASSES_ROOT (and all of its subkeys)
\HKEY_USERS\DEFAULT

Service Pack 3 Installations

Further restriction of network access to the Registry can be done on installations that have incorporated Service Pack 3 during the installation. The system Registry can be secured from anonymous (null) logons when they attempt to connect to specific named pipes. These pipes can be blocked, but exceptions can be made in the key during its installation.

```
[HKEY_LOCAL_MACHINE\SYSTEM\CurrentControlSet\Services\
LanManServer\Parameters]
"NullSessionPipes" = multi_sz: "Add the named pipes you wish to exclude from
the restriction, separated by commas. If spaces exist in the pipe name, enclose
the name in quotes"
```

> **Author's Note**
>
> *This registry edit cannot be applied during the unattended installation process because it possesses a data type of REG_MULTI_SZ. These data types cannot be applied using REGEDIT.EXE, making it an edit that must be done manually.*

Anonymous logons, by default, possess the capability to browse both domain usernames and available shares. This can be restricted on systems that have incorporated Service Pack 3 during the installation. To disable this type of access, use the following edit:

```
ANONBRWS.REG
REGEDIT4
[HKEY_LOCAL_MACHINE\SYSTEM\CurrentControlSet\Control\Lsa]
"RestrictAnonymous" = dword:00000001
```

Administrators wishing to inform or warn users concerning network policy can display legal warnings during the login sequence to ensure that users are forewarned of the consequences, should they misuse their session.

```
WARNING.REG
REGEDIT4
[HKEY_LOCAL_MACHINE\SOFTWARE\Microsoft\Windows NT\Current Version\Winlogon]
"LegalNoticeCaption" = "Caption Heading Here"
"LegalNoticeText" = "Your Message Text Here"
```

> **Tip**
>
> *By default, Windows NT Workstation displays the Shut Down button option on the login screen. This can represent a potential hazard, should a user attempt to gain unauthorized access to the local file system through the use of a bootable disk. It would be advisable, in situations that require heightened security, to prepare the target workstations by setting the system BIOS so that booting from disk is disabled, further securing the workstation.*

To disable the display of the Shut Down button, use the following edit:

```
NOCLOSE.REG
REGEDIT4
[HKEY_LOCAL_MACHINE\SOFTWARE\Microsoft\Windows NT\CurrentVersion\Winlogon]
"ShutdownWithoutLogon" = "0"
```

The logon sequence can be further secured by restricting the display of the last authenticated user's logon name. This can be done by using the following edit:

```
NOUNAME.REG
REGEDIT4
[HKEY_LOCAL_MACHINE\SOFTWARE\Microsoft\Windows NT\CurrentVersion\Winlogon]
"DontDisplayLastUserName" = "1"
```

After a user has completed a session, if he possesses the ability to shut down the system, both his login credentials, system page file, and, if used, roaming profile can be removed from cache. Though the login credentials and system page file are secured even after a user has logged out, a heightened security model may require their deletion. The roaming profile, however, is not as secure, and should be deleted in stricter security environments.

The following edits are used to clear the system once a user has logged out:

```
CLRLOGIN.REG
REGEDIT4
[HKEY_LOCAL_MACHINE\SOFTWARE\Microsoft\Windows NT\CurrentVersion\Winlogon]
PAGEFILE.REG
REGEDIT4
[HKEY_LOCAL_MACHINE\SYSTEM\CurrentControlSet\Control\SessionManager\
Memory Management]
"ClearPageFileAtShutdown"=dword:00000001
ROAMING.REG
REGEDIT4
[HKEY_LOCAL_MACHINE\SOFTWARE\Microsoft\Windows NT\CurrentVersion\Winlogon]
"DeleteRoamingCache" = dword:00000001
```

Chapter 7

System Policies and User Profiles

This chapter covers:

- The role of System Policies
- Installing and using the System Policy Editor, POLEDIT.EXE
- An explanation of NT's default policy templates
- Creating custom policy templates
- Using System Policies for security
- Modifying the NT's default User profile
- Customizing users' profiles

After reading this chapter, you should be able to do the following:

- Understand the role of System Policies in a network's security framework
- Apply and edit System Policies
- Create and deploy your own policy templates
- Customize the default User profile during the unattended install process
- Modify users' profiles remotely

The Role of System Policies

With all of the fascination over the system Registry, it's very tempting to manually edit its contents; however, a real danger exists in doing so. Registry edits can be poorly or improperly written and can even be incorrect. When misapplied, such edits can leave a system damaged beyond repair. In addition, the sheer number of edits that must be made to further modify or secure a single system, let alone 100, can quickly become difficult to keep track of, especially on networks in which mixed security settings are controlled through the Registry. The danger not only lies in an experienced administrator making these types of changes. Curious users, beta software installers, and even hackers can all wreak havoc on an unprotected NT system Registry.

Therefore, a system administrator should devise a way to implement certain Registry modifications that prevent users from making changes to important parts of the desktop, network, and operating system environment, if not completely restrict access to the Registry altogether.

This is where System Policies fit in. *System Policies* provide an administrator with the ability to make changes to Registry values that affect workstation and network security based on User, Group, or Machine affiliations. But System Policies are not restricted solely to enhancing security. You can also use them to install software or printers, modify existing applications or operating system parameters, and even control user environment variables. Policies' versatile nature makes their use extremely attractive. But System Policies should not be seen as the catch-all tool for network administration. In fact, you should scrutinize their use carefully due to the scope of changes that they can make.

When deciding whether to use System Policies to secure NT workstations, you should consider the following:

- Is a System Policy the best way to implement the desired change?
- Should configuration changes be made through Group affiliation or be applied individually?
- Would creating security be better served through a User rights restriction or NTFS permission change?
- Is security on your network always changing, or does it remain fairly constant?

These are only a few things to consider when you opt to implement System Policies to alter or enhance security on your network. Implementing System Policies can be as complex as making manual edits to workstations due to the number of multiple configurations that are allowed based on User, Machine, and Group membership.

The System Policy Editor, POLEDIT.EXE

The System Policy Editor, POLEDIT.EXE, is a tool used to create custom operating system environment variables and enforce restrictions on workstations through Registry modifications. It is located on the Windows NT Server Distribution CD-ROM under \CLIENTS\SRVTOOLS\WINNT\I386 (or

Chapter 7: System Policies and User Profiles 187

Processor Type) subdirectory. Alternatively, you can obtain the latest version from Service Pack 3 by extracting it with the /X switch.

The editor can be installed by simply running the SETUP.BAT that is included with the installation files in the subdirectory. The editor can also be installed by copying the contents of the POLEDIT.EXE subdirectory on the CD-ROM to the desired directory on the target workstation and copying the .ADM template files to the \%SYSTEMROOT%\INF subdirectory.

System Policies can be used to manipulate key, value, and string settings in the system Registry of an NT workstation. The System Policies are stored in a .POL file, which enables an administrator to initiate changes to a system Registry through the GUI of the System Policy Editor. Workstations on a network can be configured to accept System Policies from a network file server during login. This capability gives administrators the power of remote update and control, and it enables them to initiate global changes to systems on the network from a single location.

Policies can be tailored to provide default settings for both users and machines, which affect everyone, or specific settings, which affect individual users, groups, and machines. Figure 7.1 shows the System Policy Editor.

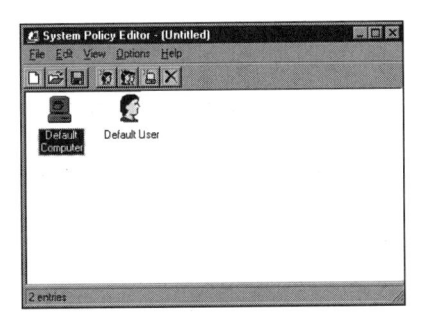

Figure 7.1. *System Policy Editor.*

As you can see, as the System Policy Editor opens it has icons for both the default User and Machine accounts. This capability makes it possible for you to place policy options and restrictions either on specific user accounts or on individual machines. Policies can also be applied to groups of users, allowing for the grouping of options tailored to a specific user community.

Figure 7.2 illustrates a more detailed use of the Policy Editor.

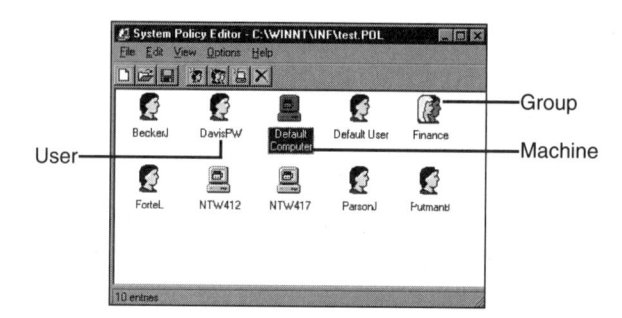

Figure 7.2. *Custom System Policy for machines, users, and groups.*

System Policies can be *layered*—that is, more than one policy can exist at the same time and can be ordered hierarchically, which makes it possible for a multipolicy environment to exist. Users, groups, and machines may be defined in more than one policy. You can set the precedence of each policy to overwrite the settings for objects in another policy, creating an elaborate structure of security and environment variables for machines, groups, and specific users.

System Policy Templates

With a System Policy, an administrator can do the following:

- Control which programs a user may use

- Restrict access to certain Control Panel functions and Registry editing tools

- Deny certain users the ability to shut down the system or save changes to the environment upon exiting the system

But this only represents a fraction of what policies can do. Windows NT ships with three standard policies, which are by default stored in the %SystemRoot%\Inf subdirectory. These templates store the following predetermined Registry settings, which may be used in a System Policy:

- The WINNT.ADM file contains custom settings unique to Windows NT desktops.

- The WINDOWS.ADM contains settings unique to Windows 95 desktops.

- The COMMON.ADM file contains settings that are shared by both operating system types.

By default, the COMMON.ADM and WINNT.ADM are loaded.

Tip

If you have Windows 95 clients on your network, System Policies for these clients must be created on a Windows 95 computer. The same rule applies to Windows NT. A policy created on a Windows NT machine can only be used on Windows NT systems.

Default Computer Policy Options

Table 7.1 contains a comprehensive listing of the configuration options available in the default policy templates COMMON.ADM and WINNT.ADM. The table defines the policy option, identifies which .ADM template file it is found in, gives the definition of the policy option, and indicates the workstation administration category or categories under which it belongs.

Table 7.1. Default Computer Policy Options

Policy	Policy Option	Function	Category
Network/ (COMMON.ADM)	System Policies Update/Remote Update	Defines the network location of the System Policy to be used; can be set to use the Automatic path or a defined Manual update path.	Security
System/ (COMMON.ADM)	SNMP/ Communities SNMP/Permitted Managers SNMP/Traps for public Community	Sets SNMP communities. Sets permitted managers. Sets traps for public communities.	Management
	Run/	Specifies a command that runs during system startup—similar to using the Startup group option, only not visible to users without Registry access.	
Windows NT Network/ (WINNT.ADM)	Sharing/Create Hidden Drive Shares (Workstation) Sharing/ Create Hidden Drive Shares (Server)	Creates or removes hidden drive shares to the root of each system drive using the <drive letter>$ along with the Admin$ share to the root of \%SystemRoot%.	Management/ Remote Update/ Security

continues

Table 7.1. Continued

Policy	Policy Option	Function	Category
Windows NT Printers/ (WINNT.ADM)	Disable Browse Thread on this Computer	Disables the sharing of printer information to other Print servers.	Management/ Remote Update/ Security
	Scheduler Priority	Sets scheduling priority for print jobs.	
	Beep for Error Enabled	System beeps every 10 seconds when a print error is encountered.	
Windows NT Remote Access/ (WINNT.ADM)	Max. Number of Unsuccessful Authentication Retries	Sets the number of remote Authentication retries before disabling the account.	Management/ Security
	Max. Time Limit for Authentication	Sets the time limit for returning an authentication response.	
	Wait Interval for Callback	Sets the time delay for the system to attempt a callback.	
	Auto Disconnect	Sets the time delay for disconnecting when detecting system inactivity.	
Windows NT Shell/ (WINNT.ADM)	Custom Shared Folders/Program Folder	Defines an alternative location for the storage or use of programs.	Management/ Remote Update/ Security
	Custom Shared Folders/Desktop Icons	Defines an alternative location for desktop icons.	
	Custom Shared Folders/Start Menu	Defines an alternative location for the Start menu.	
	Custom Shared Folders/Startup Folder	Defines an alternative location for the Startup folder.	

Chapter 7: System Policies and User Profiles

Policy	Policy Option	Function	Category
Windows NT System/ (WINNT.ADM)	Logon/Logon Banner	Displays warning or other information during the logon.	Remote Update/ Security
	Management/ Logon/Enable Shutdown from Authentication Dialog Box	Enables/disables the Shutdown button on the logon screen during startup.	
	Do not Display Last User Name	Disables/enables the display of the last user logon name.	
	Run Logon Scripts Synchronously	Sets the system to wait to process the logon script before starting the user's profile shell. If set in the user policy, the user policy takes precedence.	
	File System/Do not create 8.3 Filenames for Long Filenames	Disables the use of the DOS 8.3 naming convention for defining long filenames.	
	File System/ Allow Extended Characters in 8.3 Filenames	Permits extended characters in 8.3 naming convention filenames.	
	Do not Update LastAccess Time	Does not update the last access time for files; it can increase the system's performance.	
Windows NT User Profiles/ (WINNT.ADM)	Delete Cached Copies of Roaming Profiles	Removes copies of roaming profiles upon logout.	Management/ Security
	Automatically Detect Slow Network Connections	Detects slow network connections to the logon server.	
	Slow Network Connection Timeout	Sets the amount of time before the system issues a slow connection warning.	
	Timeout for Dialog Boxes	Sets the amount of time for timing out dialog boxes over a network connection.	

Default User Policy Options

Table 7.2 describes the default user policy options.

Table 7.2. Default User Policy Options

Policy	Policy Option	Function	Category
Control Panel/ (COMMON.ADM)	Display/ Restrict Display	Optionally deny access to the following display options: Deny Access to the Display Icon, Hide the Background Tab, Hide the Screen Saver Tab, Hide the Appearance Tab, and Hide the Settings Tab.	Management/ Security
Desktop/ (COMMON.ADM)	Wallpaper	Specify the location of the desired wallpaper background; the option exists to tile the image as well.	Management
	Color Scheme	Choose a default color scheme for users.	
Shell/ (COMMON.ADM)	Restrictions/ Remove Run from the Start Menu	Disables the Run option on the Start menu. Removes Control Panel and printers from Settings from the Settings option.	Management/ Security
	Restrictions/ RemoveFolders		
	Restrictions/ Remove Taskbar from Settings	Removes the Taskbar command from the Settings option.	
	Restrictions/ Remove the Find Command	Removes the Find option from the Start menu.	
	Restrictions/ Hide Drives in My Computer	Hides all drives from My Computer/ Explorer.	
	Restrictions/ Hide Network Neighborhood	Hides the Network Neighborhood icon.	

Chapter 7: System Policies and User Profiles 193

Policy	Policy Option	Function	Category
	Restrictions/ No Entire Network in Network Neighborhood	Restricts browsing of the entire network.	
	Restrictions/ No Workgroup Contents in Network Neighborhood	Restricts browsing of workgroup contents.	
	Restrictions/ Hide All Items on the Desktop	Removes all items from the desktop.	
	Restrictions/ Disable the Shut Down Command	Denies access to shut down the system.	
	Restrictions/ Don't Save Settings on Exit	Does not save any changes to the system upon exit.	
System/ (COMMON.ADM)	Restrictions/ Disable Registry Editing Tools	Denies access to Registry editing tools on the local system.	Management/ Security
	Restrictions/ Run Only Allowed Windows Apps	Permits administrators to create a list of local/network applications that the user may run.	
Windows NT Shell/ (WINNT.ADM)	Custom User Interface/ Custom Shell	Permits administrators to specify an optional shell command other than Explorer.	Management/ Remote Update/ Security
	Custom Folders/ Custom Program Folder	Defines an alternative location for the storage or use of programs.	
	Custom Folders/ Custom Desktop Icons	Defines an alternative location for Desktop icons.	
	Custom Folders/ Hide Start Menu Subfolders	Additional security to hide Start menu subfolders when using a Custom Programs folder or Desktop icons.	

continues

Table 7.2. Continued

Policy	Policy Option	Function	Category
	Custom Folders/ Custom Startup Folder	Defines an alternative location for the Startup folder.	
	Custom Folders/ Custom Network Neighborhood	Defines an alternative location for using a custom Network Neighborhood.	
	Custom Folders/ Start Menu	Defines an alternative location for the Start menu.	
	Restrictions/Only Use Approved extension security. Shell Extensions	Enforces shell	
	Restrictions/ Remove File Menu from Explorer	Restricts access to the File menu in Explorer.	
	Restrictions/ Remove Common Program Groups from Start Menu	Removes the Common program group from the Start menu.	
	Restrictions/ Disable Context Menus from the Taskbar	Restricts the context menus on the taskbar.	
	Restrictions/ Disable Explorer's Default Context Menu	Restricts the default Context menus in Explorer.	
	Restrictions/ Remove "Map Network Drive" and "Disconnect Network Drive" options	Denies users the ability to either map new network connections or remove preset ones.	
	Restrictions/ Disable Link File Tracking	Does not resolve .LNK extensions during startup.	
Windows NT System/ (WINNT.ADM)	Parse AUTOEXEC. BAT	Adds the environment variables contained in the AUTOEXEC.BAT to the user's environment.	Management/ Remote Update/ Security

Policy	Policy Option	Function	Category
	Run Logon Scripts Synchronously	Sets the system to wait to process the logon script before starting the user's profile shell. If set in the computer policy for the system being logged in to, the computer policy takes precedence.	
	Disable Task Manager	Disables use of the Task Manager.	
	Show Welcome Tips at Logon	Enables/disables the display of NT's Welcome tips at startup.	

Policy Option Behaviors

When implementing a policy option, the following guidelines in Table 7.3 dictate how the policy option behaves.

Table 7.3. Policy Options

Policy	Policy Option	Function
Box Checked	Option Enabled in the Target Registry	The corresponding option is enabled in the target system's Registry. A reboot of the system is normally required for the change to take effect.
Box Cleared	Option Deleted from the Target Registry	The corresponding option is removed from the target system's Registry. A reboot of the system is normally required for the change to take effect.
Box Grayed	Option Unchanged in the Target Registry	The corresponding option is ignored. Leaving the option filled provides faster processing of the System Policy, making for a swifter logon sequence.

Distributing System Policies

You can place a System Policy on the logon server (naming the policy NTCONFIG.POL and placing it in the NETLOGON share on an NT server or SYS:PUBLIC\ on a NetWare server) to automatically update any NT workstation that logs in to it. System Policies can play a role in the unattended installation process by securing, maintaining, and updating NT systems because many of the functions supported by System Policies offer options for remote update, installation, and maintenance of Windows NT.

But System Policies can be located on individual workstations as well. You can copy a System Policy of your own design to the \%SYSTEMROOT% during the unattended process by placing it in the \$OEM$\$$ subdirectory of the DSP. You can create the policy itself to reference this location in the Default Computer/Network/System Policies Update/Remote update option of the System Policy. In this way, the local policy loads automatically each time the workstation is booted.

As your skill with their use grows, you may want to create policies of your own, incorporating custom additions to policies that you currently use. Windows NT's System Policy Editor supports the use of multiple policy templates (.ADM files), so adding policy templates of your own design is easy. Creating .ADM files, however, does require practice and considerable testing. The next section covers how to customize your own policy templates.

Creating a Custom Policy File

When you are looking at the options available with NT's standard policies, the choices present a host of configuration options. These options present a broad range of applications within an unattended installation. But the available default options may not suit your current installation or security needs. You may want to create a custom policy instead of creating additional registry edits to use during an unattended installation. But tracking all of the manual edits that you may be making to systems on your network can become a cumbersome and time-consuming task.

System Policies can provide you with a single, consolidated listing of many of the edits you may want to make, all in an easy-to-use format. System Policies also present administrators with the option of creating both unique system- and user-specific changes. But creating custom ADMs can be difficult to master at first. It may require some additional time to test their validity before you actually deploy them. After you create and properly apply them, System Policies can provide an easy way to modify existing and new systems on your network.

It is important to note that when you are creating a custom policy file, certain limitations restrict their functionality:

- Policy options are restricted to the HKEY_LOCAL_MACHINE and HKEY_CURRENT_USER subtrees of the Registry. Any modification that can be made in either of these two sections of the Registry can be created in a custom System Policy. Modifications are limited only by the second restriction.

Chapter 7: System Policies and User Profiles 197

- Only edits which use specific data types can be used within a System Policy. These edits include the following: REG_SZ, REG_EXPAND_SZ, and REG_DWORD types. Registry modifications that use REG_MULTI_SZ and REG_BINARY types are not supported in System Policies. If you are familiar with the system Registry, you may know that this limitation is not great because many of the most desirable edits that can be made to the Registry exist in either HKEY_LOCAL_MACHINE or HKEY_CURRENT_USER and involve using REG_SZ or REG_DWORD data types.

With that in mind, let's look at how registry edits are transformed into options in a policy template.

Example 1: Restricting Anonymous Users

In this first example, we'll take a look at a simple registry edit that enhances a post–Service Pack 3 NT workstation's security by preventing anonymous users from viewing active account names and available shares. The registry edit, named RESTRICT.REG, is as follows:

```
REGEDIT4

[HKEY_LOCAL_MACHINE\SYSTEM\CurrentControlSet\Control\Lsa]
"RestrictAnonymous" = "1"
```

This edit can be placed in the installation process by using a statement in the CMDLINES.TXT file, as follows:

```
[Commands]
".\REGEDIT /S .\RESTRICT.REG"
```

In this way, the Registry change can be pushed down to the target workstation during the automated installation, enhancing its security.

The next example shows the same registry edit, this time in the format it would appear in as a custom policy template:

```
CLASS MACHINE

CATEGORY  "Windows NT Additional Security"

POLICY "Restrict Anonymous Browsing"
KEYNAME "System\CurrentControlSet\Control\Lsa"
        VALUENAME "RestrictAnonymous"
        VALUEON NUMERIC 1
        VALUEOFF DELETE
PART "A check here will deny Anonymous browsers the ability"
TEXT       END PART
           PART "to list Domain Usernames and Shares, Requires SP3."
TEXT    END PART
END POLICY
END CATEGORY    ;Windows NT Additional Security
```

198   Part II: Advanced Configuration of an Unattended Installation

To restrict anonymous users, follow these steps:

1. Save this example as SAMPLE1.ADM to the \INF subdirectory of \%SystemRoot%. Then open POLEDIT.EXE and select the Options and Policy Template menu option.

2. The Policy Template Options window appears (see Figure 7.3). Select Add, which enables you to browse for the file SAMPLE1.ADM in the directory in which it was originally saved.

Author's Note

For this example, the two default policy templates, COMMON.ADM and WINNT.ADM, were removed to better view the custom .ADM file.

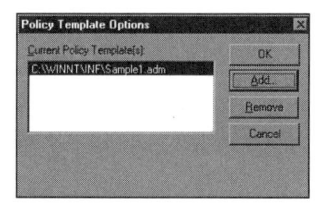

Figure 7.3. *Adding the sample template file.*

3. After selecting the custom file, click OK. Select File and then New Policy from the drop-down menu.

4. Double-click on the Default Computer icon to view the new policy option, Restrict Anonymous Browsing (see Figure 7.4).

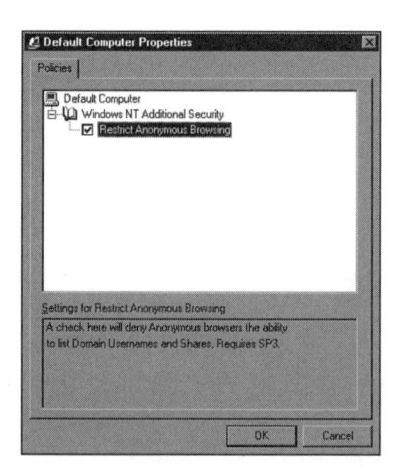

Figure 7.4. *New policy option.*

Taking a second look at our policy contents, we can identify the elements of the registry edit and identify some of the instructional code surrounding it:

```
CLASS MACHINE

CATEGORY  "Windows NT Additional Security"

POLICY "Restrict Anonymous Browsing"
KEYNAME "System\CurrentControlSet\Control\Lsa"
        VALUENAME "RestrictAnonymous"
        VALUEON NUMERIC 1
        VALUEOFF DELETE
PART "A check here will deny Anonymous browsers the ability"
TEXT        END PART
                PART "to list Domain Usernames and Shares, Requires SP3."
TEXT      END PART
END POLICY
END CATEGORY     ;Windows NT Additional Security
```

CLASS MACHINE identifies which key in the Registry will be modified with the preceding categories and policies. The two options here are MACHINE and USER. MACHINE identifies the Registry key HKEY_LOCAL_MACHINE, and USER identifies the Registry key HKEY_CURRENT_USER.

```
CATEGORY  "Windows NT Additional Security"
```

This line helps to group policies in a logical fashion. Registry edits that pertain to security can all be placed in the CATEGORY for security. The category name appears in quotation marks.

```
POLICY "Restrict Anonymous Browsing"
```

This line identifies the beginning of the POLICY option to the Policy Editor. The policy type appears in quotation marks.

```
KEYNAME "System\CurrentControlSet\Control\Lsa"
```

KEYNAME identifies the Registry location where the subsequent edit takes place.

```
VALUENAME "RestrictAnonymous"
```

VALUENAME identifies the Registry value that the policy affects.

```
VALUEON NUMERIC 1
```

VALUEON is used to denote the setting that should be placed in the Registry should the POLICY option be enabled. NUMERIC identifies this particular registry edit as a DWORD value. If the value type for the edit were REG_SZ, then the entry would not require the additional option NUMERIC; it would only require that the string variable be contained in quotation marks, as in "1". 1 is the actual String value that is to be entered for the Value type.

```
VALUEOFF DELETE
```

VALUEOFF is used to disable the corresponding policy option in the target Registry. DELETE is used to remove the VALUE entirely when disabled, but VALUEOFF can require using the NUMERIC or string entry "0" options in the registry edits that may require them.

```
PART "A check here will deny Anonymous browsers the ability" TEXT      END PART
```

PART is a multifunction identifier in Policies that you can use to display information or input requirement options in the GUI of the System Policy Editor. TEXT is only one of the functional identifiers within a PART statement, denoting that the preceding information contained in quotation marks should be displayed in the lower window of the System Policy Editor. (The other function identifiers in a PART statement are NUMERIC, EDITTEXT, COMBOBOX, DROPDOWNLIST, and LISTBOX.) END PART is used to complete the PART statement. (For more information on these PART function identifiers, see Table 7.5.)

```
PART "to list Domain Usernames and Shares, Requires SP3." TEXT  END PART
```

Another PART statement, PART … TEXT   END PART, is used here to create line breaks in the displayed information to ensure that it fits in the lower window of the System Policy Editor.

```
END POLICY
```

END POLICY identifies the end of the POLICY option.

```
END CATEGORY    ;Windows NT Additional Security
```

END CATEGORY identifies the end of the Policy category.

Example 2: Creating an Autologon Policy Option

Next is a second, more complex example of a registry-edit-turned-policy-option. Here NT's autologon feature is used to bypass the system login prompt at boot with a predetermined account name and password. Following is the modified registry edit, AUTOLOG.REG, which sets the account, password, and selected domain in the Registry.

```
REGEDIT4

[HKEY_LOCAL_MACHINE\SOFTWARE\Microsoft\Windows NT\CurrentVersion\Winlogon]
"AutoAdminLogon" = "1"
"DefaultUserName" = "Administrator"
"DefaultPassword" = "password"
"DefaultDomainName"="Domain"
```

Now here's the same registry edit used in a System Policy, SAMPLE2.ADM:

```
CLASS MACHINE

CATEGORY !!Autolog

  POLICY !!AutoAdminLogon
  KEYNAME "Software\Microsoft\Windows NT\CurrentVersion\Winlogon"
```

```
            VALUENAME AutoAdminLogon
            VALUEON "1"   VALUEOFF DELETE
        PART !!Auto_Logon_Tip1            TEXT
    END PART
        PART !!Auto_Logon_Tip2            TEXT
    END PART
        PART !!Auto_Logon_Tip3            TEXT
    END PART
        PART !!Default_UserName           EDITTEXT
    VALUENAME "DefaultUserName"
                MAXLEN 15
                    DEFAULT !!UserName_DefCaption
            END PART
PART !!Default_Password               EDITTEXT
VALUENAME "DefaultPassword"
MAXLEN 14
DEFAULT !!Password_DefCaption
END PART
        PART !!Default_Domain                 EDITTEXT
                    VALUENAME "DefaultDomainName"
                    MAXLEN 15
                    DEFAULT !!Domain_DefCaption
            END PART
END POLICY

END CATEGORY       ;Autolog
[strings]
Autolog="Windows NT Login Control"
AutoAdminLogon="Automated Logon"
Auto_Logon_Tip1="A check in this box will enable the auto-logon option"
Auto_Logon_Tip2="a Username and Password must be present, the Domain name"
Auto_Logon_Tip3="is required only if authenticating to a Domain Controller"
Default_UserName="Username"
Default_Password="Password"
Default_Domain="Domain Name"
UserName_DefCaption="Administrator"
Password_DefCaption="Password (must be non-blank)"
Domain_DefCaption="Domain Name (Only if authenticating to a Domain Controller)"
```

If we look again at this second policy example, we can see that several parts are different from the first example, most notably the use of the !! identifier and the addition of the [strings] section. The !! identifier that appears before a variable name is used to inform the Policy Editor that a corresponding line of text should be used to replace it, which is stored in the [strings] section, as in the following example:

```
CATEGORY !!Autolog

[strings]
Autolog="Windows NT Login Control"
```

Microsoft undoubtedly designed this additional functionality so that the code contained in the Policy section would not be confused or lost in lines of text.

202 Part II: Advanced Configuration of an Unattended Installation

> **Author's Note**
>
> *It is up to the individual to decide which method of providing descriptive policy information best suits his/her deployment needs.*

The next difference you may notice between these two examples is the second example's use of the PART statement and the additional function identifiers of EDITTEXT, MAXLEN, and DEFAULT. This particular Registry/Policy option requires that a username, password, and possibly a domain name be present in the Registry for the autologon sequence to function. The PART statement defines the need for a text box to be present in order for the user to input the necessary string type for this registry edit, which is denoted by the EDITTEXT identifier.

```
PART !!Default_UserName          EDITTEXT
VALUENAME "DefaultUserName"
        MAXLEN 15
            DEFAULT !!UserName_DefCaption
    END PART
```

The MAXLEN 15 option defines the maximum number of characters that may be present in the text box; a Windows NT username can only be 15 characters or fewer. The DEFAULT option is used to place default information in the text box in order to give the user further guidance about the type of information that should be placed there.

Figure 7.5 shows what the example looks like in the System Policy Editor.

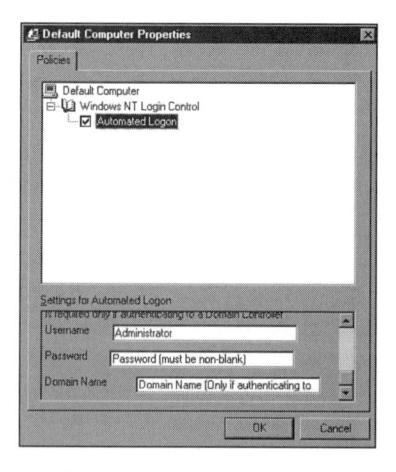

Figure 7.5. *Sample Policy template.*

Chapter 7: System Policies and User Profiles 203

> *Tip*
>
> *The file, SAMPLE2.ADM, is added to the list of policy templates in the same manner as was the first example—by first opening the System Policy Editor; choosing Options, Policy Template; and finally browsing for the file SAMPLE2.ADM.*

After you have selected SAMPLE2.ADM, choose New Policy from the File menu and double-click on the Default Computer icon. As with the first example, the WINNT.ADM and COMMON.ADM files were removed to show this example alone.

Table 7.4 highlights the available options for creating custom policies.

Table 7.4. Policy Function Identifiers

Function Identifier	Definition
CLASS type	This identifies which key in the Registry needs to be modified with the preceding categories and policies. The two options here are MACHINE and USER. MACHINE identifies the Registry key HKEY_LOCAL_MACHINE, and USER identifies the Registry key HKEY_CURRENT_USER.
CATEGORY* name	This helps to group policies in a logical fashion. Registry edits that share a common function can all be placed in the same CATEGORY. The category name may appear in quotation marks or be defined using !!VARIABLE_NAME.
END CATEGORY	This identifies the end of the Category group.
POLICY name	This identifies the beginning of the policy option to the Policy Editor. The policy type must appear in quotation marks or be defined using !!VARIABLE_NAME.
END POLICY	This identifies the end of the policy option.
PART name	This is the first portion of a multifunction statement under the POLICY option that is used to display information or input requirement options in the GUI of the System Policy Editor. (The other function identifiers in a PART statement, NUMERIC, EDITTEXT, COMBOBOX, DROP-DOWNLIST, and LISTBOX are contained in Table 7.5.)
END PART	This defines the end of PART statement.
VALUEON	This is used to denote the setting that should be placed in the Registry should the corresponding value option be enabled.
VALUEOFF	This defines the setting the value should possess when it is disabled.

continues

Table 7.4. Continued

Function Identifier	Definition
KEYNAME	This identifies the full path to the location in the Registry where the subsequent edit takes place. KEYNAME is used by subordinate CATEGORIES, POLICY, and PART variables unless KEYNAME is redefined to redirect the path for the subordinate Statement.
VALUENAME	This identifies the Registry value that the policy affects.
VALUE	This specifies the Registry value to set to a VALUENAME.
!!	This identifies a [string] value.
[strings]	This is the section header for string variables.

*CATEGORY identifiers can only appear once per category type.

Table 7.5 shows the available PART options and their functional identifiers.

Table 7.5. PART Function Identifiers

PART Function	Identifier Options	Description Identifier
CHECKBOX Denotes the use of a check box. The value if check is by default non-zero. If unchecked, the entry value is deleted.	DEFCHECK	When present, the check box is checked by default.
	VALUEON	When present, it is used to define the check box value when it is checked, with the specified value being written to the Registry.
	VALUEOFF	When present, it is used to define the check box value when it is cleared, with the specified value being written to the Registry.
	ACTIONLISTON/ ACTIONLISTOFF	It enables you to define multiple actions that affect values under the same Registry key. ACTIONLISTON defines the beginning of the parameters to be affected, and ACTIONLISTOFF ends the statement.
COMBOBOX Displays a combo box, which is an edit field plus a drop-down list entry.	DEFAULT value	If present, the corresponding value appears in the test box as an example for the required box for suggested values.
	MAXLEN value	If present, it identifies the maximum number of characters permitted in the text box.

PART Function	Identifier Options	Description Identifier
	REQUIRED	If present, the policy section containing this option cannot be used unless the requisite value has been entered for the corresponding entry.
	SUGGESTIONS/ END SUGGESTIONS	Used to present a list of optional entries that may be specified in the drop-down list.
	EXPANDABLETEXT	If present, it defines the Registry entry as REG_EXPAND_SZ instead of REG_SZ.
DROPDOWNLIST Displays a drop-down list control. The user can only choose from one of the entries supplied.	REQUIRED	If present, the policy section containing this option cannot be used unless the requisite value has been entered for the corresponding entry.
	ITEMLIST/ END ITEMLIST	Defines the list of the items contained in the DROPDOWNLIST. For example, ITEMLIST NAME *name* VALUE *value* NAME *name* VALUE *value* END ITEMLIST.
EDITTEXT Displays an edit field that accepts alphanumeric text.	DEFAULT value	If present, the corresponding value appears in the test box as an example for the required entry.
	MAXLEN value	If present, it identifies the maximum number of characters permitted in the text box.
	REQUIRED	If present, the policy section containing this option cannot be used unless the requisite value has been entered for the corresponding entry.
	EXPANDABLETEXT	If present, it defines the Registry entry as REG_EXPAND_SZ instead of REG_SZ.
LISTBOX Displays a list box with Add and Remove buttons. This is the only part type that	NOSORT	It displays the LISTBOX contents as they appear in the policy. By default, it sorts entries by their canonical names.

continues

Table 7.5. Continued

PART Function	Identifier Options	Description Identifier
can be used to manage multiple prefix values under one key.	VALUEPREFIX	It identifies the prefix to be used to determine value names. If a prefix is defined, then the prefix plus "1", "2", and so on is used. This is used in place of the default naming scheme. The prefix can be empty (""), which causes the value names to be "1", "2", and so on. This entry cannot be used with the EXPLICIT-VALUE option.
	EXPLICITVALUE	This requires not only the value data, but also the value name. This entry cannot be used with the VALUEPREFIX option.
	ADDITIVE	When present, this option merges the specified policy value with the corresponding Registry key. If missing, the entry deletes any existing duplicate entry for the specified key.
NUMERIC Displays an edit field with an optional spin control that accepts a numeric is empty.	DEFAULT value	When present, it specifies the default value for the NUMERIC entry. If DEFAULT is used but no value is specified, the entry value.
	MIN value	This is used to identify a minimum value setting. The default is 0.
	MAX value	This is used to identify a maximum value setting. The default is 9999.
	SPIN value	This specifies the used in spin control. A value of 0 disables spin control; a value of 1 is the default.
	REQUIRED	If present, the policy section containing this option cannot be used unless the requisite value has been entered for the corresponding entry.

PART Function	Identifier Options	Description Identifier
	TXTCONVERT	This converts entries into REG_SZ string values ("*entry_type*") rather than as binary values.
TEXT Displays a line of static (label)text. There is no associated Registry value with this part type.	No options available	No option definitions available.

Using System Policies for Security

Many of the security-related registry edits that have been covered in this book can be converted into a custom System Policy template and used in conjunction with NT's standard policy templates to create an extremely secure workstation environment. But it is important to understand how System Policies, and—more importantly—policy layering, can be used to create an effective network security framework.

Many first-time users of System Policies experience frustration because they do not understand how and when these policies should be applied. The most common error is making undesirable changes to either the default user or computer policies, such as disabling Registry editing tools and finding out upon reboot that their changes affect even the administrator's account on the local station.

Following are some general rules of thumb that you should apply when designing a System Policy for security:

- Rarely make changes to either of the System Policy's default accounts because they affect everyone. You should only modify either of these accounts if you are sure that you would like the change you are making to apply to all users.

- Just as with user accounts, try to manage users through group policies rather than individual policies when possible. This cuts down on the amount of administrative time spent incorporating changes or updates should they become necessary in the future.

- When possible, have workstations retrieve System Policies from the server during their logon sequence. This makes for administrative ease because a single policy file is being updated rather than multiple policy files on each machine.

- When assessing security-related changes to the Registry through System Policies, be sure to think through which types of changes should be

208   Part II: Advanced Configuration of an Unattended Installation

workstation-specific and which changes should follow the user. A restrictive policy local to a machine could include changes to the default user in order to ensure that the machine will not be tampered with, such as with an information kiosk or possibly a student computing lab.

- Use caution when layering group policies. It is important to remember that the dominant group policy nullifies policy restrictions that may exist in another System Policy of lower hierarchical value, effectively granting users or groups permissions that you may not want them to have.

- Document your System Policy configurations to help alleviate the problem of *policy clashes*, in which two policies conflict with one another. These clashes can often be difficult to resolve should a more complex policy structure be in place on your network. Documenting these configurations can go a long way toward diagnosing and resolving any policy clashes.

Following these simple guidelines when developing System Policies should help you avoid problems in your network environment.

Custom Policy Templates

Look back at the preceding chapter. It is important for you to note that you are not confined to the security options present in NT's default templates. By applying what was demonstrated in the earlier section, you can see that many of the security-related registry edits have been made into a custom policy template, SECURITY.ADM.

Figure 7.6 shows a custom policy template. This template includes enhanced security options for Windows NT Workstation, many of which rely on Service Pack 3 having been installed on the target system.

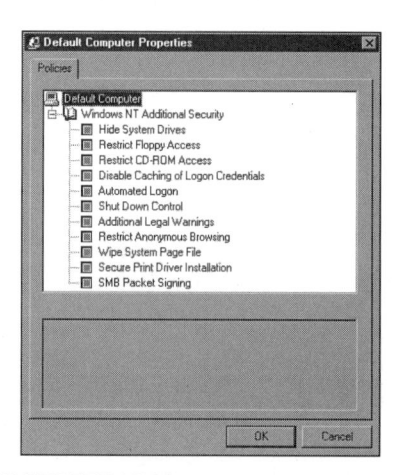

Figure 7.6. *Contents of SECURITY.ADM.*

Chapter 7: System Policies and User Profiles 209

Depending on your network environment, some of the options present in this template may not be desirable or even necessary. But this example shows how security-oriented registry edits can be grouped together and tailored in their use in either individual or group policies. Following is the code for the custom .ADM file:

```
CLASS MACHINE

CATEGORY  !!Additional_Security

KEYNAME "Software\Microsoft\Windows\CurrentVersion\Policies\Explorer"
    POLICY !!NoDrives
        PART !!Hidden_Drives_List      DROPDOWNLIST
        VALUENAME "NoDrives"
        NoSort
        ITEMLIST
            NAME "Hide All System Drives"   VALUE NUMERIC 67108863
            NAME "Hide the C Drive"         VALUE NUMERIC 67108859
            NAME "Hide the D Drive"         VALUE NUMERIC 67108855
            NAME "Hide the E Drive"         VALUE NUMERIC 67108847
    NAME "Hide the D & E Drives"     VALUE NUMERIC 67108815
        END ITEMLIST
            REQUIRED
        END PART
        PART !!NoDrives_Tip1    TEXT    END PART
        PART !!NoDrives_Tip2    TEXT    END PART
    END POLICY

    POLICY !!AllocateFloppies
    KEYNAME "Software\Microsoft\Windows NT\CurrentVersion\Winlogon"
    VALUENAME AllocateFloppies
        VALUEON "1"  VALUEOFF DELETE
        PART !!Floppy_Tip1          TEXT    END PART
        PART !!Floppy_Tip2          TEXT    END PART
    END POLICY

    POLICY !!AllocateCDRoms
    KEYNAME "Software\Microsoft\Windows NT\CurrentVersion\Winlogon"
        VALUENAME AllocateCDRoms
        VALUEON "1"  VALUEOFF DELETE
        PART !!CD_Tip1              TEXT    END PART
        PART !!CD_Tip2              TEXT    END PART
    END POLICY

    POLICY !!CachedLogonCounts
    KEYNAME "Software\Microsoft\Windows NT\CurrentVersion\Winlogon"
        VALUENAME CachedLogonCounts
        VALUEON "0"  VALUEOFF DELETE
        PART !!Cached_Logon_Tip1            TEXT    END PART
        PART !!Cached_Logon_Tip2            TEXT    END PART
    END POLICY
```

```
POLICY !!AutoAdminLogon
KEYNAME "Software\Microsoft\Windows NT\CurrentVersion\Winlogon"
    VALUENAME AutoAdminLogon
    VALUEON "1"   VALUEOFF DELETE
        PART !!Auto_Logon_Tip1          TEXT    END PART
        PART !!Auto_Logon_Tip2          TEXT    END PART
        PART !!Auto_Logon_Tip3          TEXT    END PART
        PART !!Default_UserName         EDITTEXT
VALUENAME "DefaultUserName"
            MAXLEN 15
                DEFAULT !!UserName_DefCaption
            END PART

    PART !!Default_Password             EDITTEXT
VALUENAME "DefaultPassword"
MAXLEN 14
DEFAULT !!Password_DefCaption
END PART

        PART !!Default_Domain           EDITTEXT
                    VALUENAME "DefaultDomainName"
                    MAXLEN 15
                    DEFAULT !!Domain_DefCaption
            END PART
END POLICY

POLICY !!ShutdownWithoutLogon
KEYNAME "Software\Microsoft\Windows NT\CurrentVersion\Winlogon"
    VALUENAME ShutdownWithoutLogon
    VALUEON "0"   VALUEOFF DELETE
        PART !!Shutdown_Logon_Tip1      TEXT    END PART
        PART !!Shutdown_Logon_Tip2      TEXT    END PART
END POLICY

POLICY !!LogonPrompt
KEYNAME "Software\Microsoft\Windows NT\CurrentVersion\Winlogon"
    PART !!Logon_Prompt                 EDITTEXT
VALUENAME "LogonPrompt"
MAXLEN 255
                DEFAULT !!Logon_DefCaption
            END PART

        PART !!Welcome_Prompt           EDITTEXT
                    VALUENAME "Welcome"
                    MAXLEN 255
                    DEFAULT !!Welcome_DefCaption
            END PART
END POLICY

POLICY !!RestrictAnonymous
KEYNAME "System\CurrentControlSet\Control\Lsa"
    VALUENAME "RestrictAnonymous"
    VALUEON NUMERIC 1
    VALUEOFF NUMERIC 0
```

Chapter 7: System Policies and User Profiles   211

```
PART !!Restrict_Anon_Tip1         TEXT    END PART
        PART !!Restrict_Anon_Tip2         TEXT    END PART
END POLICY

POLICY !!ClearPageFileAtShutdown
KEYNAME "System\CurrentControlSet\Control\Session Manager\Memory Management"
    VALUENAME "ClearPageFileAtShutdown"
    VALUEON NUMERIC 1
    VALUEOFF NUMERIC 0
        PART !!Clear_PageFile_Tip1         TEXT    END PART
        PART !!Clear_PageFile_Tip2         TEXT    END PART
END POLICY
POLICY !!Add_Print_Drivers
KEYNAME "System\CurrentControlSet\Control\Print\Providers\LanMan Print
Services\Servers"
    VALUENAME "AddPrintDrivers"
    VALUEON NUMERIC 1
    VALUEOFF NUMERIC 0
    PART !!Print_Driver_Tip1    TEXT    END PART
    PART !!Print_Driver_Tip2    TEXT    END PART
END POLICY

        POLICY !!RequireSecuritySignature
        KEYNAME "System\CurrentControlSet\Services\Rdr\Parameters"
            VALUENAME "RequireSecuritySignature"
            VALUEON NUMERIC 1
            VALUEOFF NUMERIC 0
            PART !!Security_Signature_Tip1    TEXT    END PART
            PART !!Security_Signature_Tip2    TEXT    END PART
        END POLICY

END CATEGORY      ;Additional_Security

[strings]
Additional_Security="Windows NT Additional Security"
NoDrives="Hide System Drives"
Hidden_Drives_List="Select which drives should be hidden:"
NoDrives_Tip1="WARNING: This policy option will conflict with the"
NoDrives_Tip2="Hide Drives policy in the COMMON.ADM policy file"
AllocateFloppies="Restrict Floppy Access"
Floppy_Tip1="A check in this box will restrict access to the Floppy Drive"
Floppy_Tip2="to anyone but the user currently using an interactive login"
AllocateCDRoms="Restrict CD-ROM Access"
CD_Tip1="A check in this box will restrict access to the CD-ROM Drive"
CD_Tip2="to anyone but the user currently using an interactive login"
CachedLogonCounts="Disable Caching of Logon Credentials"
Cached_Logon_Tip1="Disables NT's default setting of caching the Logon"
Cached_Logon_Tip2="Credentials of the last interactive login session"
AutoAdminLogon="Automated Logon"
Auto_Logon_Tip1="A check in this box will enable the auto-logon option"
Auto_Logon_Tip2="a Username and Password must be present, the Domain name"
Auto_Logon_Tip3="is required only if authenticating to a Domain Controller"
Default_UserName="Username"
Default_Password="Password"
Default_Domain="Domain Name"
```

```
UserName_DefCaption="Administrator"
Password_DefCaption="Password (must be non-blank)"
Domain_DefCaption="Domain Name (Only if authenticating to a Domain Controller)"
ShutdownWithoutLogon="Shut Down Control"
Shutdown_Logon_Tip1="A check here will not permit Windows NT to be"
Shutdown_Logon_Tip2="shutdown without a User possessing a valid login first"
LogonPrompt="Additional Legal Warnings"
Logon_Prompt="Additional Warning"
Logon_DefCaption="Enter a username and password that is valid for this system"
Welcome_Prompt="Welcome Message"
Welcome_DefCaption="This entry appears in Begin Logon, Logon Info, Locked
and Unlocked Workstation titles"
Local_System_Authority="LSA Enhancements"
RestrictAnonymous="Restrict Anonymous Browsing"
Restrict_Anon_Tip1="A check here will deny Anonymous browsers the ability"
Restrict_Anon_Tip2="to list Domain Usernames and Shares, Requires SP3."
ClearPageFileAtShutdown="Wipe System Page File"
Clear_PageFile_Tip1="A check here will clear the System Page File of any"
Clear_PageFile_Tip2="sensitive data during a system shutdown."
Add_Print_Drivers="Secure Print Driver Installation"
Print_Driver_Tip1="A check in this box restricts the installation of Print"
Print_Driver_Tip2="Drivers to Administrators and Power Users."
RequireSecuritySignature="SMB Packet Signing"
Security_Signature_Tip1="This will ensure that NT Workstation will only
connect"
Security_Signature_Tip2="to servers that support SMB Packet
Signing, requires SP3."
```

Troubleshooting

If the System Policy Editor crashes using a large custom .ADM, this may be due to the way in which NT is storing the policy in memory and may not represent a problem with the policy itself. An updated version of POLEDIT .EXE is available from Microsoft's FTP site. You should download it to replace your version of POLEDIT.

Case Study: University of Victoria's Department of Computer Science

The computing staff of the Department of Computer Science at the University of Victoria recently upgraded one of their 55-workstation instructional labs from Windows 3.11 to Windows NT Workstation 4.0. The security for these systems had to be balanced to ensure that the 32-bit applications required by the department's faculty would function properly under NT. The custom configuration also had to be secure enough to protect these systems from tampering in a high-traffic environment, requiring an exacting attention to detail. The deployment of NT workstations was further complicated by the need for the workstations to authenticate to UNIX servers.

Chapter 7: System Policies and User Profiles   213

The security solutions created for this NT deployment in a UNIX computing environment are extremely creative. The local workstations are secured through modified NTFS permissions to specific files and directories. In addition, each authenticated account receives a modified NTUSER.DAT file when its User profile is generated. The NTUSER.DAT file contains registry edits that have been pulled from custom System Policies and directly added to the profile, providing an added layer of security in the lab.

Each evening, the profiles on the local systems are removed so that any that may have been tampered with are deleted and re-created using the secured settings in the custom NTUSER.DAT file after a user logs on to the system again.

Modifying NT's Default User Profile

Every installation of Windows NT 4.0 possesses a Default User profile, which is stored in the \%SYSTEMMROOT%\PROFILES\DEFAULT USER subdirectory. This folder contains all of the default environment, Registry, and application settings that are applied to each new user's profile as it is created during their first logon session. These new settings are then saved to a folder within the \PROFILES subdirectory bearing the user's logon name.

Table 7.6 shows the subdirectories contained in every NT profile.

Table 7.6.   Profile Subdirectories

Profile Subdirectory	Purpose
Application Data	This folder houses custom information for an application that is specific to the user.
Desktop	This folder contains any custom desktop icons and shortcuts.
Favorites	This folder houses a user's favorite locations or shortcuts to program folders.
NetHood	This folder contains shortcuts to networked resources in the Network Neighborhood. This folder is hidden by default.
Personal	This folder houses information and data specific to the user. By default, it is a location where applications such as MS Word store documents created by the user.
PrintHood	This folder, which is hidden by default, contains shortcuts to Printer shares.
Recent	This folder contains shortcuts to items that have recently been accessed by the user, such as specific documents or files. This folder is hidden by default.

continues

Table 7.6. Continued

Profile Subdirectory	Purpose
SendTo	This folder houses shortcuts to floppy drives, folders, or applications.
Start Menu	This folder stores the contents of the user's customized Start menu.
Templates	This folder houses shortcuts to system or application templates. This folder is hidden by default.

In addition to these folders, a user's profile directory contains a file called NTUSER.DAT. This file stores the Registry hive HKEY_CURRENT_USER that is applied to a system's Registry during the user's logon session.

Depending on your deployment or administrative needs, you may want to add modifications to the Default User's profile so that each new user logging on to that system receives customized icons, settings, and environment variables of your making.

Creating Custom User Profiles for Use During Unattended Installation

During an installation of Windows NT, a file called DEFAULT._ is copied to the target workstation. This file is actually the HKEY_USER subtree of an NT Registry. It can be modified before an unattended installation and placed back into the installation file that is set to be used by all installations, thus becoming the default for each new account created.

To create the default file, follow these steps:

1. Set up an NT workstation so that it has the user-defined environment variables you want your users to have.

2. Attach to the directory containing NT's installation files on your DSP and locate the file DEFAULT._.

3. Use NT's EXPAND.EXE to expand the file into a temporary directory to work with it, and rename the compressed file **DEFAULT.OLD** (you may want to use EXPAND.EXE at a later date).

4. Open REGEDT32 on the Template workstation and locate the hive HKEY_USER. Highlight the keyname and then go to the Registry drop-down menu and select Load Hive.

5. Locate the file DEFAULT and double-click on it. A window appears asking you to name the new hive. Call it **NTUSER**. The new hive loads beneath HKEY_USER.

Chapter 7: System Policies and User Profiles   215

6. After the new hive is loaded, you can migrate keys and values from HKEY_CURRENT_USER to the new hive NTUSER. Highlight the desired keys and save them by choosing Registry, Save Key. Restore them to the new hive by using the Registry, Restore option.

7. After you have completed the necessary changes to the new hive, select Registry and Unload Hive.

8. A warning window prompts you, as shown in Figure 7.7. Make sure that the hive you have selected is correct and then click on Yes. This saves the new settings back to the file DEFAULT, which you can then rename DEFAULT._. Copy it back to the directory on the DSP from which you retrieved it.

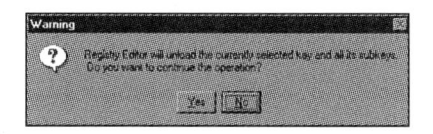

Figure 7.7. *Unloading a Registry hive.*

With this option, custom settings that you have preset in HKEY_USER can be transferred to the new systems during the unattended process, modifying every new account created to contain the new settings.

Alternatively, you can opt to modify an existing default profile on a template system and distribute it during the unattended process. The same method that was used to modify the DEFAULT file can be used to modify the NTUSER.DAT file found in the %SystemRoot%\Profiles\Default User subdirectory of the template system. This file can be loaded in REGEDT32.EXE as a new hive in HKEY_USERS and modified. It can then be unloaded and distributed to target systems using the OEM\$$\Profiles\Defaul~1 directory on the DSP, which is redefined during the unattended process by using the RENAME.TXT file with an entry such as the following:

```
[\WINNT\PROFILE\]
DEFAUL~1 = "Default User"
```

In this way, the new template is used to replace the Default User settings during the unattended installation.

As you can see, modifying the Default User profile prior to the unattended installation process can provide an administrator with an excellent tool for tweaking the user's desktop environment. Using this option, an administrator can further minimize the travel that may need to take place after an installation has completed to make those one or two extra modifications.

> **Warning**
>
> *Note that if the administrator's account on a system is damaged, deleted, or corrupted, the account is re-created using the default profile if it is not restored from an ERD or tape backup. This could be an unwanted situation should the default profile contain modifications that you do not want to pass on to the administrator's account.*

Chapter 8

Maintaining the Environment

This chapter covers:

- Preventative maintenance of NT Workstation
- Scheduling events on remote systems
- Remotely accessing and updating NT systems
- Using System Policies to control user environments
- Diagnosing problems with NT

After reading this chapter, you should be able to do the following:

- Remotely maintain Windows NT systems on a network
- Remotely schedule system updates and application installations
- Create a Network Install tab for available applications
- Set user and workstation defaults with System Policies
- Diagnose stop events

Maintenance Options for Windows NT

Second to the many difficulties intrinsic to the deployment process are those issues related to the maintenance and update of NT systems on a network. In some instances, maintenance issues can quickly outstrip installation concerns in terms of the number of problems that they create for an administrator.

But before we go any further with the last chapter of the book, we'd like to say a few final words on the subject of deploying NT because it is concerned with this chapter's primary topic—maintenance.

First, document your final working deployment—not the one that you diligently put down on paper in the preplanning stages of your deployment, but the fully functional one you just completed rolling out. Even though documentation is the bane of many an administrator's existence, it can prove to be an extremely critical element when you are faced with a problem later. Factor into your deployment plan the time you think it will take to properly document your final rollout. You'll be glad you did. Documentation can not only serve as a useful diagnostic tool, but it can aid in training new computing staff and can prove extremely valuable later when you may have to revisit your plans for a reinstallation or additional deployment of Windows NT.

Second, although it may sound much like a cliché, preventative maintenance is still the best form of maintenance around. Ensuring that your deployment takes into account the proper use of device drivers, protocols, and services, and that your user community possesses the necessary rights and permissions to function properly can go a long way toward creating a trouble-free environment. We cannot stress this point enough. An incorrectly configured installation of NT Workstation can prove to be a major maintenance headache later.

Users possessing excessive permissions to the local system can present another administrative problem. Unauthorized or improperly installed software and unwanted configuration changes represent two of the biggest maintenance issues in most computing environments, regardless of the operating system. Ensuring that users possess only the necessary rights and permissions for interactive (and, in some cases, network) login sessions and access to required applications and services also contributes to creating a more maintenance-free environment for any NT administrator.

Furthermore, testing your required set of current and new applications can make for fewer surprises later. With the tendency of applications to write program files to the \%SystemRoot% and %SystemRoot%\System32 subdirectories on the local drive, you want to be sure that these programs are not overwriting system files critical to the operating system. This is especially important when supporting legacy applications that may not be written to the newer programming standards of the 32-bit environment.

Finally, create both an update and a troubleshooting scheme. These are especially important in larger organizations. Planning the installation of system or application updates should be preceded by a proper testing phase of the update in a production environment. Finalizing a troubleshooting scheme may mean only updating your current one, but it is an important factor in the overall maintenance plan.

Case Study: Instructional Design Lab, University of Virginia School of Law

The Instructional Design Lab at University of Virginia's School of Law features a new Windows NT deployment of 13 workstations. This new lab was designed for the training section of Information Technology and Communication (ITC), the university's information technology group, in order to provide them with an up-to-date instructional environment for computer-based training.

Because the lab is relatively small—but large enough to represent a maintenance concern for just one individual—automating certain functions will minimize the total amount of time needed to maintain the environment.

In groups of five and one group of three, each workstation is scheduled at different times in the evening or early morning throughout the week to back up critical Registry information to an NT server, which is in turn backed up to tape during the server's routine backups. This makes the Registry information available to the administrator for each system should it become necessary in a diagnostic situation. The systems are also scheduled to run disk diagnostics and defragmentation routines once every two weeks at 3 a.m.

System updates are distributed through another scheduling routine, in which the workstations, again in groups of five, attach to the server and check for the existence of an update package, install it if one exists, and reboot if necessary—all without the use of Systems Management Server (SMS). In this way, many of the routine tasks of update, maintenance, and repair are scheduled to occur automatically, removing the requirement for an administrator to be physically present to perform these tasks.

The automated scheduling of these tasks also enables the administrator to process desired commands during off-peak hours so that routine maintenance neither interferes with normal class schedules, nor requires the administrator to stay late.

This chapter covers some of the maintenance options that can be remotely configured and automated to increase the total amount of work that can be accomplished by computing staff.

Maintenance and Update Logistics

After these maintenance concerns have been addressed, administrators are faced with the logistical problems of maintaining and updating Windows NT systems. A few abilities you—as the administrator—may want to automate and/or schedule are as follows:

- Remotely adding or scheduling operating system and application updates to Windows NT systems on your network.

- Remotely adding or scheduling new application installations for Windows NT systems or providing users with a menu of application/update options.

- Remotely scheduling workstations to back up critical data—such as the system Registry or entire system files—and even scheduling reboots or shutdowns.

- Remotely controlling, customizing, or restricting both user and workstation default settings, including Registry and Profile updates.

Taking another look at some of the earlier chapters on automating tasks that can occur during an unattended installation of Windows NT proves that a variety of different tools native to NT can be used for maintaining and updating the very same systems. A number of additional tools that are native to the operating system or are part of Microsoft's resource kits can extend the reach of administrators desiring remote update and maintenance capabilities on their networks.

The AT Command

A major advantage of remote administration of NT workstations is the ability to remotely schedule updates or maintenance for the operating system. Scheduling updates and maintenance can be critical. You do not want to impede the normal workflow of the user community. For example, it would probably be more desirable to schedule a remote update of 100 NT workstations to occur at 1 in the morning while no one is in the office rather than at 10 a.m. during a normal busy workday. Scheduling events remotely also removes the requirement for an administrator or computing staff member to travel to workstations, manually updating systems or performing system maintenance. The likelihood of travel is dependent upon the size, type and diversity of the network and user environment being administered.

Remotely scheduling events under Windows NT may involve using a command-line utility called *AT.EXE*. This tool is used to schedule events or commands to run on local or remote systems at desired times, and can be set to follow a scheduled pattern. Table 8.1 lists the command-line options for AT.EXE.

Table 8.1. AT *Command Options*

Usage: AT.EXE [options]
AT time /every: M, T,W, Th, F, S, Su "command"

Option	Function
"Command"	Signifies the command that is executed by AT. The command must be enclosed by quotation marks and possibly preceded by CMD.EXE should the desired event not be a .BAT, .COM, or .EXE file.
\\computername	Designates the system on which the scheduled event should be run. Used to remotely schedule services.
/delete id	Deletes a scheduled event from the queue by its ID. If no ID is specified, then all scheduled jobs currently in the queue are deleted.
/every	Specifies the date on which the event is scheduled to occur. Dates can be denoted by either the day of the week (M, T, W, Th, F, S, Su) or the day of the month (1–31). The date can also be left unspecified, signifying that the event should occur on the current date.
id	Assigns a job number to the scheduled event, starting with zero (0).
/interactive	Allows interaction of the scheduled event with the current interactive login session. Scheduled events that are not run using the /interactive switch are run as background processes.
/next::date	Runs the scheduled event on the next instance of the designated date. Multiple dates can be specified and are separated by a comma. If no date is specified, the scheduled event is run on the next instance of the day the event was scheduled on.
/yes	Used to autoconfirm AT delete commands.
time	Designates the time at which the scheduled event is to take place. The *time* should be specified using a 24-hour clock.
/?	Opens the AT help screen.

As you can see from the preceding list, an AT command can be scheduled to run on either local or remote systems. But a few initial settings must be configured or altered in order for the AT scheduling tool to function and to further customize its use:

- The Schedule service must be started on the target system in order for the AT.EXE tool to function.

- In order to remotely configure the AT command using the \\computername option, the Server service must be enabled on the target system. This does not, however, preclude locally scheduled AT commands from functioning.

- The tool is by default restricted to the Administrator group. Remote users must possess administrative equivalency on the target system. Optionally, the target system can be configured to allow system operators to enter scheduled events to occur.

AT Configuration via SCHEDULE.REG

Fortunately, the Schedule service can be remotely started and configured in a number of different ways. First, you can reconfigure the service's default during the unattended installation process so that the Schedule service is enabled to start automatically. You can change the service's startup option from Manual to Automatic using a .REG file, SCHEDULE.REG, which is referenced in the CMDLINES.TXT:

```
REGEDIT4
[HKEY_LOCAL_MACHINE\SYSTEM\CurrentControlSet\Services\Schedule]
"Start" = dword:00000002
```

After the file is created, place it in the root of the OEM subdirectory of your Distribution Share Point (DSP) and reference it in the CMDLINES.TXT as follows:

```
[Commands]
".\REGEDIT /S .\SCHEDULE.REG"
```

AT Configuration via NET START

The Schedule service can also be started through the use of a NET START command, such as NET START SCHEDULE, which can also be referenced in a server login script or RUNONCE statement. When you use this method, the Schedule service is started for that particular login session, but the Schedule service is not restarted upon reboot because the startup option for the service is still set to Manual. This particular option may be desirable to administrators who only want to enable the Schedule service for the remote update session.

Activating the Server Service on Target Systems

The next requirement for remotely issuing AT commands to NT systems on a network is that the Server service must be active on each target system that you want to remotely administer. If the Server service has been disabled or removed from the target systems, AT commands cannot be registered to remote systems. Instead, they need to be issued locally on each station, which can be accomplished by referencing AT commands in server login scripts or issuing them during unattended installations using the RUNONCE option in the target system Registry.

Modifying the Schedule Service Account

You're probably already familiar with the AT command, having used it to schedule local jobs on workstations. If you have, you are aware of its limitations, such as when you use the AT command to access networked resources. These limitations are largely due to the Schedule service's default use of the system account, which possesses administrative equivalency on the local system but only limited access on the network. In fact, the system account only possesses network credentials equivalent to the Everyone group and Anonymous or Null sessions.

In many environments, the security restrictions that may be in place on a network certainly have restricted the group Everyone's access to network resources and quite possibly have removed the capability for Anonymous or Null sessions to access or browse resources. These restrictions nullify the networking capabilities of the local system account on workstations, making it an ineffective tool for using the AT command to access networked objects.

But the system account can be replaced with a modified account of your design, which would grant the Schedule service and the AT command greater capabilities in a network environment. You could use such an account as a tool for maintaining and updating the NT systems on your network. This alteration to the operating system could even be accomplished remotely using several tools, such as the following:

- NET.EXE and REGEDIT.EXE (native to NT)
- INSTSRV.EXE (MS NT Server/Workstation 4.0 Resource Kit)
- NTRIGHTS.EXE (MS NT Server 4.0 Resource Kit, Supplement II)

With these tools, the system account is replaced, and the necessary modifications to the system account are made to allow the local system expanded access to networked resources. This can be done either during the unattended installation process of Windows NT or through a simple login script. Following is a sample batch file that can be used in unattended installations to perform the desired changes:

```
c:
cd \
cd temp
net user scheduler password /add /expires:never /passwordreq:yes
/comment:"Local Scheduling ID" /profilepath:c:\winnt\profiles\scheduler
net localgroup Administrators /add scheduler
net group "Domain Users" /add scheduler /Domain
ntrights +r SeServiceLogonRight -u scheduler
c:\temp\INSTSRV Schedule REMOVE
```

```
c:\temp\INSTSRV Schedule C:\winnt\system32\atsvc.exe -a %MachineName%\scheduler
-p password
net start Schedule
regedit /s c:\temp\schedule.reg
del c:\temp\*.* /Q
exit
```

In the preceding example, the batch file references files that have been copied to the C:\TEMP directory during the first stages of the unattended install process. The NET USER command first adds the account Scheduler to the local User Accounts database, creating the account options in the process.

The /PROFILEPATH: statement is critical. Its importance will be explained later.

The NET LOCALGROUP and GROUP statements are used to add the account to both the local Administrators group and the Domain Users group. These statements then set up the new system account to possess the local and network access credentials it needs later to schedule network jobs.

The NTRIGHTS statement grants the Scheduler ID the right to log on to the system as a service, which is critical to its use later in the command set.

The INSTSRV command removes the Schedule service and then reinstalls it by using the modified Scheduler ID and password.

The NET START command starts the Schedule service, and the REGEDIT command silently adds the file SCHEDULE.REG (referenced earlier in this chapter) to alter the default startup parameter of the Schedule service from Manual to Automatic, ensuring that with each reboot the service is started.

The final command uses DEL with a /Q switch to silently delete the contents of C:\TEMP. This command erases the files after the change has occurred and then exits the file.

Why the /PROFILEPATH Statement?

The /PROFILEPATH option keeps the Scheduler account from creating new profile folders each time the system is rebooted. The Scheduler account creates these new folders because the system recognizes the ID logging in as an actual account that possesses the logon as a Service right, so it creates a new profile folder for it. Each time the account is used to log on to the service again upon reboot, a new profile folder is created, this time with a .000 extension. As the workstation is continually rebooted, the cycle continues, creating new profile folders in sequential order—.001, .002, .003, and so on—which can fast consume disk space. In order to prevent this consumption, use the /PROFILEPATH statement when creating this account and avoid the multiple profile folder issue.

Chapter 8: Maintaining the Environment   225

Altering the AT Command Submission Control

The AT command can be configured to accept AT commands from system operators. Edit the system Registry of the target system to contain the following edit, SUBMITAT.REG:

```
REGEDIT4
HKEY_LOCAL_MACHINE\SYSTEM\CurrentControlSet\Control\Lsa
"Submit Control" = dword:00000001
```

In this way, any user logged in interactively can schedule events on the local system.

> *Tip*
>
> *To control the scheduling of AT commands when this registry edit has been added, remove or add permissions for users and/or groups from the key KEY_LOCAL_MACHINE \System\CurrentControlSet\ Services\Schedule. Removing or adding these permissions will control which users can use the AT command on the local system to schedule events.*

Remote Maintenance Capabilities of AT

After the method of starting the Schedule service and distributing AT commands has been determined, the number and types of scheduled events can include a variety of maintenance and update options. Examples include checking the integrity of the local hard disk or disks and backing up critical system information or, with NTBACKUP.EXE, even the entire system. Options could also include backing up a remote system or server for new installation packages—such as system or application updates—or for new programs. Following are a few examples showing possible remote maintenance capabilities when you use the AT command:

```
AT  00:00  /EVERY:M, W, F  \\COMPUTERNAME /INTERACTIVE
"%SYSTEMROOT%\SYSTEM32\RDISK.EXE /S-"
```

- This output schedules RDISK to back up the Registry to the \SYSTEM32\ REPAIR subdirectory (/S- denotes that no Emergency Repair Disk (ERD) is to be created in the process) of the target system at midnight every Monday, Wednesday, and Friday. This relieves the target system user from having to remember to make an ERD, while allowing you to ensure that regular backups of the system's Registry are being made. You may want to elaborate on this method because storing critical backup information on the target system may not be desirable. If you do, you can place the RDISK command in a batch file, along with a NET USE statement mapping a drive to a Server share, which is in turn used to copy the contents of \SYSTEM32\RDISK to the mapped network drive. Following is an example batch file:

226   Part II: Advanced Configuration of an Unattended Installation

```
%SYSTEMROOT%\SYSTEM32\RDISK.EXE /S-
NET USE  X: \\SERVERNAME\SHARENAME  /PERSISTENT:NO
IF NOT EXIST X:\%COMPUTERNAME% MD X:\%COMPUTERNAME%
COPY %SYSTEMROOT%\REPAIR\*.* X:\%COMPUTERNAME%
NET USE X:\ /DELETE
EXIT
```

- You can copy this batch file, here called RDISK.BAT, to the local system during an unattended installation by placing it in the \$OEM$\$$ subdirectory of the DSP and then referencing it in an AT command as follows:

  ```
  AT  00:00 /EVERY:M, W, F  \\COMPUTERNAME /INTERACTIVE
  "%SYSTEMROOT%\RDISK.BAT"
  ```

- Another example of how you can use the AT command to remotely maintenance Windows NT workstations is to schedule the remote systems to check a Server share for the existence of a system update or application install, as in the following example:

  ```
  AT  00:00 \\COMPUTERNAME  "%SYSTEMROOT%\UPDATE..BAT"
  ```

- This AT command schedules the target system to run the batch file UPDATE.BAT at midnight on the day the AT command was issued. This can easily be modified to include the /EVERY switch, causing the AT command to periodically check a server for a system update, patch, or application installation. The UPDATE.BAT file might look similar to the following:

  ```
  NET USE  X: \\SERVERNAME\SHARENAME  /PERSISTENT:NO
  X:\LATEST.BAT
  EXIT
  ```

- This output maps a network drive to the drive letter X: and then proceeds to process the file LATEST.BAT. In this way, the remote batch file, LATEST.BAT, can be altered to contain whatever system update or installation package you choose.

  Following is an example of how Service Pack 3 might be installed.

  ```
  X:\UPDATE.EXE  /F /Q
  EXIT
  ```

> *Tip*
>
> *The /F switch forces any open applications to close, and the /Q switch runs the installation in Quiet mode.*

> *Tip*
>
> *When referencing a system update, such as a service pack or a new application install, be sure to use the proper switches that allow the command to be installed using a silent or unattended installation method.*

If an application does not possess the capability to perform an unattended or silent installation, you can create a SYSDIFF package containing the customized installation of the application. You can then reference this package in the update batch file by using an /APPLY statement.

As you can see, the AT command can be used in a number of different ways to enable administrators to remotely maintain and update NT workstations on a network. The use of this extremely versatile tool is really only limited by the creativity of the administrator.

If you possess the Microsoft Resource Kit, you can also use the GUI version of the AT command, WINAT.EXE, which simply allows the scheduling of events to occur from the GUI environment. Figure 8.1 shows the WinAT interface.

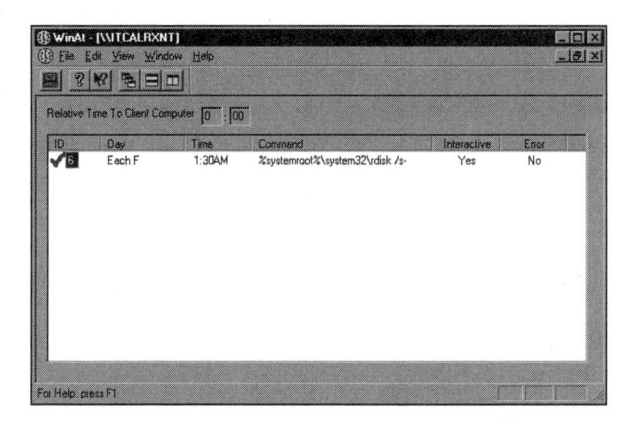

Figure 8.1. *WinAT.*

The SHUTDOWN Command

After an update or a new application has been installed or a scheduled event has been applied to a workstation, you may want to have the remote stations reboot—should the update or application not possess the capability to do so—as part of the installation process. This can be done by using either the GUI tool SHUTGUI.EXE or the command-line tool SHUTDOWN.EXE, which are both found in the Microsoft Resource Kit. The GUI version of this tool can be found in the Management Program group in the Resource Kit. Figure 8.2 shows the GUI version of the Shutdown utility.

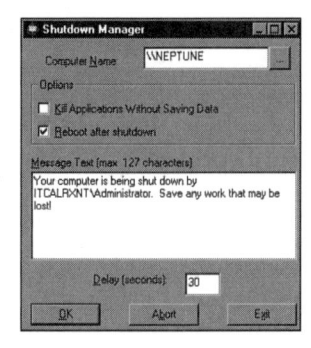

Figure 8.2. *The Shutdown Manager.*

With this utility, you can remotely force workstations to shut down and reboot.

SHUTDOWN Command-Line Options

As with the scheduling of AT commands, a remote user must possess the administrative equivalency to issue remote shutdown commands. To script the SHUTDOWN command into a batch file, use the command-line version of this tool, SHUTDOWN.EXE, which is described in Table 8.2.

Table 8.2.   SHUTDOWN Utility Options.

```
Usage: SHUTDOWN.EXE [options]
SHUTDOWN [\\COMPUTERNAME] [/A] [/C] [/L] ["MSG"] [/R] [/T:xx] [/Y] [/?]
```

Option	Function
/A	Aborts the SHUTDOWN command. This switch can only be used within the specified timeout period. Cannot be used with other switches.
/C	Forces any running applications to close.
\\COMPUTERNAME	Specifies the remote system that should process the reboot command. If no system is specified, the command is processed on the system where the shutdown command was issued.
/L	Specifies that a local shutdown should occur.
"MSG"	Allows the administrator to optionally send a message along with the shutdown command. A maximum of 127 characters can be used.
/R	Reboots the system after a shutdown.
/T:xx	Specifies the amount of time, in seconds, that the shutdown command should be delayed before processing the reboot. The default is 20 seconds.
/Y	Answers any command confirmation queries with Yes.
/?	Displays the Shutdown help screen.

Warning

Use of the /C *switch overrides any application's default setting to save data before exiting, which can result in loss of data not previously saved.*

By using this tool in conjunction with the scheduling utility AT, an administrator can remotely configure all of the NT workstations on the network to reboot at a desired time:

AT 00:45 \\COMPUTERNAME "SHUTDOWN.EXE /L /R /Y /C"

Troubleshooting Tip

Ensure that the utility SHUTDOWN.EXE exists on the local workstation so that it can be locally referenced, as in the preceding output.

With this output, administrators can remotely control updates and application installations for NT workstations on the network, including scheduling remote reboots.

Using the Network Install Tab

In some environments, administrators may want to leave the option of installing operating system updates or new applications. This can present a problem because different application and update installation files can be stored in more than one directory on a server and even on more than one server on a network. The logistical problem is to get users to install the correct or required packages. Because users possess varying levels of computing skills, they may be spending too much time searching for installation packages and storing multiple copies of an application. They may also be spending too much time updating installation files and packages in different directories or on different servers, and, in some instances, even downloading them to their local hard drives from the Internet.

To combat this problem, administrators can use an old Windows 95 trick—installing a Network Install tab in the Add/Remove Programs Control Panel. Figure 8.3 shows the Network Install tab.

With this tab, users are presented with a single menu containing pointers to installation setup files for applications and updates that may be stored in a variety of different locations. How is this done?

You can institute a Network Install tab in two ways. On an NT server, the first way is to find the APPS.INF file located in the \%SYSTEMROOT%\INF subdirectory. Open it in a text editor and add the section header [**AppInstallList**]. Beneath the header, add the application name and then its location, using either a mapped drive or UNC paths. Figure 8.4 shows an example.

230   Part II: Advanced Configuration of an Unattended Installation

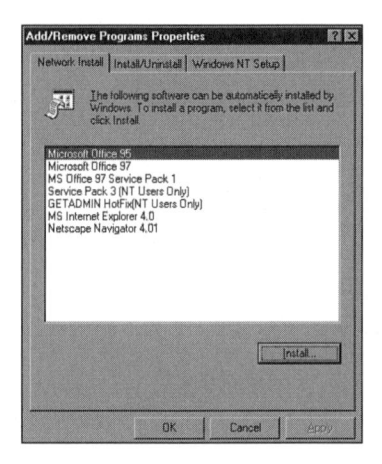

Figure 8.3. *The Network Install tab.*

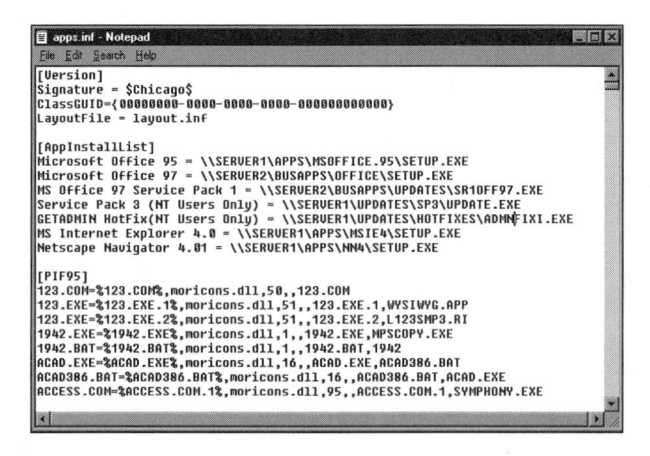

Figure 8.4. *APPS.INF file.*

In this figure, you can see the application's name as it appears in the Network Install Tab menu, followed by the path to the program or the update's setup executable. Be sure that the locations the application installs reside in are accessible to users by ensuring that they possess the correct permissions to the directories or shares.

> *Tip*
>
> *Mapped network drive letters can be referenced in the file to link drives to software installation locations, but be sure that they use persistent mappings that are available to users at all times.*

Chapter 8: Maintaining the Environment 231

After you have completed updating the file, save and close it. You can then add the following registry edit, NETINST.REG, to target workstations during an unattended installation:

```
REGEDIT4
[HKEY_LOCAL_MACHINE\SOFTWARE\Microsoft\Windows\
CurrentVersion]
"AppInstallPath" = "\\SERVERNAME\INF$\APPS.INF"
```

This output can be referenced in the CMDLINES.TXT file or added at a later date using the AT Scheduling utility or even a login script.

In this example, the \WINNT\INF directory has been flagged as shareable and made into a hidden share, denoted by the $, with Read-Only restrictions placed on it for users and Full Control for domain administrators. Users possess the ability to access the hidden share because they have Read-Only permissions to access the APPS.INF file, and domain administrators possess the ability to update the file remotely as new applications are made accessible to users. Figure 8.5 shows how the registry edit looks after it has been applied.

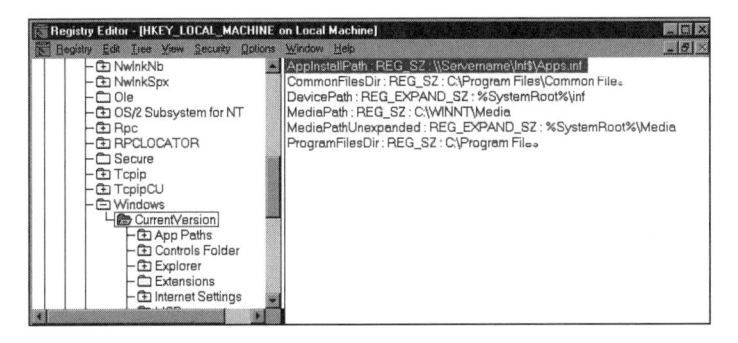

Figure 8.5. *[AppInstallPath] Registry addition.*

The second way to apply the Network Install tab is similar to the first option. In this second method, you create a file called APPS.INI, which can be placed wherever it is accessible over a network.

Open Notepad or a similar text editor and create the file APPS.INI. As in the first example, simply add the [AppsInstallList] section header to the file and then add the names and locations of the setup programs you want to be available. Figure 8.6 shows an example APPS.INI file:

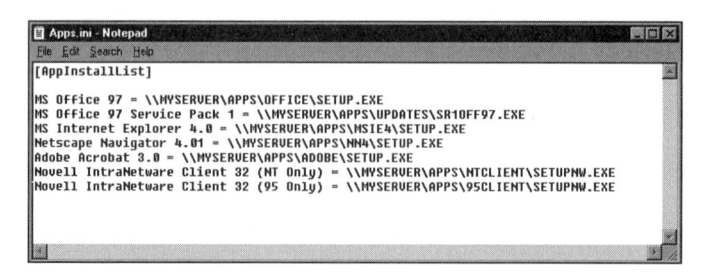

```
┌─ Apps.ini - Notepad ─────────────────────────────────────── _ ■ × ┐
│ File  Edit  Search  Help                                           │
│ [AppInstallList]                                                   │
│ MS Office 97 = \\MYSERVER\APPS\OFFICE\SETUP.EXE                    │
│ MS Office 97 Service Pack 1 = \\MYSERVER\APPS\UPDATES\SR1OFF97.EXE │
│ MS Internet Explorer 4.0 = \\MYSERVER\APPS\MSIE4\SETUP.EXE         │
│ Netscape Navigator 4.01 = \\MYSERVER\APPS\NN4\SETUP.EXE            │
│ Adobe Acrobat 3.0 = \\MYSERVER\APPS\ADOBE\SETUP.EXE                │
│ Novell IntraNetware Client 32 (NT Only) = \\MYSERVER\APPS\NTCLIENT\SETUPNW.EXE │
│ Novell IntraNetware Client 32 (95 Only) = \\MYSERVER\APPS\95CLIENT\SETUPNW.EXE │
│                                                                    │
└────────────────────────────────────────────────────────────────────┘
```

Figure 8.6. *APPS.INI.*

Next, place the APPS.INI file in a network-accessible location, ensuring that users possess Read-Only privileges to the file and to the referenced directories containing the install files. Then add the following registry edit, NETINST2.REG, to the target systems you want to have the Network Install tab:

```
REGEDIT4
[HKEY_LOCAL_MACHINE\SOFTWARE\Microsoft\Windows\
CurrentVersion]
"AppInstallPath" = "\\SERVERNAME\LOCATION\APPS.INI"
```

With this method, access to the \INF subdirectory on an NT server is not necessary. Also, the APPS.INI file can be placed in, say, the SYS:PUBLIC directory of a Novell server, making it accessible to logged-in users.

Controlling User Environments

As mentioned earlier in the chapter, preventative maintenance can go a long way toward ensuring that systems stay up and running. This argument can be extended to include customized control over a user's desktop and network environments.

It is important to make the distinction between these kinds of restrictions and those made in earlier chapters. Chapters 6, "Securing Desktop Environments," and 7, "System Policies and User Profiles," were concerned with securing the user's environment from threats related to data security and intrusion. This chapter's restrictions are designed to make a less volatile desktop, leaving users with the tools required to accomplish their tasks while ensuring the integrity of the operating system.

These are very similar topics, but an administrator who may be restricting a user from accessing the network Control Panel may not be concerned about that same user accessing sensitive data.

Securing a Workstation with System Policies

As we saw in Chapter 6, one of the most useful methods for securing an NT workstation from changes is the use of System Policies. When you apply the WINNT.ADM and COMMON.ADM templates, a System Policy can be used to inhibit users from accessing or changing system settings in a number of different ways. Some of the more useful Policy options are detailed in the following sections.

DEFAULT COMPUTER/SYSTEM/RUN

The Run option permits administrators to remotely set an application or update to run automatically when a workstation is started.

DEFAULT COMPUTER/WINDOWS NT SHELL/CUSTOM SHARE FOLDERS

- Custom Shared Programs Folder
- Custom Shared Desktop Icons
- Custom Shared Start Menu
- Custom Shared Startup Folders

These four options can be extremely valuable when an administrator wants to create custom shared desktop environments for users who are machine-centric.

DEFAULT USER/SHELL/RESTRICTIONS

- Remove Run Command
- Remove Folders from Settings
- Remove Taskbar from Settings

These options on the Start menu can be used to create a more secure desktop environment. The Remove Folders from Settings option removes the Control Panel folder.

- Hide Drives in My Computer
- Hide Network Neighborhood
- No Entire Network in Network Neighborhood
- No Workgroup Contents in Network Neighborhood

These options can provide varying levels of restrictions. Hiding the drives on a system from a user can restrict the browsing of the local file system. The options regarding the Network Neighborhood help prevent a user from browsing network objects to which an administrator may not want a user to have access.

- Disable Shutdown Command
- Don't Save Settings at Exit

These options help prevent a user from making changes to the local system that an administrator may not want to allow. This option can be used to allow interactive logins to have more control during their session but to not retain the changes upon exit; instead, the interactive logins return the system to its original state.

DEFAULT USER/SYSTEM/RESTRICTIONS
- Disable Registry Editing Tools
- Run only Allowed Windows Applications

Disabling Registry editing tools makes it impossible for a user to make manual changes to the local system Registry. This is an extremely helpful policy option. Running only allowed applications further restricts users from access to locally installed applications.

DEFAULT USER/WINDOWS NT SHELL/CUSTOM USER INTERFACE

The Custom Shell option can be useful if an administrator wants to use a customized shell other than EXPLORER.EXE during a user's session. Alternatives might be Internet Explorer, which could be used to set access restrictions on an organization's information kiosk.

DEFAULT USER/WINDOWS NT SHELL/CUSTOM FOLDERS
- Custom Programs Folder
- Custom Desktop Icons
- Hide Start Menu Subfolders
- Custom Startup Folders
- Custom Network Neighborhood
- Custom Start Menu

These options can all be used individually or together to create a customized User profile. These policy options can be used in conjunction with the Run Only Allowed Windows Applications option, which can further restrict access to local and network applications.

DEFAULT USER/WINDOWS NT SHELL/RESTRICTIONS
- Only Use Approved Shell Extensions
- Remove Common Program Groups from Start Menu

- Disable Context Menus for the Taskbar
- Disable Explorer's Default Context Menu
- Remove the "Map Network Drive" and "Disconnect Network Drive" Options

These restrictions help to deny access to configuration options an administrator may not want the user to change. Removing Common Groups from Start Menu can be helpful in preventing certain users from easily accessing information from the available options.

DEFAULT USER/WINDOWS NT SYSTEM

- Disable Task Manager (Service Pack 3)
- Show Welcome Tips at Logon

Disabling Task Manager has its advantages and disadvantages. If it is not accessible, a user may not be able to quit a program that has locked up. Show Welcome Tips at Logon can be helpful if an administrator has created customized tips for users and wants to re-enable the option if it is disabled during the unattended installation process.

Securing a Workstation via the Control Panel

In addition to using these options in the standard System Policies, an administrator can restrict access to the configurable options found in the Control Panel. If the volume containing the installation of Windows NT is NTFS, set the permission for the file you want to restrict to **Deny Access** for the user you do not want to have access to change settings. In this way, an administrator can restrict access to certain icons for users or groups, while allowing others access to them.

If the file system is FAT, rename the .CPL on which you want to restrict access to .OLD or some other file extension (see Table 8.3).

Table 8.3. .CPL Files and Corresponding Control Panel Icons

.CPL File	Control Panel Icon
ACCESS.CPL	Accessibility Options
APPWIZ.CPL	Add/Remove Programs
CONSOLE.CPL	Console
DESK.CPL	Display
DEVAPPS.CPL	PC Card (PCMCIA), SCSI Adapters, and Tape Devices
INETCPL.CPL	Internet

continues

Table 8.3. Continued

.CPL File	Control Panel Icon
INTL.CPL	Regional Settings
JOY.CPL	Joystick
MAIN.CPL	Fonts, Keyboard Mouse, and Printers
MLCFG32.CPL	Mail (may not be present if Exchange has been removed)
MMSYS.CPL	Multimedia
MODEM.CPL	Modems
NCPA.CPL	Network
ODBCCP32.CPL	ODBC
PORTS.CPL	Ports
RASCPL.CPL	Dial-up Monitor
SRVMGR.CPL	Server, Services, and Devices
SYSDM.CPL	System
TELEPHON.CPL	Telephony
TIMEDATE.CPL	Date/Time
UPS.CPL	UPS

Tip

If you have installed TWEAKUI from the Microsoft PowerToys tools, ensure that interactive users possess Read-Only access to the file TWEAKUI.CPL or an error occurs during boot.

More on Defining User Settings

We have now thoroughly considered the use of restrictions or specific configurations intended to prevent users from changing settings that an administrator may want to remain a certain way. Now we'll take a look at some of the more helpful settings that can enhance a user's environment, including the following:

- Creating Your Own Custom Tips at Startup
- Setting the Default Internet Homepage

These options can be extremely helpful to new users of NT, who might need additional guidance or assistance after an upgrade has occurred or who are using NT for the very first time.

Creating Your Own Custom Tips at Startup

Creating your own custom tips at startup can be helpful in providing network-specific information that a user may need when working on a NT workstation.

Customized tips can contain any kind of information, including who to contact if a user gets stuck.

Windows NT's default tips reside in the KEY_LOCAL_MACHINE\ SOFTWARE\Microsoft\Windows\ CurrentVersion\Explorer\Tips (see Figure 8.7). Each tip is numbered, so you can choose any of the following:

- Replacing an existing tip.
- Creating a new one.
- Adding a tip using the next available number.

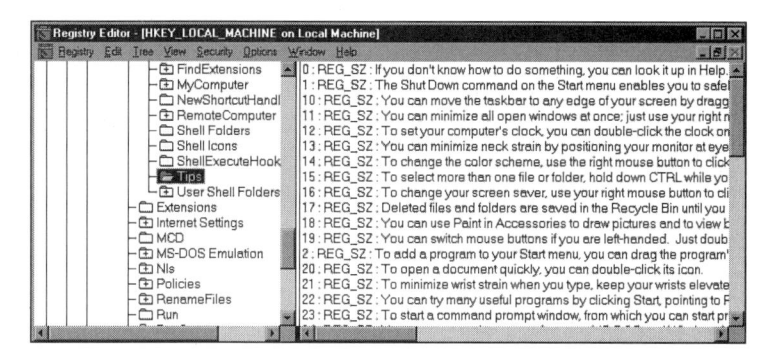

Figure 8.7. *Registry tip location.*

Each tip is entered as a REG_SZ value. It can be added as part of the unattended process by simply creating the desired tip and adding the Registry entry or entries in a .REG file referenced in the CMDLINES.TXT on the DSP.

Setting the Default Internet Homepage

Another helpful default setting is configuring the default Internet startup page. This startup page can be extremely helpful when used in conjunction with an organization's Internet/intranet Web site, which may contain addition help files, information, or resources to which a user may require access. It can also be a guide to an easily created HTML-based online tutorial for Windows NT.

By default, MS Internet Explorer is configured to point to the following file: F:\Program Files\Plus!\Microsoft Internet\docs\home.htm, but it can be reset using the following registry edit, DEFBROWS.REG:

```
REGEDIT4\.DEFAULT\
[HKEY_USERS\DEFAULT\Software\Microsoft\Internet Explorer\Main]
"Start Page" = "http://yourhomepage.com/userhelp.html"
```

This edit can be applied during an unattended installation or added to the default policy should you choose to edit it prior to an unattended installation. (See Chapter 7 for more information on editing and customizing the default user profile.)

Restoring NT Workstation

Even with the best of precautions, maintenance, and testing, problems occur. Routinely reviewing the event logs of remote workstations on your network can and will go a long way toward giving you an early warning should a problem be brewing. Incorporating the review of remote event logs into your weekly schedule may be advisable, especially if your user community requires excessive or administrative rights to the local workstation but is not careful about the system's health. Viruses, badly written device drivers, and new applications—to name a few—can all lead to an NT system exhibiting aberrant behavior, even winding up in the Stop Event screen, affectionately referred to as a *BSOD*, or *Blue Screen of Death*.

This last section does not delve deeply into the methods of analyzing stop events. It instead briefly covers how to analyze a BSOD, shows the correct steps to take to attempt a recovery, and reviews some of the possible options for restoring the system.

Diagnosing a Stop Event

Stop events are actually error traps that are built into the operating system. They are designed to monitor the various components of the operating system for problems, halting the system when an error is detected in order to avoid any further difficulties from occurring and to prevent data corruption.

Many first-time users are literally thrown into a frenzy when they encounter a stop event, with all of its cryptic information presented on a nice bright blue background. We have been surprised to note how many users quickly reboot their system, hoping to clear the offensive event. Sometimes rebooting resolves the current failure, but sometimes it does not (which is another reason why you should periodically review event logs).

The first thing to determine when diagnosing a stop event is to consider what had changed on the failing system. Ask the users if they attempted a configuration change or recently installed a new application or if they had been experiencing system lockups or failures prior to the stop event.

If no discernible changes have been made or declared, next analyze the screen itself. The results of the process error are dumped to the screen for analysis (see Figure 8.8).

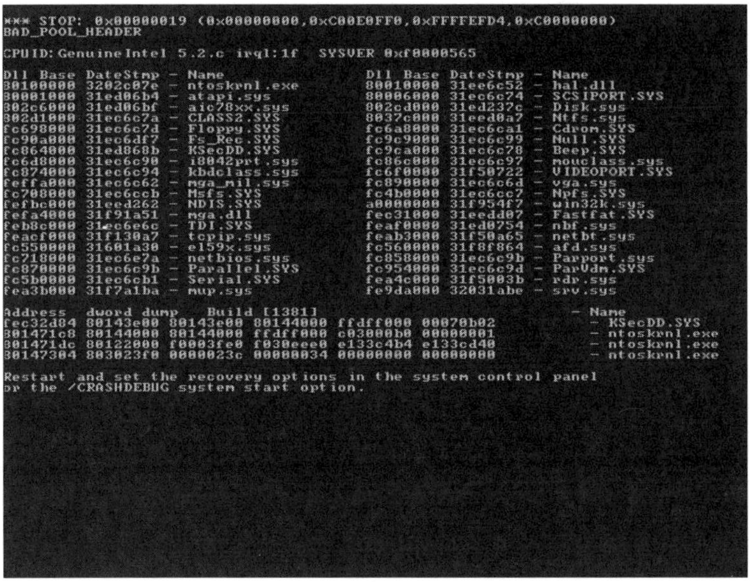

Chapter 8: Maintaining the Environment 239

Figure 8.8. *Stop event screen.*

Take special note of the stop event message STOP:, which is followed by one *Hex address* (the offending event or process event) and then three additional Hex addresses and an abbreviated message, which is the system's translation of the causal error.

BSOD error messages can be difficult to translate and can even be misleading if not properly diagnosed. An example of this might be the STOP:INACCESSIBLE_BOOT_DEVICE event, which could mean the boot sector was overwritten by another operating system installation (such as Windows 95), a bad hard drive, or even a boot sector virus. You can see why keeping accurate notes on your installation can be exceedingly helpful in the diagnosis process. They may play a factor in discovering problems that could arise later.

The sections that follow describe some common BSOD error messages and their possible meanings.

0x0000007B INACCESSIBLE_BOOT_DEVICE

As the error indicates, the system's boot device is inaccessible. Possible problems causing this error to occur are the following:

- Error accessing the hard disk
- Disk controller error or misconfiguration
- Boot sector virus

- Device driver failed to initialize the boot device
- SCSI termination error
- Unrecognizable data on disk

0x00000051 REGISTRY_ERROR
As the error message states, the system encountered an incorrect parameter while processing the system's Registry. This could mean anything from a corrupted system Registry to disk or data corruption.

0x0000000A IRQL_NOT_LESS_OR_EQUAL
A device or service process attempted to access pageable memory at a process internal request level (IRQL) that was higher than permitted. Because a process can only access objects that have priorities equal or lower in priority to its own, the system halts, generating the error. This stop event is generally caused by a bad device driver attempting to access an improper address.

0x0000001E KMODE_EXCEPTION_NOT_HANDLED
When this stop event occurs, pay attention to the exception address. It can usually be used to trace the process that caused the trap.

0x00000077 KERNEL_STACK_INPAGE_ERROR
This error means that the requested page of kernel data could not be read. This could be the result of anything from a bad block in memory to a hard disk controller error. Address ranges of 0xC000009C and 0xC000016A appearing with this error could indicate a bad block on the hard disk. An address of 0xC0000185 could indicate two devices in contention for the same IRQ, improper SCSI termination, or possibly a bad SCSI cable.

0x0000007F UNEXPECTED_KERNEL_MODE_TRAP
This error indicates an error trap that occurred in privileged processor mode and identifies a kernel trap it should not be attempting to use or catch. This usually points to corrupt file system drivers or possibly bad RAM.

> *Tip*
>
> *One of the best sources for identifying BSOD error messages is Microsoft's Knowledge Base, located at **http://www.microsoft.com**, which is being continually updated and refined. When searching for a stop event, enter **STOP** as the search string.*

Resolving BSOD Errors

After you've identified the error, it usually points you in the direction of your next step. If the error points to a recent change in the Registry, the system can be rebooted. You can attempt to use the Last Known Good Configuration option by pressing the Spacebar when presented with the option.

If you succeed in accessing the system properly, immediately open the Event Viewer and check to see which service or device failed, causing the stop event.

If this attempt fails, you can try to run the system in VGA mode, which starts the system using the /SOS switch in the BOOT.INI file. Again, if this works, access the Event Viewer to see what caused the problem.

Modifying the BOOT.INI File

If this attempt also fails, you can attempt to modify the BOOT.INI file to access some additional diagnosis options. You can even take a Core Dump of the system, which can, if you are extremely at a loss for a solution, be sent off to Microsoft for diagnosis. Table 8.4 shows some of the additional switches that may be used in the BOOT.INI file, which can be useful in diagnosing problems.

Table 8.4. Additional BOOT.INI Switches.

Option	Function
/BASEVIDEO	Boots the system with a standard VGA driver at 640×480 resolution. Great for troubleshooting the loading of an incorrect or incompatible video driver.
/BAUDRATE=nnnn	Specifies the baud rate you should use for debugging.
/CRASHDEBUG	Enables automatic recovery and restart. Can be enabled through the system program Control Panel. Great if you want your server to automatically restart but not so great if you need to see the stop event screen to diagnose your failure.
/DEBUG	Loads the debugger so that dumps can be made if a crash occurs.
/DEBUGPORT=comx	Specifies the port you should use during a debugger session. Used with /BAUDRATE and /DEBUG.
/NODEBUG	No debugging information stored.

continues

Table 8.4. Continued

Option	Function
/MAXMEM:n	Specifies the maximum amount of memory NT will use. Helpful for diagnosing bad RAM or mismatched SIMMs. Here's a tip: Don't go below 12MB or NT does not start.
/NOSERIALMICE= [com x ¦ com x,y,z]	Disables the mouse. Helpful if you have port/driver conflicts between a modem and a mouse.
/SOS	Displays drivers as they load. Helpful for identifying those drivers that fail to play well with others.

To modify the BOOT.INI file, first remove the read-only attribute from the file using ATTRIB.EXE as follows:

ATTRIB -R C:\BOOT.INI

After it is removed, the BOOT.INI file can be opened in a standard text editor and modified (see Figure 8.9).

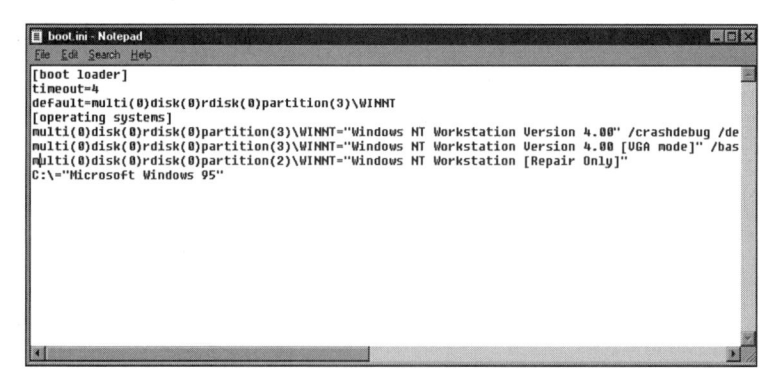

Figure 8.9. *Modifying the BOOT.INI file.*

Alternative Diagnosis Options

If the diagnosis modifications to the BOOT.INI file fail to provide insight into the problem, an ERD can be attempted, should one exist. (See the section, "The AT Command," earlier in the chapter.)

To use an ERD, you must first boot the system with the NT installation disks and select the Repair option. When prompted, follow the required steps to restore the Registry from the disk. If this still fails, you can attempt to refresh the system files using the retail installation CD-ROM, but this could present a problem if you have service packs installed. Because service packs contain both updated system files and Registry additions, refreshing the system can cause more harm than good. Refreshing the installation can also inadvertently overwrite any OEM-supplied drivers you may have installed, further complicating the problem.

At this point, if a backup of the system exists, you should attempt a restore. If it does not exist, you can try accessing the installation of Windows NT if it is on a FAT partition. Booting with a standard DOS bootable disk, you can attempt to locate the offending file, delete or rename it, and then attempt a second boot. But if the installation of NT resides on an NTFS volume, it is inaccessible from DOS. You can try installing a second copy of NT to a different directory, boot to it to access the first installation, and attempt to locate the problem.

If you still cannot rectify the problem using one of these methods, a reinstallation or restoration from tape backup, if available, may be required.

Diagnosing stop events can be a time-consuming process. Carefully examining the information regarding the event and any changes that occurred prior to the event usually provides the requisite information to successfully correct the problem.

Part III
Appendices

A Native NT Tools

B Useful Registry Edits

C Windows NT Services and Protocols

D Cloning NT

Appendix A

Native NT Tools

This appendix contains command summaries for the tools native to Windows NT that have been presented in this book. You may choose to use these tools during your unattended installation. This appendix is not intended to be all-inclusive, nor is it intended to be a definitive source of information regarding these tools.

CACLS.EXE

This command-line utility is extremely useful for displaying and modifying the Access Control Lists (ACLs) of the files and directories contained within an NTFS volume. When these ACLs are used in a batch file, an administrator can globally reset permissions on a workstation or server.

Usage: CACLS [options]

Option	Function
/t	Change the rights of specified files in the current directory and subdirectories for the username(s) or group(s) specified.
/e	Add changes to ACL instead of overwriting previous ACLs.
/c	Continue changing ACLs even when there are errors.
/g username:right	Grant the username(s) or group(s) one of the following rights: Read Change Full Control

continues

continued

Option	Function
/r `username`	Revoke rights for the username(s) or group(s) specified.
/p `username:right`	Replace a right specified for the username(s) or group(s) specified. The optional values are as follows: None Read Change Full Control
/d `username`	Denies access for the username(s) or group(s) specified.

Recognizing CACLS Output

When using CACLS.EXE to view ACLs for files and directories, some of the permission sets displayed may be preceded by code contained in parentheses:

- (OI)
- (IO)
- (CI)

These sets appear after the User or Group but before the permission variable. They denote the Inheritance settings for the files or directories in question, which are as follows:

Code	Definition
Object Inherit (OI)	Files created in the specified directory inherit the designated right.
Container Inherit (CI)	Subdirectories created under the specified directory inherit the designated right.
Inherit Only (IO)	Does not apply to the specified directory—only to existing subdirectories.
Objects	Represent files.
Containers	Represent directories.

SYSDIFF.EXE

SYSDIFF, Microsoft's SystemDifference tool, was designed to assist administrators in configuring multiple workstations during an unattended installation. With SYSDIFF, administrators can import the settings from one workstation, creating a *package* (image file) out of them, and then distribute them to other workstations during the deployment process. SYSDIFF also possesses the capability to create a "mirror" directory structure of the sample workstation on a Distribution Share Point (DSP) that contains all of the imported changes, applications, and settings that will be imported. You can access this mirror structure during the unattended process in order to import the configuration options it contains.

Usage: SYSDIFF [*Options*]

Option	Function
/SNAP	Used to take a preliminary "snapshot" of an NT system, which is later used to compare against. /SNAP records the differences. SYSDIFF /SNAP <*Snap Filename*>.IMG.
/DIFF	Used after a snapshot has been taken and the changes made to the operating system have been completed. The changes are then recorded in a difference file. SYSDIFF /DIFF <*Snap Filename*>.IMG <*Diff Filename*>.IMG.
/APPLY	Used to apply a recorded difference file to a target system. SYSDIFF /APPLY <*Diff Filename*>.IMG.
/LOG	Used to create a log file when the /SNAP and /DIFF options are used. SYSDIFF /LOG:<*Logfile name*>.LOG /SNAP <*Snap Filename*>.IMG.
/U	Used to generate Unicode text files. This switch is usable with any of SYSDIFF's options.
/DUMP	Used as a diagnostic tool. Use of this switch converts the contents of the difference image file into a readable output file. SYSDIFF /DUMP <*Diff Filename*>.IMG <*Dump Filename*>.DMP.

continues

continued

Option	Function
/INF	Used after a difference file has been generated. It takes the content of the image file and does four things with it: 1. Generates an installation .INF file containing Registry and file/directory information needed to install the contents of the difference file. 2. Creates a mirror directory structure taken from the recorded image contained within the difference file and places it in a usable format in the OEM subdirectory of a DSP, where it can be referenced during an unattended installation. 3. Creates $$RENAME.TXT files (when necessary) within the newly created directory structure to properly convert shortened filenames back to their original long names during the installation process. 4. Adds the appropriate information into the CMDLINES.TXT file, either appending an existing CMDLINES.TXT or creating a new one. SYSDIFF /INF *<Diff Filename>*.IMG *<OEM Location>*.
/M	Used during the unattended process when an /APPLY statement is used to install the difference image to the target system. When specified, this switch causes the installation of the difference image to be applied to the Default User profile of the Target system rather than the current user's profile. In this way, all new profiles created receive the update, rather than just the current user. SYSDIFF /INF /M *<Diff Filename>*.IMG *<OEM Location>*.

Option	Function
/C:Commentary	Used in conjunction with the /DIFF statement when creating an image file, this optional switch is used to inform the user what difference package is being applied. SYSDIFF /DIFF /C:"Netscape Package"<Snap Filename>.IMG <Diff Filename>.IMG.

REGEDIT.EXE and REGEDT32.EXE

Usage: REGEDIT /S <Registry Edit>.REG

One of the two native Registry editing tools available with Windows NT, REGEDIT.EXE is the only native tool that you can use to apply registry edits (.REG files) during the unattended installation process or during system updates. You can apply these edits using the /S or Silent option. Following is an example of this tool's use in the CMDLINES.TXT:

```
[Commands]
".\REGEDIT /S .\REGFILE.REG"
```

> *Caution*
>
> *You can use REGEDIT.EXE to apply only REG_SZ, REG_DWORD, and REG_EXPAND_SZ Registry modifications, not to install REG_BINARY or REG_MULTI_SZ edits.*

The REGEDT32.EXE Registry tool is used for manual editing of the system Registry.

> *Caution*
>
> *Misuse of Registry editing tools can result in serious, possibly irreparable, damage to a system's Registry, resulting in the need for a reinstallation of the Registry (from backup) or the operating system itself.*

AT.EXE

The AT Scheduling tool may be one of the most beneficial items native to Windows NT that is in an administrator's software toolkit. With it, an administrator can, either remotely or locally, schedule events that perform installation, maintenance, and system update routines.

Part III: Appendices

Usage: AT.EXE [*options*]

AT *time* /every: M, T,W, Th, F, S, Su "*command*"

Option	Function
Command	Signifies the command to be executed by AT. The command must be enclosed by quotation marks and possibly be preceded by CMD.EXE should the desired event not be a .BAT, .COM, or .EXE file.
\\computername	Designates the system on which the scheduled event should be run. Used to remotely schedule services.
/delete	Deletes a scheduled event from the queue by its ID. If no ID is specified, then all scheduled jobs currently in the queue are deleted.
/every	Specifies the date on which the event is scheduled to occur. Dates can be denoted by either the day of the week (M, T, W, Th, F, S, Su) or the day of the month (1-31). The date can also be left unspecified, signifying that the event should occur on the current date.
id	Assigns a job number to the scheduled event, starting with zero (0).
/interactive	Allows interaction of the scheduled event with the current interactive login session.
/next:*date*	Runs the scheduled event on the next instance of the designated date. Multiple dates can be specified and are separated by a comma. If no date is specified, the scheduled event is run on the next instance of the day on which the event was scheduled.
/yes	Autoconfirms AT delete commands.
time	Designates the time at which the scheduled event is to take place. Time should be specified using a 24-hour clock.
/?	AT help screen opens.

It is important to note that the AT command-line tool, by default, uses the system account to process scheduled events through the Scheduler service. This means that for access to the AT scheduled event, the same rights and permissions granted to the local system account are given. The system account on the local workstation possesses the following credentials:

Appendix A: Native NT Tools 253

User:	System	Pseudo-Group—local group scope
Default owner:	Administrators	Local group
Groups belonging to:	Administrators	Local group
	Everyone	Pseudo-Group—local group scope

This type of access grants the system account the necessary rights to process almost any desired local commands. But in the context of network requests, the system account possesses a much more restrictive set of credentials, using a null session for access. Following are the null session credentials:

User:	Everyone	Pseudo-Group
Default owner	Everyone	Pseudo-Group
Groups belonging to:	Anonymous logon	Pseudo-Group—Local group scope
	Network	Pseudo-Group—Local group scope

As you can see from the preceding group membership, the local system account's network access is determined by the permissions and rights that the Anonymous, Everyone, and Network groups possess on a network. Also, the group Everyone represents the common session context that exists between the permissions and rights. When AT events are scheduled on a target system involving network requests, access to a requested networked resource is precluded by the group Everyone's being granted permission to the resource.

For environments in which the scheduling of events is desired but heightened security has restricted the group Everyone's access to networked resources, the system account for the Scheduler service can be replaced with a manufactured local account. This account can be added to a global group possessing access to the desired network resources. One example is creating an ID on a domain possessing the requisite permissions for access to networked resources and then adding it to the target workstation's local Administrator's group during the unattended installation.

You can then use the following code to modify the Schedule service during the unattended process. Simply use the MS Resource Kit tool INSTSRV.EXE in a batch file that is referenced with a RUNONCE statement in the Registry, along with a .REG file in the CMDLINES.TXT file:

```
[Commands]

".\REGEDIT /S .\CHGSCHED.REG"
```

The .REG file, SHGSCHED.REG, looks like the following:

```
REGEDIT4
[HKEY_LOCAL_MACHINE\SOFTWARE\Microsoft\Windows\CurrentVersion\RunOnce]
"RunThis" = "C:\\TEMP\\SCHEDULE.BAT"
```

The preceding edit calls the batch file SCHEDULE.BAT, which you can copy to the directory C:\TEMP during the unattended installation by creating the subdirectory \C\TEMP within the OEM subdirectory on the DSP. Along with the following batch file, copy NET.EXE, INSTSRV.EXE (from the NT Server Resource Kit), NTRIGHTS.EXE (from the NT Server Resource Kit, Supplement II), and the file SCHEDULE.REG into this directory.

> **Note**
>
> For you to use this option during the unattended process, the target system must be automatically logged on to the domain with an ID that possesses the capability to add users to global groups.

```
SCHEDULE.BAT

c:
cd \
cd temp
net user scheduler password /add /expires:never /passwordreq:yes
/comment:"Local Scheduling ID" /profilepath:c:\winnt\profiles\scheduler
net localgroup Administrators /add scheduler
net group "Domain Users" /add scheduler /Domain
ntrights +r SeServiceLogonRight -u scheduler
c:\temp\INSTSRV Schedule REMOVE
c:\temp\INSTSRV Schedule C:\winnt\system32\atsvc.exe -a %MachineName%\scheduler
-p password
net start Schedule
regedit /s c:\temp\schedule.reg
del c:\temp\*.* /Q
```

In the preceding example, the file SCHEDULE.BAT uses a series of commands to modify the Schedule service. The NET USER command adds the ID scheduler to the target system. This command also adds the password, ensures that the account never expires, and creates the path on which the ID's profile is stored. This last statement, denoted by the /PROFILEPATH option, is extremely important. Without the /PROFILEPATH option—in which the schedule ID is used to replace the system account in the Schedule service—the workstation is rebooted each time a new profile folder is created, starting with a folder extension of .000, then .001, .002, and so on. This can become a problem should the continual creation of duplicate profile folders make the system run out of disk space. When the /PROFILEPATH option is in place, the new ID uses a stated path on which the profile is stored and does not continually re-create new profile folders.

The next two NET statements, NET LOCALGROUP and NET GROUP, add the ID to the local Administrator's group and to the global group Domain Users, respectively.

The NTRIGHTS tool (explained in Chapter 6, "Securing Desktop Environments") is used to grant the Scheduler ID permission to "Logon as a Service" (SeServiceLogonRight), which is necessary if the ID will be used to replace the System ID as the account used with the Schedule service.

The INSTSRV strings are used to first remove the Schedule service and then to reinstall the service using the modified scheduler account. It is important to include the %MachineName% or %ComputerName% option when specifying the account to be used; otherwise, the service reinstallation does not succeed.

The NET START command is used to restart the modified Schedule service, and the REGEDIT statement processes the SCHEDULE.REG file to reset the default startup parameters for the Schedule service from Manual to Automatic. Following is the required edit, SCHEDULE.REG:

```
REGEDIT4
[HKEY_LOCAL_MACHINE\SYSTEM\CurrentControlSet\Services\Schedule]
"Start" = dword:00000002
```

The final line deletes the contents of C:\TEMP and exits the batch file. Be sure to include the /Q switch in the DEL command so that it processes the deletion request in Quiet mode and thus does not require user intervention.

In this way, the Scheduler service can be reinstalled during the unattended process to use an ID that has been tailored to provide the necessary access to network resources. This same ID can be reconfigured using the User Manager for Domains to provide greater or lesser access, whichever the network administrator requires.

NET.EXE

The most versatile of command-line tools available to an administrator is NET.EXE. Because many of the commands available do not require confirmation, NET.EXE can be used easily in batch files or scripts to perform remote, automated functions.

```
NET [Options] [Switches]

NET Options:

ACCOUNTS ¦ COMPUTER ¦ CONFIG ¦ CONTINUE ¦ FILE ¦ GROUP ¦ HELP ¦ HELPMSG ¦
LOCALGROUP ¦ NAME ¦ PAUSE ¦ PRINT ¦ SEND ¦ SESSION ¦ SHARE ¦ START ¦ STATISTICS
¦ STOP ¦ TIME ¦ USE ¦ USER ¦ VIEW

NET ACCOUNTS [Option]
```

This option is used to modify the configurable elements governing user and group accounts on a system.

Switch	Definition
None	Displays the system's current user account settings.
/DOMAIN (NT Workstation only)	Forces the command to occur on the domain's primary domain controller.
/FORCELOGOFF:{Minutes¦No}	Sets the number of minutes to wait before logged-on users are disconnected, should their accounts possess time restrictions. Setting this switch to No enables users to remain logged on but does not permit them to log back on during the time restriction should they log off. The default value is No.
/LOCKOUTDUR:{Minutes}	Sets the account lockout duration when a user surpasses the value set in /LOCKOUTTHR: for unsuccessful logon attempts.
/LOCKOUTTHR:{Attempts¦NEVER}	Sets the number of unsuccessful logon attempts an account is permitted to process before locking itself. NEVER, which disables account lockout, is the default.
/LOCKOUTWIN:{Minutes}	Sets the time window in which the lockout threshold number is monitored. If the lockout threshold is exceeded within the time window, the account is disabled for the account lockout duration value.
/MAXPWAGE:{Days¦UNLIMITED}	Sets the amount of time a password is valid on a system; the default is 90 days. The valid range of days for which an account can have a valid password is from 1 to 49,710. The number of days cannot be less than the minimum password age. UNLIMITED disables the time limit.

Switch	Definition
/MINPWAGE:{Days}	Sets the minimum amount of time a password is valid on a system; the default is 0 (disabled).
/MINPWLEN:{Number}	Sets the minimum password length; the default is 6. The valid range is from 0 to 14.
/SYNC (domain controllers only)	Synchronizes the User/Group Accounts database with the primary domain controller.
/UNIQUEPW:{Number}	Sets the number of password changes that need to occur before a password can be used. The maximum is 8 changes.

NET COMPUTER [Option]

This command creates a computer account for an NT server or workstation on a domain.

Switch	Definition
\\Computername	Name of the system being modified.
/ADD	Adds the computer account to the domain.
/DEL	Deletes the computer account from the domain.

NET CONFIG SERVER [Option]

This command modifies Server service variables:

Switch	Definition
None	Displays the current Server service properties.
/AUTODISCONNECT:{Time}	Sets the amount of time an account can remain connected and inactive before it is automatically disconnected; the default is 15 minutes. The valid range is from 1 to 65,355, with −1 disabling the autodisconnect feature.
/SRVCOMMENT:"Remarks"	Adds a comment that appears with the Server's entry in Server lists.
/HIDDEN:{yes¦no}	Hides a server's entry from the Server lists; the default is yes.

NET CONFIG WORKSTATION [Option]

This command modifies the Workstation service variables that relate to COM devices.

Switch	Definition
None	Displays the workstation COM values.
/CHARCOUNT:{Bytes}	Specifies the amount of data in bytes that are collected before the data is released to a communication device. If /CHARTIME: is also used, the option value that is met first is acted upon. The range is from 0 to 65,535 bytes; the default is 16 bytes.
/CHARTIME:{Msec}	Sets the number of milliseconds that must transpire before you send the data to a communication device. If /CHARCOUNT is also used, the option value that is met first is acted upon. The range is from 0 to 65,535,000 ms; the default is 250 ms.
/CHARWAIT:{Seconds}	Sets the number of seconds an NT system waits for a communication device to become available. The available range is from 0 to 65,535 seconds; the default is 3,600 seconds.

NET CONTINUE [Servicename]

This option resumes a service that has been paused by using NET PAUSE.

NET FILE [Option]

This option displays open files and their lock status.

Switch	Definition
None	Lists open files and their corresponding lock statuses.
ID Number	Provides detailed information regarding a particular file's status when its ID is specified.
/CLOSE	Closes an open file (spe..ed by the ID) and removes the file lock.

NET GROUP [Option]

This command is used to create, delete, and manage global groups in a domain.

Switch	Definition
None	Displays global groups in the domain.
"Groupname"	When specified, denotes the group which is to be added, deleted, modified, or viewed, depending on additional variables in the NET GROUP command string. Quotation marks should be used when specifying a group.
Username [...]	Denotes the username(s) that should be added or removed from the specified groupname. If multiple names are listed, they should be separated be single spaces.
/ADD	Adds a global group or adds a username to a group. The specified username must exist before it is added to a group.
/COMMENT:"Remark"	Adds up to a 48-character comment string to the group. Comments must be enclosed in quotation marks.
/DELETE	Deletes a global group or deletes a username from a group.
/DOMAIN (NT Workstation only)	Forces the command to occur on the domain's primary domain controller.

NET HELP [Option]

This command offers you help in finding specific commands or topics.

> *Tip*
>
> *When displaying information on the command line, such as with a* NET /? *statement, pause the information that streams by if it cannot fit within the DOS window. Simply place a* ¦MORE *at the end of the string.*

Switch	Definition
None	Displays available help topics.
Command	When specified, displays help for the designated Command. For example, NET HELP GROUP displays the command options for NET GROUP.
/?	Displays the correct syntax for the command.
Services	Displays information on services and how they can be modified using NET commands.
Syntax	Displays the correct method of using command-line strings.

NET HELPMSG [Error Number]

When a four-digit error message is displayed in Windows NT, a more detailed explanation of the error may be available. To use the NET HELPMSG command, type the error number after NET HELPMSG.

NET LOCALGROUP [Option]

This command is used to modify or view local groups on a system.

Switch	Definition
None	Displays the server/workstation name and the names of the local groups on the system.
"Groupname"	Displays the members of the group specified.
Username [...]	Denotes the username(s) that should be added or removed from the specified groupname. If multiple names are listed, they should be separated by single spaces. If the username is a member of another domain, specify the domain name preceding the user ID.
yes/ADD	Adds a local group, adds a username(s) to a group, or adds a global group to a local group.
/COMMENT:"Remark"	Adds up to a 48-character comment string to the group. Comments must be enclosed in quotation marks.
/DELETE	Deletes a local group, a username(s), or a global group from a local group.
/DOMAIN (NT Workstation only)	Forces the command to occur on the domain's PDC.

NET NAME [*Option*]

This command adds, deletes, or displays the messaging name (or alias) of an NT system. This ID is used for the reception of messages that use the Messenger service.

Switch	Definition
None	Displays the current messaging names for a system.
/ADD	Adds a new messaging name, which can be up to 15 characters. Typing **NET NAME** *<newname>* causes a messaging alias to be added.
/DELETE	Removes a messaging alias from a computer.

NET PAUSE [*Service*]

The NET PAUSE command halts a running service. NET PAUSE /HELP shows the correct names of services.

NET PRINT [*Option*]

The command is used to control print jobs in shared print queues.

Switch	Definition
\\computername\sharename	Specifies the name of the system sharing the printer and the share name of the printer.
Job	Specifies the numerical ID of the print job.
/DELETE	Deletes the specified print job from the shared queue.
/HOLD	Holds the specified print job in the shared queue.
/RELEASE	Releases a print job that has been put on hold.

NET SEND [*Option*] Message

This command is used to transmit messages to users on a network. Broadcast messages can have up to 128 characters.

Switch	Definition
Name	The user, computer or messaging alias to which the message should be sent. If the name is a computer name that contains spaces, enclose the alias in quotation marks.
*	Sends the message to all of the members in your group.
/DOMAIN:{Domain Name}	Sends the message to the domain name specified.
/USERS	Sends the message to all users connected to the server.

NET SESSION [Option]

This command is used to view active sessions on a system. Sessions can be shared files, directories, printers, or any other networked resource.

Switch	Definition
None	Displays a list of active sessions currently connected to the system.
\\ComputerName	Specifies the remote system that will be observed.
/DELETE	Deletes a connected session. It can be used with the \\ComputerName option.

NET SHARE [Option]

This command tool allows for the viewing or creation of shares on a system.

Switch	Definition
None	Displays the list of currently available shares on a system.
Sharename	Displays information about the specified share. When used with the Drive:Path option, it is also used to name a new share.
Drive:Path	Specifies the location of the directory that will be shared.

Switch	Definition
/DELETE	Deletes an active share.
/REMARK:"Comment"	Adds a comment to the share.
/UNLIMITED	Removes any restriction on a share that limits the number of simultaneous connections to that share.
/USERS:{Number}	Limits the number of simultaneous connections to a share.

NET START [*Service*]

This NET START command, when used alone, displays the services currently running on a system. When a service name is specified, NET START starts the service.

NET STATISTICS [Workstation or Server]

This command displays network information for either the Workstation or Server services on a system.

NET STOP [*Service*]

Like NET START, this command is used to control services on a system. It stops a running service.

NET TIME [*Option*]

This command is used to synchronize the time between systems on a network.

Switch	Definition
\\Computername	Specifies the name of the system with which the time will be synchronized.
/DOMAIN:{Domain Name}	Specifies the domain to be synchronized with.
/SET	Synchronizes the local system time with the designated server or domain.
/yes	Autoconfirms synchronization when used in conjunction with the /SET switch.

NET USE [Option]

This command controls connections to networked resources.

Switch	Definition
None	Displays current connections.
Devicename	Specifies the device that will be connected. There are two types of devices, disk drives (D–Z) and Printers (LPT1–LPT3). Using an asterisk in place of an actual device name specifies the next available device.
*	Produces a password prompt. In this way, the password is not displayed.
\\ComputerName\Sharename	Specifies the server name and the desired share. The server name can have up to 15 characters in its name.
Volume	Used to specify a NetWare volume name. Requires either the Client service for NetWare (NT Workstation) or the Gateway service for NetWare (NT Server).
Password	Specifies the password in clear text for a password-protected share.
/DELETE	Deletes an active network resource connection.
/HOME	Connects users to their home directory on a server, should one exist.
/PERSISTENT:{yes¦no}	yes specifies that the connection is saved even after a reboot. no means that if the connection is lost, the system does not attempt to restore it. (However, if the connection is active when a reboot is specified, the connection is restored.)
/USER:{Domain\}Username	Specifies that a username other than the current active logon is used to connect to the desired resource.

NET USER [Options]

This command is used to modify or view user accounts on a system.

Switch	Definition
None	Displays users on a system or a domain.
Username	Lists the account settings for the ID specified.

The following commands must be preceded by the Username option.

Switch	Definition
Password	The word placed after the username is used as the password for that account. Here Password can be substituted for any desired password (under 14 characters).
*	Produces a password prompt. In this way, the password is not displayed.
/ACTIVE:{yes¦no}	yes enables the account; no disables the account. The default is yes.
/ADD	Adds the specified username as a new account on the system.
/COMMENT:"Remarks"	Adds up to a 48-character comment string to the account. Comments must be enclosed in quotation marks.
/COUNTRYCODE: {Number}	Denotes the country code for the account so that the specified language files for Help screens and error messages are displayed. When you enter a value of 0, the country code of the system the account is being installed to is used.
/DELETE	Deletes the specified account.
/DOMAIN (NT Workstation only)	Forces the command to occur on the domain's PDC.
/EXPIRES: {Date¦NEVER}	Specifies the date the account expires. Dates can be entered using the following formats: 11/09/97 Nov. 9 November, 9,1997 11/9 (Omitting the year defaults to the next occurrence of the specified date.) NEVER means the account does not expire.

continues

continued

Switch	Definition
`/FULLNAME:"User's Name"`	Inserts the user's full name.
`/HOMEDIR:{Path}`	Sets the path to the designated user's directory. The path must exist.
`/HOMEDIRREQ:{yes¦no}`	Sets whether a home directory is required or not.
`/PASSWORDCHG:{yes¦no}`	Sets whether a user is permitted to change his/her own password; the default is `yes`.
`/PASSWORDREQ:{yes¦no}`	Sets whether a password is required for an account or not.
`/PROFILEPATH:{Path}`	Sets the path for the storage location of a user's profile.
`/SCRIPTPATH:{Path}`	Sets a path for the user's logon script. Path should be relative to `%SystemRoot%`.
`/TIMES:{Times¦ALL}`	Specifies the time and days of the week a user can access the system. Time is expressed in one hour increments, either on a 12- or 24-hour clock. Use of the 12-hour clock requires the use of AM or PM. Days can either be spelled out (Monday) or abbreviated (M). Multiple entries must be separated by colons, and no spaces should exist in the data string. Example: `/TIMES:T,7AM-7PM:Wednesday,07:00-19:00:` Using ALL removes any time restrictions; ALL is the default.
`/USERCOMMENT:"Remark"`	An additional comment field.
`/WORKSTATIONs:`	Sets the workstations on a `{Computername [...]¦*}` network the account is permitted to use. Up to eight stations can be specified, each separated by a comma. Use of the asterisk permits the account to access all systems.

NET VIEW [*Option*]

This command is used to display available resources on a network.

Switch	Definition
None	Lists servers in the domain.
\\ComputerName	Displays the available networked resources on the designated server.
/DOMAIN: {Domain Name}	Displays a list of domains, or, when specifying a domain, all of the computers in the domain.
/NETWORK:NW	Displays a listing of servers on a NetWare network. If a server name is specified, the available resources for that server are displayed.

POLEDIT.EXE

This GUI tool creates System Policies using .ADM templates. The tool is found on the NT Server CD-ROM under \CLIENTS\SRVTOOLS\WINNT\I386 (or Processor Type).

Appendix B

Useful Registry Edits

This appendix contains the registry edits that appear in the chapters of this book. It also contains additional registry edits that may prove useful to an administrator or deployer of NT.

> **Warning**
>
> *Using registry edits incorrectly can cause serious problems—particularly corruption of the Registry—that may make it necessary to reinstall Windows NT. Use these registry edits in the manner in which they are intended and ensure that a valid, up-to-date Emergency Repair Disk exists for a system when testing the use of these edits.*

Chapter 5, "Installing Additional Applications"

```
LOGON.REG:

REGEDIT4
[HKEY_LOCAL_MACHINE\SOFTWARE\Microsoft\Windows NT\CurrentVersion\Winlogon]
"DefaultUserName" = "Administrator"
"AutoAdminLogon" = "1"
"DefaultPassword" = ""
"DefaultDomain" = ""MyDomainName"
```

This edit permits an administrator to configure a system to automatically insert a username and password and thus bypass the logon prompt at system startup. In order for users or administrators to bypass the autologon when it is enabled, they must first log on and then log out of the system by holding down the Shift key as the Logon as a Different User option is selected. This action presents the user with the standard Logon dialog box.

> **Warning**
>
> *Use of this registry edit places the username and password in clear text in the Registry. If certain users possess the capability to view the Registry, they are able to read the entry, possibly compromising security.*

MSOFFICE.REG:

```
REGEDIT4
[HKEY_LOCAL_MACHINE\SOFTWARE\Microsoft\Windows\CurrentVersion\RunOnce]
"RunThis" = "C:\\Temp\\Msoffice.bat"
```

This edit processes a batch file that contains the installation string needed to start the setup process for MS Office.

NETWARE.REG:

```
REGEDIT4
[HKEY_LOCAL_MACHINE\SOFTWARE\Microsoft\Windows\CurrentVersion\RunOnce]
"RunThis" = "C:\\Temp\\Novell.bat"
```

This edit is used to begin the installation of the Novell IntranetWare Client 32.

NOSRVLST.REG:

```
REGEDIT4
[HKEY_LOCAL_MACHINE\SYSTEM\CurrentControlSet\Services\Browser\Parameters]
"MaintainServerList" = "No"
```

This edit disables a workstation from becoming a backup master browser. The default is `auto` for workstations and `yes` for servers. When setting the `MaintainServerList` option to `no`, you must also disable the browser service.

BROWSER.REG:

```
REGEDIT4
[HKEY_LOCAL_MACHINE\SYSTEM\CurrentControlSet\Services\Browser]
"Start" = dword:00000004
```

This edit disables the browser service on an NT workstation. It is used in conjunction with the NOSRVLST.REG edit.

NOSERVER.REG:

```
REGEDIT4
[HKEY_LOCAL_MACHINE\SYSTEM\CurrentControlSet\Services\LanmanServer]
"Start" = dword:00000004
```

This edit disables the Server service on an NT workstation, which is enabled by default. Ensure that the BROWSER.REG edit is used in conjunction with this edit or the Service Control Monitor displays an error.

Chapter 6, "Securing Desktop Environments"

SECURITY.REG:

```
REGEDIT4
[HKEY_LOCAL_MACHINE\SOFTWARE\Microsoft\Windows\CurrentVersion\RunOnce]
"RunThis" = "c:\\batch\\cacls.bat"
```

This edit uses the RUNONCE option to process a batch file that contains the CACLS tool, which resets NTFS security on a target system during the unattended process.

ADDUSERS.REG:

```
REGEDIT4
[HKEY_LOCAL_MACHINE\SOFTWARE\Microsoft\Windows\CurrentVersion\RunOnce]
"RunThis" = "c:\\batch\\addusers.bat"
```

This edit also uses the RUNONCE option to process a batch file. The batch file this option processes contains a series of NET commands that add users to the target system during the unattended process. If you need to process multiple commands, such as CACLS.BAT and ADDUSERS.BAT, add the contents of both to one batch file.

WINREG.REG:

```
REGEDIT4
[HKEY_LOCAL_MACHINE\SYSTEM\CurrentControlSet\Control\SecurePipeServers\]
"Winreg"
```

Adding security to the winreg key in the following edit determines which users will have access to the local system Registry from the network.

ANONPIPE.REG:

```
REGEDIT4
[HKEY_LOCAL_MACHINE\SYSTEM\CurrentControlSet\Services\LanManServer\Parameters]
"NullSessionPipes" = multi_sz:" , "
```

> *Tip*
>
> *Add the named pipes you want to exclude from the security restrictions imposed by the winreg key. Enclose the entries in quotes and separate multiple entries with commas.*

> *Note*
>
> *This registry edit cannot be added using REGEDIT.EXE; it must be added manually.*

Part III: Appendices

ANONBRWS.REG:

```
REGEDIT4
[HKEY_LOCAL_MACHINE\SYSTEM\CurrentControlSet\Control\Lsa]
"RestrictAnonymous" = dword: 00000001
```

This key, a Post SP3 registry edit, is used to disable anonymous browsing of a system or a network's resources.

WARNING.REG:

```
REGEDIT4
[HKEY_LOCAL_MACHINE\SOFTWARE\Microsoft\Windows NT\Current Version\Winlogon]
"LegalNoticeCaption" = "Caption Heading Here"
"LegalNoticeText" = "Your Message Text Here"
```

This edit is used to display a legal notice during the logon sequence to warn users of the risks due to inappropriate use of the system or the network.

NOCLOSE.REG:

```
REGEDIT4
[HKEY_LOCAL_MACHINE\SOFTWARE\Microsoft\Windows NT\CurrentVersion\Winlogon]
"ShutdownWithoutLogon" = "0"
```

This edit resets an NT Workstation's Shutdown options from the logon prompt, disabling a user's capability to shut down a system without first authenticating to it. This edit is set up by default on NT Server but not Workstation.

NOUNAME.REG

```
REGEDIT4
[HKEY_LOCAL_MACHINE\SOFTWARE\Microsoft\Windows NT\CurrentVersion\Winlogon]
"DontDisplayLastUserName" = "1"
```

This edit disables the display of the last username that authenticated to a system, making it more difficult for potential hackers to guess usernames and passwords for a system.

CLRLOGIN.REG:

```
REGEDIT4
[HKEY_LOCAL_MACHINE\SOFTWARE\Microsoft\Windows NT\CurrentVersion\Winlogon]
"CachedLogonsCount"=dword:00000000
```

This edit disables the caching of a user's logon and network credentials.

PAGEFILE.REG:

```
REGEDIT4
[HKEY_LOCAL_MACHINE\SYSTEM\CurrentControlSet\Control\SessionManager\Memory Management]
"ClearPageFileAtShutdown"=dword:00000001
```

This edit wipes the system pagefile clean of data during the shutdown process.

ROAMING.REG:

```
REGEDIT4
[HKEY_LOCAL_MACHINE\SOFTWARE\Microsoft\Windows NT\CurrentVersion\Winlogon]
"DeleteRoamingCache" = dword:00000001
```

This edit deletes copies of roaming profiles after a user has logged off of the system, removing the potential for tampering or spying of potentially sensitive information that is stored in the profile's NTUSER.DAT file.

Chapter 7, "System Policies and User Profiles"

RESTRICT.REG:

```
REGEDIT4
[HKEY_LOCAL_MACHINE\SYSTEM\CurrentControlSet\Control\Lsa]
"RestrictAnonymous" = "1"
```

This Post SP3 edit disables anonymous user access to a system.

Chapter 8, "Maintaining the Environment"

SCHEDULE.REG:

```
REGEDIT4
[HKEY_LOCAL_MACHINE\SYSTEM\CurrentControlSet\Services\Schedule]
"Start" = dword:00000002
```

This edit resets the startup parameters for the Schedule service from `Manual` to `Automatic`.

SUBMITAT.REG:

```
REGEDIT4
HKEY_LOCAL_MACHINE\SYSTEM\CurrentControlSet\Control\Lsa
"Submit Control" = dword:00000001
```

By default, only members of the Administrator's group possess access to schedule AT commands on a system. This registry edit permits ordinary users to submit AT commands.

NETINST.REG:

```
REGEDIT4
[HKEY_LOCAL_MACHINE\SOFTWARE\Microsoft\Windows\
CurrentVersion]
"AppInstallPath" = "\\SERVERNAME\INF$APPS.INF"
```

This edit is used to set up target systems so that they use the Network Install tab in the Add/Remove Programs option of the Control Panel. Ensure that the APPS.INI file is accessible in the INF directory by creating a hidden share named INF$, and ensure that it contains the correct location of the applications you want to make accessible to users.

```
NETINST2.REG:

REGEDIT4
[HKEY_LOCAL_MACHINE\SOFTWARE\Microsoft\Windows\
CurrentVersion]
"AppInstallPath" = "\\SERVERNAME\LOCATION\APPS.INI"
```

This edit is used to set up target systems so that they use the Network Install tab in the Add/Remove Programs option of the Control Panel. Ensure that the APPS.INI file is accessible and that it contains the correct location of applications you want to make accessible to users.

```
TIPS.REG:

REGEDIT4
[HKEY_LOCAL_MACHINE\SOFTWARE\Microsoft\Windows \CurrentVersion\Explorer\Tips]
"0" = "My First Tip Here"
"1" = "My Next Tip Here"
"2" = "Here's Another Tip"
```

This edit permits you to reset existing tips or create new ones, starting with the number 50.

```
NOWELCM.REG

REGEDIT4
[HKEY_CURRENT_USER\SOFTWARE\Microsoft\Windows\CurrentVersion\Explorer\Tips]
"DisplayInitialTipWindow"=dword:00000000
"Show"=hex:00,00,00,00
"Next"=hex:03,00
```

This edit disables the display of the welcome page altogether.

```
DEFBROWS.REG:

REGEDIT4\.DEFAULT\
[HKEY_USERS\DEFAULT\Software\Microsoft\Internet Explorer\Main]
"Start Page" = "http://yourhomepage.com/userhelp.html"
```

This edit enables you to reset the default startup page of Internet Explorer during the unattended installation process.

Appendix C

Windows NT Services and Protocols

Windows NT provides a variety of services and protocols that can be installed and configured during the unattended deployment process. Understanding the correct usage of network protocols and system services is essential to creating a streamlined installation of Windows NT that will work for you in any networking environment.

Windows NT Workstation's Default Services

The following services are installed by default during the setup process:

- Service: Alerter
- Startup: Automatic

This service is used in conjunction with the Messenger service to alert select users and computers of administrative alerts on the local system.

- Service: ClipBook Server
- Startup: Manual

This service supports ClipBook Viewer, which allows remote ClipBook viewers to see local pages.

- Service: Computer Browser
- Startup: Automatic

This service maintains a list of available servers on a network for both users and programs to access.

- Service: Directory Replicator
- Startup: Manual

This service replicates files and directories between computers on a network.

- Service: Event Log
- Startup: Automatic

This service maintains logs of application, security, and system events on the local system.

- Service: Messenger
- Startup: Automatic

This service sends and receives messages sent by the Alerter service or administrators.

- Service: Net Logon
- Startup: Automatic

This service is used for pass-through authentication to a domain controller when a workstation participates in a domain.

- Service: Network DDE
- Startup: Manual

This service provides network transport for Dynamic Data Exchange (DDE) conversations on a network. This service also provides security for these exchanges.

- Service: Network DDE DSDM
- Startup: Manual

The DDE Shared Database Manager (DSDM) is used by the Network DDE service to manage shared DDE conversations.

- Service: NT LM Security Support Provider
- Startup: Manual

This service provides security for RPC programs that do not use named pipe transports.

- Service: Remote Procedure Call (RPC) Locator
- Startup: Automatic

This service manages the RPC name service database. Programs that require RPC functionality use this service.

- Service: Remote Procedure Call (RPC) Service
- Startup: Automatic

This service is the RPC subsystem that provides the endpoint mapper and other RPC services.

- Service: Schedule
- Startup: Manual

This service enables the AT command for the scheduling of events on the system.

- Service: Server
- Startup: Automatic

This service accepts and fulfills I/O requests from the network. It provides RPC support, as well as other server services, such as File & Print Services and named pipe sharing.

- Service: Spooler
- Startup: Automatic

This service is known as the printer spooling service.

- Service: UPS
- Startup: Disabled

When used, this service manages the Uninterruptible Power Supply (UPS).

- Service: Workstation
- Startup: Automatic

This service provides network communications and connections.

Windows NT Protocols

The following protocols are available under Windows NT:

- AppleTalk
- Data Link Control (DLC)
- NetBIOS Extended User Interface (NetBEUI)
- NWLink IPX/SPX Compatible Transport

- NWLink NetBIOS
- Point-to-Point Tunneling Protocol (PPTP)
- STREAMS protocol
- Transmission Control Protocol/Internet Protocol (TCP/IP)

AppleTalk

This protocol is used on AppleTalk networks to connect Macintosh/Apple systems together. When used with NT Workstation and NT Server, it allows NT and Apple systems to share data and printers.

Data Link Control (DLC)

The DLC protocol is primarily used to access IBM mainframe computers. It is not designed for general networking on Windows NT. This protocol is also used to access printers that are connected directly to a LAN, such as printers using JetDirect cards. DLC is a bridgeable protocol, but it is not routable.

NetBIOS Extended User Interface (NetBEUI)

NetBEUI is a protocol designed for use on small LANs of 20 to 200 workstations. It does not travel across routers, but it supports both connectionless and connection-oriented traffic on a single network segment. This protocol, which requires no configuration, is the default protocol for MS LAN Manager and Windows 3.11 and 95.

NWLink IPX/SPX Compatible Transport

This protocol is Microsoft's version of the Internetworking Packet eXchange (IPX) and Sequenced Packet eXchange (SPX) transport protocols that are used on Novell networks. It is needed to communicate with NetWare servers that are not using NWIP.

NWLink NetBIOS

NWLink NetBIOS supports NetBIOS communication between NetWare servers and Windows NT.

Point-to-Point Tunneling Protocol (PPTP)

The Point-to-Point Protocol (PPP) is used to create Virtual Private Networks (VPNs) over networks or the Internet between Remote Access Service (RAS) clients and servers. It does so by creating encrypted "tunnels" between the RAS-enabled systems.

STREAMS Protocol

The STREAMS protocol is an enhanced network transport on Windows NT that manages symmetric multiprocessing computers. UNIX systems that use STREAMS networking can be ported to NT using this protocol.

Transmission Control Protocol/Internet Protocol (TCP/IP)

TCP/IP is fast becoming the standard protocol on networks, mainly due to TCP/IP's use for Internet connectivity. As organizations increase their activity over the Internet, the desire to move to a single protocol for both internal and external communication becomes greater. The common protocol capabilities between operating systems such as UNIX, Macintosh, and Windows, as well as the protocol's scalability over larger LANs and WANs make the move to using a single protocol even more desirable.

Appendix D

Cloning NT

A great controversy exists among newsgroups, periodicals, and the Internet regarding the issue of cloning full-blown installations of Windows NT. To date, the process of cloning full installations of Windows NT is unsupported by Microsoft, as stated in their Knowledge Base article Q162001, "Do Not Disk Duplicate Installed Versions of Windows NT." In this article, Microsoft states that it does not support disk-duplicated installations of Windows NT because the unique security ID, or *SID*, is compromised by the disk duplication process, which clones the SID.

This appendix looks at a different type of cloning method that Microsoft approves when you are deploying Windows NT.

The Security ID (SID)

The SID is used as the machine's unique identifier to an NT domain controller. It is also used in generating a network access token for the requesting system. When disk-duplicated workstations exist in the same domain, an environment is created in which machines possessing the same SID attempt to access a domain controller for authentication. The domain controller authenticates the first system correctly but refuses access to the other workstations possessing the same SID. The domain controller interprets these duplicated workstations as unauthorized systems attempting to access the network using the SID of an already authenticated system.

Some administrators have discovered what they believe to be a solution to the problem of cloning full-blown installations of NT. They have installed NT Workstation as a member of a workgroup, and after cloning and installing each system, added it to the domain. The premise behind this solution is that the 96-bit machine SID is modified after the system is added to a domain, thereby supposedly bypassing the problem of duplicate SIDs.

This solution, however, can pose a problem. What this plan does not take into account is that the local workstation SID is still the same. This solution also does not take into account that the default account—and any account created on the local system prior to adding NT Workstation to the domain—possesses the same duplicate security IDs, with only the last four digits designating a new ID.

NT workstations with the Server service enabled have experienced all sorts of erratic behavior, including random system lockups.

The second problem with this type of solution is that it is not truly an unattended process. *Disk duplication* means traveling to each system after the cloning process is complete, manually adding each system to the domain and removing the "unattended" out of the automated installation process.

Finally, disk duplication methods almost certainly remove the systems that use such methods from the upgrade path to Windows NT 5.0. NT 5.0 is promising an integration of Kerberos-based security, which is purported to rely on the locally generated SID for access to network resources, so the disk-duplicated systems may not be upgradable.

Cloning NT After Text-Mode

The alternative to cloning full-blown installations of NT is cloning installations of Windows NT that have been halted just after completing the text-mode phase of the setup process. This supported method ensures that the necessary files for installing NT are copied to the local drive that will be cloned. The SID for the workstation has not been generated yet because it is generated during the GUI phase of the install process.

This alternative method permits administrators to shorten the installation process as it occurs at the target system because it only has to complete the GUI phase of setup. It also enables administrators to make any last-minute modifications to the installation if necessary.

To halt an installation of NT after the completion of the text-mode portion of setup or to add or modify the following key in the UNATTEND.TXT file, use the following output:

```
[Unattended]

NoWaitAfterTextMode = 0
```

> **Note**
>
> *The previous output is only a portion of the UNATTEND.TXT file.*

After the system halts, it can be rebooted, this time with a bootable network-capable disk. This disk interrupts the installation process. By booting with such a disk, an administrator can access any cloning technology and copy the Windows NT disk image to a Distribution Share Point (DSP) on a server.

This partial install can then be accessed remotely from a target workstation by using a bootable network disk, copying down the installation using the same cloning software, and rebooting the system without the bootable disk. The system should then boot into the GUI portion of the installation, generating the unique SID, while at the same time installing any specialized applications and settings you predetermined in your custom automated setup.

GHOST

One excellent disk-cloning tool is *GHOST*, which is available from **http://www.ghostsoft.com**. Of the products currently available for disk duplication, the current version of GHOST is one of the best tested. GHOST, which supports the resizing of NTFS partitions, can be scripted in batch files. It comes with a thorough, well laid out manual describing the disk duplication process, including a section specifically dedicated to the cloning of Windows NT systems and some detailed examples.

Following is an example of GHOST being used in the AUTOEXEC.BAT of a bootable disk:

```
;AUTOEXEC.BAT
path=a:\net
a:\net\net initialize
a:\net\netbind.com
a:\net\umb.com
a:\net\tcptsr.exe
a:\net\tinyrfc.exe
a:\net\nmtsr.exe
a:\net\emsbfr.exe
a:\net\net start
net use z: \\Server\Share
echo Installing Disk Image
a:
ghost-clone,mode=load,src=z:\NTDISK.IMG,dst=1,-sure
```

In the preceding example, the MS Client for DOS 3.0 is used to connect to an NT server using TCP/IP. MS Client then maps Z: to the network share containing the disk image NTDISK.IMG and automatically starts the application of the disk image to the target system.

Tips for Using Cloned Disk Images

Some important things to consider when using cloned disk images of NT are as follows:

- Disk duplication methods require that an administrator or computing staff member travel to the target system to apply the disk image by using a bootable disk.

- Cloned images of customized NT installations can range anywhere from 120 to 400+MB in size, and multiple customized installations can exceed a gigabyte or more of server disk space.

- Disk images, due to their size as one contiguous file (often exceeding 400MB when applications are added to a custom install), consume network bandwidth. GhostSoft recommends that over a medium-speed network/server, a maximum of 5 to 10 concurrent copies to target systems should occur. On a high-speed network/server, that number increases to 10 to 20.

- Before needed changes can be made to cloned disk images, they must be brought down to the target system. They must then be modified before the GUI phase of the installation is permitted to continue. This process may be necessary should updated drivers or services need to be added. Recloning an installation image may be necessary should a complete overhaul of the install be required.

Consider carefully before using cloning tools in the installation process. Be sure that the decision to use them is weighed against maintenance and update issues that may arise later.

> *Author's Note*
>
> *Microsoft recently announced (*Info World, *16 March 1998, Volume 20, Issue 11) that members of its "select" customer group (1,000 will have access to Microsoft-developed cloning tools that circumvent the troublesome elements associated with cloning. Known as "SysClone," these tools will likely solve many of the problems encountered when developing unattended installations of Windows NT.*

Glossary of Terms

Access Control Entry (ACE)   Determines the specific access or auditing permissions to an object within an Access Control List (ACL).

Access Control List (ACL)   Identifies permissions for users and groups to specific files and directories.

Administrator   One of two default local user accounts created during the installation of Windows NT. Used for the administration of the local system.

administrative equivalency   Rights and permissions inherited by a user account that has been added to the Administrator's or Domain Administrator's group.

Answer file   Refers to the UNATTEND.TXT, or similar file, that contains the keys and values used during an automated installation of Windows NT. It can also refer to any file containing responses to program queries requiring user input.

AppleTalk   A network protocol used on Apple networks. NT systems, both Workstation and Server, can use this protocol to share data and printers.

attributes   The properties of a file. Indicate whether a file is a compressed, hidden, read-only, or system file, as well as whether or not a change has occurred since it was last backed up.

authentication   The validation process used to ensure that an account's credentials are valid for the system being accessed.

Backup Domain Controller (BDC)   An NT server configured to maintain a copy of domain user and security information, which is updated on the primary domain controller (PDC) and distributed among the BDCs within the domain.

bandwidth   The difference between the highest and lowest frequencies available for network signals. Typically used to describe the data carrying capacity of a network, which is expressed in bits per second (bps).

boot partition   Volume containing the installation of Windows NT.

browse list A list of available networked resources that is maintained by the Master Browser. Available to servers and workstations so that the resources can be viewed and accessed.

client A system that accesses resources advertised by another system, which is generally referred to as a server.

Client Service for NetWare An optional service provided with Windows NT Workstation that allows authentication to NetWare servers (2.x and above) and their advertised resources.

Data Link Control (DLC) Network protocol available under NT Server and Workstation that provides the system with access to resources such as HP JetDirect cards and IBM mainframe computers.

device driver Software written to allow a Windows NT system to communicate with a piece of installed hardware.

Discretionary Access Control List A mutable list that delineates which users and groups are granted or denied access to a resource or function.

domain A grouping of computers whose access to networked resources is centrally controlled and administered through a common database stored on an NT server, which is known as a primary domain controller (PDC).

Domain Name Service (DNS) A service that maps host names to IP addresses so that systems on a network can be easily identified and referred to when requesting access to resources.

dword A four-byte hexadecimal data type.

Dynamic Host Configuration Protocol (DHCP) A protocol designed to allow a system to request a dynamically assigned IP address and related information from a DHCP server. This protocol removes the need to manually configure IP addresses for systems on a network and further removes the possibility of IP addressing conflicts.

Emergency Repair Disk (ERD) Created with the RDISK command under Windows NT, it is used to back up critical Registry and environment information that can be used to restore the system should a problem arise.

File Allocation Table (FAT) Format option under Windows NT that incorporates the use of a table or linked list to track disk segment usage for data storage. Also known as *FAT16* or *FAT32*, which are the two implementations of the FAT file system.

File and Print Services for NetWare (FPNW) A service for NT Server that allows the server to advertise itself on a network as a NetWare 3.12 server. This service enables those clients using NetWare client software to access the server as if it were a Novell server.

File Transfer Protocol (FTP)   A TCP/IP-based service that allows for the transfer of files between remote systems on a network or over the Internet.

folder   A GUI name for an icon that identifies a directory in a file system.

Gateway Service for NetWare   An optional service available under NT Server that permits the server to connect to NetWare resources on a network. This service enables NT clients running only MS Client software to access NetWare objects.

global account   Term used in an NT Domain Model to describe an account that has access to resources in the domain.

graphical user interface (GUI)   Any programmatic shell that provides a user with a graphical interface with which that user can use, modify, or otherwise manipulate the operating system or software.

Hardware Compatibility List (HCL)   A listing of hardware devices that are supported under NT and are therefore capable of being used in the operating system.

hexadecimal   A numbering system based on 16 characters, 0 through 9 and A through F (with A representing 10 and F representing 15).

hive   A section of the Registry that appears as files on your system. It supports a subtree of the NT Registry containing specific keys, subkeys, and values relevant to a section of operating system functionality.

Hotfix   An update released by Microsoft to correct a specific problem found in the NT operating system.

Hypertext Markup Language (HTML)   A scripting language designed to create hypertext documents. It is often presented in the form of pages for the Web.

Hypertext Transport Protocol (HTTP)   The TCP/IP-based protocol used on the Web to transfer HTML-based content.

interactive logon   A logon session that occurs at the local console of an NT system, as opposed to a *network logon*, which occurs from a remote location and accesses resources on an NT system.

Internet Information Server (IIS)   An optional service provided with NT Server that allows NT to offer Internet-based services such as Web, FTP, and Gopher Server.

InterProcess Communication (IPC)   A multitasking function that permits two services or tasks to transfer information between one another.

LMHOSTS file   A text file that contains mappings of NetBIOS names to IP addresses of systems on a network.

local account   On Windows NT systems, any account that is granted access to local, or system-specific, resources only.

local area network (LAN)   A network covering a relatively small geographic area, as opposed to a WAN, which covers a wider area.

logon script   A file assigned to a user account that runs at logon to set various elements of the client's environment. It is referenced as a client that attaches to a server; the server contains commands designed to set the client's environment variables for the established session.

Master Browser   In a Windows network, the system that maintains the browse list of networked resources available. The position of Master Browser status is normally reserved for a primary domain controller, but it can be given to any Windows-based computer that achieves Master Browser status by election.

Messenger service   Used to send or receive messages between Windows NT systems. Often used in conjunction with the Alerter service.

NetBIOS Extended User Interface (NetBEUI)   A small, non-routable network protocol designed primarily for use in small, departmental LANs of 1 to 200 clients. NetBEUI can be configured in Token Ring environments to use Token Ring Source Routing.

network adapter   A hardware device that permits a computer to connect to a network. Also known as a Network Adapter Card, Network Card, NetCard, or Network Interface Card (NIC).

Network Basic Input/Output System (NetBIOS)   An application programming interface (API) used to network application programs.

network logon   An authenticated session to an NT system attached to a network from a remote location.

NT File System (NTFS)   A file system unique to NT that permits extensive security, extremely large volumes, and long filenames.

Nwlink IPX/SPX   An optional network protocol under Windows NT that is used to connect to NetWare environments.

password   A string of characters that are often used in conjunction with an ID to restrict access to resources.

Primary Domain Controller (PDC)   The NT server in the domain model that processes client logins and manages the account database for the domain. Only one PDC can exist in a domain.

Glossary of Terms 289

Registry   A hierarchical database that maintains the configuration information of a Windows NT or 95 system.

Remote Access Service (RAS)   An optional networking service under Windows NT that permits users to remotely access network resources via dial-in connections.

remote administration   The control and administration of one computer from another computer on a network.

Remote Procedure Call (RPC)   A service that permits the transfer and acceptance of remote service requests over a network connection.

Schedule service   A service that is used to enable the AT scheduling tool. This service allows permitted users to execute programs or tasks at specified times.

security ID (SID)   A unique string that identifies a user, group, or machine to a security system. No two SIDs can be alike.

Server service   An NT service that provides file and print services, named pipe sharing, and RPC support.

service pack   A Microsoft released program that provides a host of updates and fixes for the NT operating system.

share   A networking function that permits resources such as directories and printers to be shared over a network.

silent installation   A program installation option that permits the application to be installed without user intervention.

subnet   A portion of a network on which each system shares a common addressing scheme. Used to segment a network for any number of administrative or network-related purposes.

System Difference file   An image file created using Microsoft's System Difference tool, SYSDIFF.EXE. Difference files are used to distribute certain types of applications and configuration options to NT systems on a network.

system account   The account used by the Windows NT subsystem to perform certain administrative tasks on the local system.

System Policy   A template of settings created with the System Policy Editor. This template is stored in a .POL file that is used to modify or restrict a logon session based on User, Group, or Machine.

SystemRoot or %SystemRoot%   The directory containing Windows NT's system files. By default it is the \WINNT directory.

Task Manager   Accessed during an authenticated interactive logon session to a Windows NT system either by using Ctrl+Alt+Delete or right-clicking the Start menu. This session management tool provides a user with the ability to start, stop, or run applications or processes and to view CPU and memory utilization.

Transmission Control Protocol/Internet Protocol (TCP/IP)   A suite of networking protocols developed by DARPA for the creation of worldwide networks. Now it is typically associated with Internet access because it can provide access between systems on a network and the Internet. Extremely useful protocol for use in multi-platform and operating system environments.

Unattended   Refers to an installation option that permits a network administrator to automate the setup of Windows NT. It can also refer to an application installation option that does not require user intervention.

Unattended-aware   Refers to an installation file (.INF) that can be used during an unattended installation to install the desired device or service without requiring a user's input.

Uniqueness Database File (UDF)   A file containing user or machine-specific information that can be referenced during an unattended installation to further customize an NT system.

Universal Naming Convention (UNC)   An established method of referencing resources on a network. Usually consists of the server name preceded by two backslashes, and a share name preceded by one backslash.

wide area network (WAN)   A series of local area networks (LANs) interconnected across a large area, such as a city or between cities.

Workstation service   A service under Windows NT used to provide network connectivity or communication services.

Index

Symbols

OEM directory, CMDLINES.TXT file, 131-134
OEM subdirectory, 21-22
$$ subdirectory, 22
$$RENAME.TXT file, 22, 33
\I386 directory,
   network adapter files, locating on, 90, 92-94
   "Unattended-Aware" network adapter drivers, 105-106, 108

A

Accept CommunityName=(community names) variable, Answer files, 65
Accept Contact Name=(name) variable, Answer files, 65
Access Control Lists, *see* ACLs
accessories, adding and removing (Windows NT), 120-123
ACLs (Access Control Lists), 10
   displaying and modifying with CACLS.EXE, 247
      recognizing CACLS output, 248
Administrator group, security, 162
AdvServerType=, NT Server, 73
Alerter, NT Workstation default service, 275
alpha-based processors, installation directories, 20
anonymous browsing, disabling, registry edit, 272
anonymous users
   access, disabling, registry edit, 273
   restricting, custom policy files, 197-200
Answer files, 35, 37-38
   decimal values, driver startup parameters, 100-101
   different environments, 69-70, 72-73
   headers
      ConfigureAtLogon, 55-56
      [(Services Section)], 63-64
      [(STREAMS)], 62
   [GuiUnattended], 52
   [MassStorageDrivers], 46
   [Unattended], 43
   NT Server, 73, 76, 78
      AdvServerType=, 73
      AutoMode=, 74
      GopherRoot=(gopher root directory), 75
      InstallADMIN=, 75
      InstallFTP=, 75
      InstallGOPHER=, 75
      InstallHTMLA=, 76
      InstallINETSTP=, 74
      InstallW3SAMP=, 76
      InstallWWW=, 75
   replacing settings with UDFs (Uniqueness Database files), 85
   troubleshooting, 78
   variables, 38
      Any Host=, 65
      AssignSameNetworkNumber=, 68
      Attended=, 57
      AtuomaticNetworkNumbers=, 67
      AutoConfirm=, 55
      Background=Back.bmp, 51
      Banner=, 51
      ClientCanRequestIPAddress=, 67
      ClientsCanRequestIpxNode Number=, 68
      ComputerType=HAL TYPE [,OEM] Retail, 43-44
      ConfirmHardware=, 41
      DefaultLocation, 64
      !DefaultScriptOptions=, 64
      DetectAdapters=, 58
      DeviceType=Modem, 68
      DHCP=Yes | No, 61
      DialinProtocols=, 66
      DialoutProtocols=, 66
      FileSystem=, 40
      Install Driver=, 55
      IpxClientAccess=, 67
      KeyboardLayout=Keyboard Layout, 46
      Logo=Logo.bmp, 51
      monitor settings, 55

Answer files

NetBEUIClientAccess=, 66
NoWaitAfterGUIMode=, 40
NoWaitAfterTextMode=, 39
NtUpgrade=, 41
OemBlankAdminPassword, 53
OemPreinstall=, 39
OemSkipEULA=, 39
OemSkipWelcome, 52
OverwriteOemFilesOn Upgrade=, 43
PortName=, 68
PortUsage=, 68
Send Authentication=, 65
StorageDriverDescription=OEM or Retail, 46
TargetPath=, 42
TcpIpClientAccess=, 67
Win31Upgrade=, 42
Windows NT Setup Manager, 36
Any Host= variable, Answer files, 65
AppleTalk, Windows NT protocol, 278
applications
adding to installation
.BAT files, 137-138
.REG files, 135-137
IntranetWare Client 32, 139-144
SYSDIFF.EXE, 145-148, 150
installing, Reboot Mode Definitions, 143
removing
Briefcase, 123
MS Exchange and Explorer, 125-126
Welcome Screen, 124-125
Windows NT, 123
AssignSameNetworkNumber= variable, Answer files, 68
AT command
registry edit, 273
remote maintenance capabilities, 225, 227
Schedule, NT Workstation default service, 277
scheduling updates and maintenance, 220-221
NET START, 222
submission control, altering, 225
AT.EXE, 251-255
ATALK=(ATALK Parameters) variable, Answer files, 61
Attended= variable, Answer files, 57
AutoConfirm= variable, Answer files, 55
autologon
bypassing, registry edit, 269
LOGON.REG, 136
policy option, custom policy files, 200-201, 203

automated deployments, LeaveAlone option, 41
automated installation
Answer files, 35-38
applications, adding to
.BAT files, 137-138
.REG files, 135-137
IntranetWare Client 32, 139-144
SYSDIFF.EXE, 145-148, 150
netcard, goto skipoptions line, 110
NT Server, 73, 76, 78
Automatic Client Upgrade (IntranetWare Client 32), automating installation of, 142-143
AutomaticNetworkNumbers= variable, Answer files, 67
AutoMode=, NT Server, 74

B

Background=Back.bmp variable, Answer files, 51
.BAT files, applications, adding to installation, MSOFFICE.BAT, 137-138, 166
batching, files or scripts
multiple custom configurations, startup parameters, 87
NET.EXE, 255-257
NET COMPUTER [Option], 257
NET CONFIG SERVER [Option], 257
NET CONFIG WORKSTATION [Option], 258
NET CONTINUE [Servicename], 258
NET FILE [Option], 258
NET GROUP [Option], 259
NET HELP [Option], 259
NET HELPMSG [Error Number], 260
NET LOCALGROUP [Option], 260
NET NAME [Option], 261
NET PAUSE [Service], 261
NET PRINT [Option], 261
NET SEND [Option] Message, 261
NET SESSION [Option], 262
NET SHARE [Option], 262
NET START [Service], 263
NET STATISTICS [Workstation or Server], 263
NET STOP [Service], 263
NET TIME [Option], 263
NET USE [Option], 264
NET USER [Options], 265-266
NET VIEW [Option], 267
setup, MS Office, 270

BitsPerPel=8 variable, Answer files, 55
Blue Screen of Death (BSOD), see Stop Events
BOOT.INI file, modifying to restore NT Workstation, 241-242
Briefcase, removing, 123
BROWSER.REG, 151
browsers
    disabling backup master, registry edit, 270
    disabling service on NT workstation, registry edit, 270
    elections, 13
    registry edit, 272
    traffic, 12
BSOD (Blue Screen of Death), see Stop Events

C

C subdirectory, 22
caching, disabling logon and credentials, registry edit, 272
CACLS.EXE, 247
    recognizing CACLS output, 248
case sensitivity, UDFs (Uniqueness Database files), %1 variable, 88
case studies
    security, Pinkerton Security Agency, 160
    Windows NT
        deploying, 14-15
        DSPs (Distribution Share Points), 23-24
ClientCanRequestIPAdress= variable, Answer files, 67
ClientsCanRequestIpxNode Number= variable, Answer files, 68
ClipBook, NT Workstation default service, 275
cloning methods
    after text-mode phase, 282-283
    cloned disk images, 284
    full-blown installations of Windows NT, 281
    GHOST, 283
CMDLINES.TXT files, 33
    registry edits, 150
        BROWSER.REG, 151
        NOSERVER.REG, 151
        OEM directory, 131-134
        testing .REG files, 152
COMMON.ADM
    default computer policy options, 189
    default user policy options, 192, 195
    policy option behaviors, 195

[Component] Section, TXTSETUP.OEM file, 116
Community Name=(community name) variable, Answer files, 65
Computer Browser, NT Workstation default service, 276
ComputerType=HAL TYPE [,OEM] Retail variable, Answer files, 43-44
CON2PRT.EXE, printers, installing and configuring, 158
ConfigureAtLogon header, Answer files, 55-56
[Config.KeyName] Section, TXTSETUP.OEM file, 118
configuring
    multiple workstations, SYSDIFF.EXE, 249-250
    NT networking, case study, 38
ConfirmHardware= variable, Answer files, 41
Control Panel, controlling user environments, 235-236
crashing, System Policy Editor, 212
CreateComputerAccount=(Username, Password) variable, Answer files, 58
creating System Policies, POLEDIT.EXE, 267
customizing
    installations (multiple)
        batch files, 87
        case study, 85
        UDFs (Uniqueness Database files), 82-85
    NT Workstation installations, Setup program options, 86-88, 90
    policy files
        autologon policy option, 200-201, 203
        PART function identifiers, 204, 207
        policy function identifiers, 203-204
        restricting anonymous users, 197-200
    policy templates for security (System Policies), 208, 210-212
    user profiles, Default User profile, 214-215

D

Data Link Control (DLC), Windows NT protocol, 278
decimal values, Answer files, driver startup parameters, 100-101
default services, NT workstation, setup process, 275-277
default settings, Internet homepage, setting, 237

294 Default User profile

Default User profile
    creating custom user profiles, 214-215
    modifying, 214
    subdirectories, 214
[Defaults] Section, TXTSETUP.OEM file, 116
DefaultLocation variable, Answer files, 64
!DefaultScriptOptions= variable, Answer files, 64
deploying Windows NT
    automating, 16
    case study, 14-15
    checklist, 17-18
    maintenance issues, 217-218
    service packs, 153-154
Deployment guide Web site, strategy, 15-16
    Guide to Automating Windows NT Setup, 38
desktops
    controlling user environments, 232
        Control Panel, 235-236
        System Policies, 233-235
    defining user environments
        custom tips at startup, creating, 236
        default Internet homepage, 237
DetectAdapters= variable, Answer files, 58
DetectCount=(number of detection attempts) variable, Answer files, 59
DeviceType=Modem variable, Answer files, 68
DHCP=Yes | No variable, Answer files, 61
Dialin Protocols= variable, Answer files, 66
dialog boxes, Answer files, 35
Dialout Protocols= variable, Answer files, 66
directories, DSPs (Distribution Share Points), 19
    accessing
        NetWare networks, 28
        remotely, 25
        UNIX systems, 28-29
        in Windows NT domains, 25-26
    case study, 23-24
    creating, 20-21
    required subdirectories, 21-23
    troubleshooting, 24
    see also subdirectories
Directory Replicator, NT Workstation default service, 276
disabling backup master browsers, registry edit, 270

disks
    drives, subdirectories, 22
    duplicating
        method, 40
        problems associated with, 282
        performance, FAT partitions, 40
[Disks] Section, TXTSETUP.OEM file, 115
display adapters, see video adapters
DISPLAY subdirectory, 22
distribution methods, designing, 81
Distribution Share Point directory, 35
DLC (Data Link Control), Windows NT protocol, 278
[(DLC Parameters)] header, Answer files, 62
DLC=(DLC Parameters) variable, Answer files, 61
DNSName=(DNS domain name) variable, Answer files, 62
DNSServer=(IP Addresses) variable, Answer files, 62
domain controllers, SID (Security ID), 281
driver libraries, Windows NT
    \DRVLIB.NIC Subdirectory, 94-98
    \I386 Directory, 90, 92-94
drivers, installing specialized
    Registry data types, 119-120
    TXTSETUP.OEM file, 115-118
\DRVLIB.NIC Directory, "Unattended-Aware" network adapter drivers, 108-109
DRVLIB.NIC subdirectory, 21
\DRVLIB.NIC subdirectory, network adapter files, locating on, 94-98
DSPs (Distribution Share Points), 19
    accessing
        NetWare networks, 28
        remotely, 25
        UNIX systems, 28-29
        in Windows NT domains, 25-26
    case studies, 23-24
    creating, 20-21
    subdirectories
        $$, 22
        OEM, 21-22
        DISPLAY, 22
        drive letters, 22
        NET, 23
        TEXTMODE, 23
    troubleshooting, 24
DWORD Editor, decimal and hexadecimal values, 101

E

Emergency Repair Disk
  registry edits, 269
  testing .REG files, 152
End-User License Agreement (EULA), 36, 39
environments, mixed client and network,
  using UDFs (Uniqueness Database files),
  82-83
ERD, using to restore NT Workstation, 242
errors, 78
  codes
    registry edits, 150
    SYSDIFF, 148, 150
  messages
    INACCESSIBLE BOOT DEVICE, 239
    IRQL NOT LESS OR EQUAL, 240
    KERNEL STACK INPAGE ERROR, 240
    KMODE EXCEPTION NOT HANDLED, 240
    REGISTRY ERROR, 240
    resolving BSOD errors, 241
    unattended installation, network adapters, 112
    UNEXPECTED KERNEL MODE TRAP, 240
EULA (End-User License Agreement), 36, 39
Event Log, NT Workstation default service, 276
events, scheduling, AT.EXE, 251-255
Everyone group, 11
  security, 161-162
    NTFS volumes, 163-165
    Registry, 180-181

F

FAT partitions, sizes, 40
files
  .BAT, 166
  batching
    NET.EXE, 255-257
    NET COMPUTER [Option], 257
    NET CONFIG SERVER [Option], 257
    NET CONFIG WORKSTATION [Option], 258
    NET CONTINUE [Servicename], 258
    NET FILE [Option], 258
    NET GROUP [Option], 259
    NET HELP [Option], 259
    NET HELPMSG [Error Number], 260
    NET LOCALGROUP [Option], 260
    NET NAME [Option], 261
    NET PAUSE [Service], 261
    NET PRINT [Option], 261
    NET SEND [Option] Message, 261
    NET SESSION [Option], 262
    NET SHARE [Option], 262
    NET START [Service], 263
    NET STATISTICS [Workstation or Server], 263
    NET STOP [Service], 263
    NET TIME [Option], 263
    NET USE [Option], 264
    NET USER [Options], 265-266
    NET VIEW [Option], 267
CMDLINES.TXT, 33
copying before modifying, 123
custom policy, creating
  autologon policy option, 200-201, 203
  Part function identifiers, 204, 207
  policy function identifiers, 203-204
  restricting anonymous users, 197-200
.REG, 165
$$RENAME.TXT, 22, 33
SYSDIFF.EXE, 33-34
UNATTEND.TXT, 32
WINNT.EXE, 32
WINNT32.EXE, 32
[Files.component.ID] Section, TXTSETUP.OEM file, 117-118
FileSystem= variable, Answer files, 40
FTPRoot=(ftp root directory), NT Server, 75

G

Gateway=(gateway address) variable, Answer files, 62
GetAdmin hacker program, 162-163
GHOST, cloning methods, 283
Gopher Root=(gopher root directory), NT Server, 75
groups
  Administrator, security, 162
  Everyone, 11
    security, 161-165, 180-181
  permissions
    creating, 173
    default, 174-177
    modifying, 177-178
GuestAccountName=(name), NT Server, 76
GuestAccountPassword=(password string), NT Server, 76
[GuiUnattended] header, Answer files, 52

H

hacker programs, GetAdmin, 162-163
HAL (Hardware Compatibility List), 8
hardware requirements, Windows 95 and Windows NT, 8
headers, Answer files
    ConfigureAtLogon, 55-56
    [(Services Section)], 63-64
    [GuiUnattended], 52
    [MassStorageDrivers], 46
    [Unattended], 43
hexadecimal values, Registry, driver startup parameters, 100-101
Hot fixes, 11-12
    applying, 154

I

[(IIS Parameters)], NT Server, 74
I/O requests, Server, NT Workstation default service, 277
.IMG files
    direct application to difference files, 147
    expanding with /INF, 147-148
INACCESSIBLE BOOT DEVICE error message, 239
INETSRV subdirectory, 20
INETSTP=(Internet server parameters section) variable, Answer files, 63
.INF files
    adding and removing accessories, Windows NT, 120-123
    comparing with manufacturers', 102-103
    goto skipoptions line, 110
    OEM-supplied, scripting "Unattended-Aware," 111-112
    testing custom or modified, 145
/INF switch, expanding .IMG files with, 147-148
InstallAdapters=(install adapters section) variable, Answer files, 58
InstallADMIN=, NT Server, 75
installations
    multiple, customizing
        batch files, 87
        case study, 85
        UDFs (Uniqueness Database files), 82-85
    startup parameters, Windows NT, WINNT.EXE and WINNT32.EXE, 86-88, 90
    types, NT accessories, 121
    see also installing
InstallDC=(domain name), NT Server, 74
InstallDir=(Internet services install directory), NT Server, 75
InstallDriver= variable, Answer files, 55
InstallFTP=, NT Server, 75
InstallGOPHER=, NT Server, 75
InstallHTMLA=, NT Server, 76
InstallINETSTP=, NT Server, 74
installing
    CMDLINES.TXT file, 131-134
    drive other than C, 43
    IntranetWare Client 32, 139
        SETUPAPI.DLL, 143-144
    MS Office 97
        MSOFFICE.REG, 137
        MSOFFICEBAT, 137-138
    network adapter drivers, error messages, 112
    OEM-supplied network adapter drivers, 103-105
    operating system simultaneously, OEM-supplied network adapter drivers, 90, 99
    printers
        CON2PRT.EXE, 158
        SYSDIFF image files, 155-156
    specialized drivers
        Registry data types, 119-120
        TXTSETUP.OEM file, 115-118
    specialized video adapters, 113-114
    System Policy Editor, 186, 188
    Windows NT
        automatically, 21-23, 32-34
        case study, 23-24
        cloning methods, 281
        default, 9, 12
        DSPs (Distribution Share Points) troubleshooting, 24, 26, 28-29
        protocols, 12
        push installations, 29-31
        services, 12-13
    see also installations
InstallInternetServer=(IIS Parameters), NT Server, 74
InstallProtocols=(protocols section) variable, Answer files, 58
InstallW3SAMP=, NT Server, 76
InstallWWW=, NT Server, 75
Intel-based processors, installation directories, 20
Internet Explorer, resetting default startup page, registry edit, 274

native tools   297

IntranetWare Client 32
    applications, adding to installation
        Automatic Client Upgrade, 142-143
        SETUPAPI.DLL, 143-144
        SETUPNW.EXE /U method, 141
        UNATTEND.TXT method, 139-140
    Web site, 139
IPAddress=(Ip address) variable, Answer files, 62
[(IPX Parameters)] header, Answer files, 61
IpxClientAccess= variable, Answer files, 67
IRQL NOT LESS OR EQUAL error message, 240

J-K

JoinDomain=(Domain Name) variable, Answer files, 57
JoinWorkgroup=(Workgroup name) variable, Answer files, 57

KERNEL STACK INPAGE ERROR error message, 240
KeyboardLayout=Keyboard Layout variable, Answer files, 46
[KeyName] Section, TXTSETUP.OEM file, 118
KMODE EXCEPTION NOT HANDLED error message, 240
KRegistry
    security, 178-179
        Everyone group, 180-181
        REGSEC and SECADD utilities, 179-180
        Service Pack 3 installation, 182-183

L

LeaveAlone option, automated deployments, 41
legal notices, displaying, registry edit, 272
[LicenseFilePrintData], NT Server, 74
Limit Host=(host names) variable, Answer files, 65
LimitTo=(netcard inf option) variable, Answer files, 59
Location=(computer location) variable, Answer files, 65
Logo=Logo.bmp variable, Answer files, 51
LOGON.REG, 136

M

maintenance options
    automating and scheduling, 219
        AT command, 220-222
        Network Install tab, 229-232
        SHUTDOWN command, 227
        SHUTDOWN command-line options, 228-229
    case study, Instructional Design Lab (University of Virginia School of Law), 219
    deploying NT, 217-218
[MassStorageDrivers] header, Answer files, 46-47
Messenger, NT Workstation default service, 276
Microsoft
    Web sites
        Guide to Automating Windows NT Setup, 38
        Knowledge Base, 240
        Office, installing, 138
        Windows NT, cloning issue, 281
MIPs-based processors, installation directories, 20
MS Exchange, disabling installation of, 125-126
MS Explorer, disabling installation of, 125-126
MS Office, setup process batch file, 270
MSOFFICE.BAT, 137
    installation files, handling, 138
MSOFFICE.REG, 137

N

native tools
    AT.EXE, 251
    REGEDIT.EXE, 251
    REGEDT32.EXE, 251
    SYSDIFF.EXE, 249-250
    AT.EXE, 252-255
    CACLS.EXE, 247
        recognizing CACLS output, 248
    NET.EXE, 255-257
        NET COMPUTER [Option], 257
        NET CONFIG SERVER [Option], 257
        NET CONFIG WORKSTATION [Option], 258
        NET CONTINUE [Servicename], 258
        NET FILE [Option], 258
        NET GROUP [Option], 259

298 native tools

NET HELP [Option], 259
NET HELPMSG [Error Number], 260
NET LOCALGROUP [Option], 260
NET NAME [Option], 261
NET PAUSE [Service], 261
NET PRINT [Option], 261
NET SEND [Option] Message, 261
NET SESSION [Option], 262
NET SHARE [Option], 262
NET START [Service], 263
NET STATISTICS [Workstation or Server], 263
NET STOP [Service], 263
NET TIME [Option], 263
NET USE [Option], 264
NET USER [Options], 265-266
NET VIEW [Option], 267
POLEDIT.EXE, 267
NBF=(Netbeui Parameters) variable, Answer files, 61
NET commands, RUNONCE option, processing with registry edit, 271
Net Logon, NT Workstation default service, 276
NET subdirectory, 22-23
[(Netcard Inf option=(netcard parameter section)] variable, Answer files, 59
NET.EXE, 255-256
NET COMPUTER [Option], 257
NET CONFIG SERVER [Option], 257
NET CONFIG WORKSTATION [Option], 258
NET CONTINUE [Servicename], 258
NET FILE [Option], 258
NET GROUP [Option], 259
NET HELP [Option], 259
NET HELPMSG [Error Number], 260
NET LOCALGROUP [Option], 260
NET NAME [Option], 261
NET PAUSE [Service], 261
NET PRINT [Option], 261
NET SEND [Option] Message, 261
NET SESSION [Option], 262
NET SHARE [Option], 262
NET START [Service], 263
NET STATISTICS [Workstation or Server], 263
NET STOP [Service], 263
NET TIME [Option], 263
NET USE [Option], 264
NET USER [Options], 265-266
NET VIEW [Option], 267
[(NetBeui Parameters)] header, Answer files, 61

NetBEUIClientAccess= variable, Answer files, 66
[(netcard parameter section)] header, Answer files, 59-60
NETMON=(Netmon Parameters section) variable, Answer files, 63
NetWare, accessing DSPs (Distribution Share Points), 28
[(NetWare Client Parameters)] header, Answer files, 64
Network Administration model, 9
Network DDE DSDM, NT Workstation default service, 276
[Network] header, Answer files, 58
Network Install tab
    automating and scheduling maintenance, 229-232
    registry edit, 274
networks
    adapter drivers
        determining parameters, 98, 100-101
        installing OEM-supplied, 103-105
        replacing CD-ROM's with manufacturer's, 102-103
        scripting "Unattended-Aware," 109-111
        unattended installation, error messages, 112
        \DRVLIB.NIC Directory, "unattended-aware," 108-109
        \I386 Directory, "unattended-aware," 105-106, 108
    adapter files
        locating on \DRBLIB.NIC subdirectory, 94-98
        locating on \I386 directory, 90, 92-94
    NetWare, accessing DSPs (Distribution Share Points), 28
NOSERVER.REG, 151
Novell IntranetWare Client 32
    installation, registry edit, 270
    Web site, 139
NoWaitAfterGUIMode= variable, Answer files, 40
NoWaitAfterTextMode= variable, Answer files, 39
NT, see Windows NT
NTFS volumes
    permissions
        default, 163, 165
        Everyone group, 161-163
    security, 165
        CACLS utility, 166, 172
        resetting with RUNONCE option, registry edit, 271

registry edits 299

NTRIGHTS utility, 177-178
NtUpgrade= variable, Answer files, 41
NWLink IPX/SPX Compatible Transport, Windows NT protocol, 278
NWLink NetBIOS, Windows NT protocol, 278
NWLNKIPX=(IPX Parameters) variable, Answer files, 61
NWWKSTA=(NetWare Client Parameters section) variable, Answer files, 63

O

OEM-supplied network adapter drivers
    installing, 103-105
    operating systems, installing, 90, 99
    replacing CD-ROM's with manufacturer's, 102-103
OemBlankAdminPassword variable, Answer files, 53
OemPreinstall= variable, Answer files, 39
OemSkipEULA= variable, Answer files, 39
OemSkipWelcome variable, Answer files, 52
operating systems
    installing simultaneous instances, 90, 99
    environment variables, creating, POLEDIT.EXE, 186, 188
    32-bit, 8
    Windows NT, 9
OverwriteOemFilesOn Upgrade= variable, Answer files, 43

P-Q

PCs (power), installation directories, 20
permissions
    groups
        Administrator, 162
        creating, 173
        default, 174-177
        Everyone, 161-165, 180-181
        modifying, 177-178
    NTFS volumes, 163
        .BAT file, 166
        .REG file, 165
        CACLS utility, 166, 172
    Registry, 178-181
        Service Pack 3 installation, 182-183
    users
        creating, 173
        default, 174-177
        modifying, 177-178
Pinkerton Security Agency, 160

POLEDIT.EXE, 186, 188, 267
policy layering for security (System Policies), 208
PortName= variable, Answer files, 68
PortSections=(RAS Ports Section) variable, Answer files, 66
PortUsage= variable, Answer files, 68
printers
    installing and configuring, 155-156, 158
    spooling service, Spooler, NT Workstation default service, 277
processors, installation directories, 20
protocols
    Windows NT, 278-279
    Windows NT installation, 12
[(Protocols Section)] header, Answer files, 60
Push installations, 29-31

R

RAS (Remote Access Server), 9
[(Ras Ports Section)] header, Answer files, 68
[(RasParameters)] header, Answer files, 66-68
RAS=(Ras Parameters) variable, Answer files, 63
[(RASPPTP)] header, Answer files, 62
RASPPTP=(Ras PTPP Parameters) variable, Answer files, 61
Reboot Mode Definitions, installing applications, 143
.REG files, 165
    applications, adding to installation, 135
        LOGON.REG, 136-137
    testing, 152
REGED32T.EXE, 251
REGEDIT.EXE, 251
Registry
    data types, 119-120
    hexadecimal values, driver startup parameters, 100-101
    network adapter drivers, determining startup parameters, 98, 100-101
    security, 10-11
    System Policies, assessing security-related changes to, 208
    workstations, enforcing restrictions, POLEDIT.EXE, 186, 188
Registry Device startup parameters, 152
registry edits
    anonymous browsing, disabling, 272
    anonymous user access, disabling, 273
    applying, REGEDIT.EXE or REGEDT32.EXE , 251

AT commands, increasing access, 273
autologon, bypassing, 269
browsers, disabling, 270
CMDLINES.TXT files, 150
   BROWSER.REG, 151
   NOSERVER.REG, 151
editing manually, disadvantages, 185
incorrect use of, 269
Internet Explorer, default startup page, resetting, 274
legal notices, displaying, 272
Network Install tab, 274
Novell IntranetWare Client 32 installation, 270
NT workstation, Server service, disabling, 270
NTFS security, resetting, RUNONCE option, 271
Schedule service, resetting startup parameters, 273
security issues
   caching of logon and credentials, disabling, 272
   last username, disabling display of, 272
   roaming profiles, deleting, 273
   winreg key, 271
setup process batch file, MS Office, 270
Shutdown options, resetting, 272
system pagefile, deleting data from, 273
testing .REG files, 152
tips, resetting or creating, 274
troubleshooting, error codes, 150
welcome page, disabling display of, 274
REGISTRY ERROR error message, 240
REGSEC utility, 179-180
Remote Access Server (RAS), 9
Remote Procedure Call (RPC) Locator or Service, NT Workstation default service, 277
retail drivers, network adapter files, locating on
   \DRVLIB.NIC subdirectory, 94-98
   \I386 directory, 90, 92-94
rights, *see* permissions
roaming profiles, deleting, registry edit, 273
RPC (Remote Procedure Call) Locator or Service, NT Workstation default service, 277
RUNONCE option, processing NET commands, registry edit, 271
   NTFS security, resetting registry edit, 271

S

SAMBA, 28-29
SAP=(SAP Parameters section) variable, Answer files, 63
Schedule, NT Workstation default service, 277
   service account
      modifying, 223-224
      /PROFILEPATH Statement, 224
   startup parameters, resetting registry edit, 273
ScopeID=(scope ID) variable, Answer files, 62
scripting "Unattended-Aware"
   network adapter drivers, 109-111
   OEM-supplied .INF files, 111-112
scripts, batching
   NET.EXE, 255-257
   NET COMPUTER [Option], 257
   NET CONFIG SERVER [Option], 257
   NET CONFIG WORKSTATION [Option], 258
   NET CONTINUE [Servicename], 258
   NET FILE [Option], 258
   NET GROUP [Option], 259
   NET HELP [Option], 259
   NET HELPMSG [Error Number], 260
   NET LOCALGROUP [Option], 260
   NET NAME [Option], 261
   NET PAUSE [Service], 261
   NET PRINT [Option], 261
   NET SEND [Option] Message, 261
   NET SESSION [Option], 262
   NET SHARE [Option], 262
   NET START [Service], 263
   NET STATISTICS [Workstation or Server], 263
   NET STOP [Service], 263
   NET TIME [Option], 263
   NET USE [Option], 264
   NET USER [Options], 265-266
   NET VIEW [Option], 267
SECADD utility, 179-180
security
   case studies
      Pinkerton Security Agency, 160
      University of Victoria's Department of Computer Science, 212
   custom policy templates (System Policies), 208, 210-212
   default settings, 160
      Everyone group, 161-162
      hacker intrusions, 162-163

[(STREAMS)] header, Answer files   301

hot fixes, 11-12
NTFS volumes
　.BAT file, 166
　.REG file, 165
　CACLS utility, 166, 172
　default permissions, 163, 165
　Everyone group, 163
　options, 159-160
　permissions, users and groups, 173-178
　policy layering (System Policies), 208
　Registry, 10-11, 178
　　Everyone group, 180-181
　　REGSEC and SECADD utilities, 179-180
　　Service Pack 3 installation, 182-183
　　restricting anonymous users, custom policy files, 197-200
　service packs, 11-12
　System Policies, 185-186
　Windows NT Security Handbook, 161
Security ID (SID), cloning methods, 281-282
security issues
　Answer files, usernames and passwords, 58
　caching of logon and credentials, disabling registry edit, 272
　last username, disabling display of registry edit, 272
　registry edits, bypassing autologon, 270
　roaming profiles, deleting registry edit, 273
　winreg key, registry edit, 271
Send Authentication= variable, Answer files, 65
Server, NT Workstation default service, 12-13, 277
　NT workstation, disabling registry edit, 270
　SAMBA, 28-29
Service Pack 3, Registry, 182-183
Service packs, 11-12, 153
　Hotfixes, applying, 154
services, Windows NT installation, 12-13
[(Services Section)] header, Answer files, 62, 64
Setup Manager, Answer files, 36
setup process, NT workstation, default services, 275-277
SETUPAPI.DLL, IntranetWare Client 32, automating installation, 143-144
SETUPNW.EXE /U, IntranetWare Client 32, automating installation, 141

SHUTDOWN command
　scheduling updates and maintenance, 227
　utility options, 228-229
shutdown
　options, NT Workstation, resetting on registry edit, 272
　process, system pagefile, deleting data from registry edit, 273
SID (Security ID), cloning methods, 281-282
[(Snmp Parameters)] header, Answer files, 64
[(STREAMS)] header, Answer files, 62SNMP=(SNMP Parameters) variable, Answer files, 63
Software Service startup parameters, 152
Spooler, NT Workstation default service, 277
Start menu, updating with application's Program group, CMDLINES.TXT, 133-134
startup
　custom tips, creating, 236
　parameters
　　network adapter drivers, determining manually, 98, 100-101
　　Registry Device and Software Service, 152
　　troubleshooting, adapter errors and custom scripts, 126
　　UDFs (Uniqueness Database files), 82
　　WINNT.EXE and WINNT32.EXE, 86-88, 90
　　scripts, UNATTEND.TXT and .UDB files, 89
StaticAddressBegin=(BeginIPAddress) variable, Answer files, 67
StaticAddressEnd=(EndIPAddress) variable, Answer files, 67
STCPIP=(Simple TCPIP parameters section) variable, Answer files, 63
Stop Events, diagnosing, 238
　INACCESSIBLE BOOT DEVICE, 239
　IRQL NOT LESS OR EQUAL, 240
　KERNEL STACK INPAGE ERROR, 240
　KMODE EXCEPTION NOT HANDLED, 240
　REGISTRY ERROR, 240
　resolving BSOD errors, 241
　UNEXPECTED KERNEL MODE TRAP, 240
storage performance, FAT partitions, 40
StorageDriverDescription = OEM or Retail variable, Answer files, 46
[(STREAMS)] header, Answer files, 62

STREAMS, Windows NT protocol, 279
STREAMS=(Streams Parameters)
  variable, Answer files, 61
subdirectories
  DRVLIB.NIC, 21
  INETSRV, 20
  required in DSPs (Distribution Share
    Points)
    $$, 22
    OEM, 21-22
    DISPLAY, 22
    drive letters, 22
    NET, 23
    TEXTMODE, 23
  see also directories
Subnet=(subnet address) variable, Answer
  files, 62
SYSDIFF
  image files, printers, installing and configuring, 155-156
  troubleshooting, timestamp, 149
SYSDIFF.EXE, 33-34, 249-250
  applications, adding to installation,
    145-146
    direct application of .IMG files, 147
    error codes, 148, 150
    expanding .IMG files with /INF, 147
system administrators
  automating and scheduling
    maintenance, 219
    AT command, 220-222
    Network Install tab, 229-232
    SHUTDOWN command, 227
    SHUTDOWN command-line options,
      228-229
  System Policies, 185-186
System Difference Tool, 33, 145
system pagefile, deleting data, registry edit,
  273
System Policies
  controlling user environments
    DEFAULT COMPUTER/WINDOWS
      NT SHELL/CUSTOM SHARE
      FOLDERS, 233
    DEFAULT USER/SHELL/
      RESTRICTIONS, 233
    DEFAULT USER/SYSTEM/
      RESTRICTIONS, 234
    DEFAULT USER/WINDOWS NT
      SHELL/CUSTOM FOLDERS, 234
    DEFAULT USER/WINDOWS NT
      SHELL/CUSTOM USER
      INTERFACE, 234

DEFAULT USER/WINDOWS NT
  SHELL/RESTRICTIONS, 234
DEFAULT USER/WINDOWS NT
  SYSTEM, 235
  Run option, 233
creating POLEDIT.EXE, 267
creating custom policy files, 197
  autologon policy option, 200-201, 203
  PART function identifiers, 204, 207
  policy function identifiers, 203-204
  restricting anonymous users, 197-200
custom policy templates, security, 208,
  210-212
deciding when to use, 185-186
Editor, POLEDIT.EXE, 186, 188
policy layering for security, 208
templates, 188
  policy option behaviors, 195
  default computer policy
    options, 189
  default user policy options, 192, 195
System Policy Editor, crashing, 212

T

TargetPath= variable, Answer files, 42
[(Tcpip Parameters)] header, Answer files, 61
TcpIpClientAccess= variable, Answer files, 67
TCPPRINT=(TCPIP Printing Parameters
  section) variable, Answer files, 63
templates, System Policy, 188
  default computer policy options, 189
  default user policy options, 192, 195
  policy option behaviors, 195
temporary install directory, 41
text editors, Answer files, 36-37
text-mode phase, cloning methods, 282-283
TEXTMODE subdirectory, 22-23
32-bit operating systems, 8
tips
  creating custom at startup, 236
  resetting or creating registry edit, 274
Traps=(IP addresses) | (IPX addresses)
  variable, Answer files, 65
troubleshooting, 9
  .REG files, 153
  Answer files, 78
  DSPs (Distribution Share Points), 24, 26,
    28-29
  FAT partitions, disk and storage
    performance, 40
  registry edits, error codes, 150

SYSDIFF, timestamp, 149
temporary install directory, 41
UDBs, startup parameters, adapter errors and custom scripts, 126
TXTSETUP.OEM
   installing specialized
      drivers, 115
      video adapters, 113-114
   [Component] Section, 116
   [Config.KeyName] Section, 118
   [Defaults] Section, 116
   [Disks] Section, 115
   [Files.component.ID] Section, 117-118
   [KeyName] Section, 118

U

.UDB files
   contents of sample, 84-85
   creating, 82-83
   startup scripts, 89
UDBs, troubleshooting, 126
UDFs (Uniqueness Database files)
   case study, 85
   contents of sample .UDB files, 84-85
   creating .UDB files, 82-83
   replacing Answer file settings, 85
UNATTEND.TXT, 35, 37-38
   different environments, 69-70, 72-73
   installing OEM-supplied network adapter drivers, 103-105
   IntranetWare Client 32, automating installation of, 139-140
   startup scripts, 89
   variables, 38
      !DefaultScriptOptions=, 64
      Any Host=, 65
      AssignSameNetworkNumber=, 68
      Attended=, 57
      AutoConfirm=, 55
      AutomaticNetworkNumbers=, 67
      Background=Back.bmp, 51
      ClientCanRequestIPAddress=, 67
      ClientsCanRequestIpxNode Number=, 68
      ComputerType=HAL TYPE [,OEM] Retail, 43-44
      ConfirmHardware=, 41
      DefaultLocation, 64
      DetectAdapters=, 58
      DeviceType=Modem, 68
      DHCP=Yes | No, 61
      DialinProtocols=, 66
      DialoutProtocols=, 66
      FileSystem=, 40
      InstallDriver =, 55
      IpxClientAccess=, 67
      KeyboardLayout=Keyboard Layout, 46
      Logo=Logo.bmp, 51
      monitor settings, 55
      NetBEUIClientAccess=, 66
      NoWaitAfterGUIMode=, 40
      NoWaitAfterTextMode=, 39
      NtUpgrade=, 41
      OemBlankAdminPassword, 53
      OemPreinstall=, 39
      OemSkipEULA=, 39
      OemSkipWelcome, 52
      OverwriteOemFilesOnUpgrade=, 43
      PortName=, 68
      PortUsage=, 68
      Send Authentication=, 65
      StorageDriverDescription=OEM or Retail, 46
      TargetPath=, 42
      TcpIpClientAccess=, 67
      Win31Upgrade=, 42
   Windows NT Setup Manager, 36
UNATTEND.TXT file, 32
"Unattended-Aware"
   network adapter drivers\DRVLIB.NIC Directory, 108-109
   scripting, 109-111
   \I386 Directory, 105-106, 108
   OEM-supplied .INF files, scripting, 111-112
[Unattended] header, Answer files, 39, 41-43
unattended installation, Default User profiles, creating custom, 214-215
UNEXPECTED KERNEL MODE TRAP error message, 240
Uninterruptible Power Supply (UPS), NT Workstation default service, 277
Uniqueness Database files, *see* **UDFs**
UNIX systems, accessing DSPs (Distribution Share Points), 28-29
UPDATE.EXE, service packs
   command-line options, 153-154
   Hotfixes, applying, 154
updating system
   automating and scheduling, 219
      AT command, 220-222
      AT command submission control, altering, 225
      Network Install tab, 229-232

304 updating system

Schedule service account, modifying, 223-224
SHUTDOWN command, 227
SHUTDOWN command-line options, 228-229
upgrading Windows NT, WINNT32.EXE, startup parameters, 86-88, 90
UPS (Uninterruptible Power Supply), NT Workstation default service, 277
user access, anonymous, disabling registry edit, 273
user environments
    controlling, 232
    Control Panel, 235-236
    DEFAULT COMPUTER/WINDOWS NT SHELL/CUSTOM SHARE FOLDERS, 233
    DEFAULT USER/SHELL/ RESTRICTIONS, 233
    DEFAULT USER/SYSTEM/ RESTRICTIONS, 234
    DEFAULT USER/WINDOWS NO SHELL/CUSTOM FOLDERS, 234
    DEFAULT USER/WINDOWS NT SHELL/CUSTOM USER INTERFACE, 234
    DEFAULT USER/WINDOWS NT SHELL/RESTRICTIONS, 234
    DEFAULT USER/WINDOWS NT SYSTEM, 235
    Run option, 233
    System Policies, 233-235
    defining
        custom tips at startup, creating, 236
        default Internet homepage, 237
Username, last, disabling display of registry edit, 272
users
    anonymous
        access, disabling, registry edit, 273
        restricting, custom policy files, 197-200
    permissions
        creating, 173
        default, 174-177
        modifying, 177-178
utilities
    NTRIGHTS, 177-178
    REGSEC, 179-180
    SECADD, 179-180

V

variables
    Answer files, 38
        Accept Community Name=(community names), 65
        Any Host=, 65
        AssignSameNetworkNumber=, 68
        ATALK=(ATALK Parameters), 61
        Attended=, 57
        AutoConfirm=, 55
        AutomaticNetworkNumbers=, 67
        Background=Back.bmp, 51
        ClientCanRequestIPAddress=, 67
        ClientsCanRequestIpxNode Number=, 68
        ComputerType=HAL TYPE [,OEM] Retail, 43-44
        ConfirmHardware=, 41
        DefaultLocation, 64
        !DefaultScriptOptions=, 64
        DetectAdapters=, 58
        DeviceType=Modem, 68
        DHCP=Yes | No, 61
        DialinProtocols=, 66
        DialoutProtocols=, 66
        FileSystem=, 40
        InstallDriver=, 55
        IpxClientAccess=, 67
        KeyboardLayout=Keyboard Layout, 46
        Location=(computer location), 65
        Logo=Logo.bmp, 51
        monitor settings, 55
        NetBEUIClientAccess=, 66
        NoWaitAfterGUIMode=, 40
        NoWaitAfterTextMode=, 39
        NtUpgrade=, 41
        NWLNKIPX=(IPX Parameters), 61
        OemBlankAdminPassword, 53
        OemPreinstall=, 39
        OemSkipEULA=, 39
        OemSkipWelcome, 52
        OverwriteOemFilesOn Upgrade=, 43
        PortName=, 68
        PortUsage=, 68
        SAP=(SAP Parameters section), 63
        Send Authentication=, 65
        SNMP=(SNMP Parameters), 63
        StorageDriverDescription=OEM or Retail, 46
        TargetPath=, 42
        TcpIpClientAccess=, 67
        Win31Upgrade=, 42

video adapters, installing, 113-114
VRefresh=60 variable, Answer files, 55

W

warnings, displaying legal notices, registry edit, 272
Web sites
   GHOST, 283
   Microsoft
      Guide to Automating Windows NT Setup, 38
      Knowledge Base, 240
   Novell, IntranetWare Client 32, 139
   SAMBA, 29
   security, 178
Welcome page, disabling display, registry edit, 274
Welcome Screen, removing, 124-125
Win31Upgrade= variable, Answer files, 42
Windows 95
   hardware requirements, 8
   System Policies, 189
Windows NT
   accessories, removing, 120-123
   advantages, 7
   cloning full-blown installations, 281
   cloning methods
      after text-mode phase, 282-283
      cloned disk images, 284
      GHOST, 283
   deploying
      automating, 16
      case study, 14-15
      checklist, 17-18
      strategy, 15-16
   disadvantages, 7
   hardware requirements, 8
   installing
      automatically, 21-23, 32-34
      case study, 23-24
      default, 9, 12
      DSPs (Distribution Share Points)
         troubleshooting, 24, 26, 28-29
      protocols, 12
      push installations, 29-31
      services, 12-13
   LM Security Support Provider, NT Workstation default service, 276
   migrating to, case study, 134-135
   networking, configuring, case study, 38
   pros and cons, 9

   protocols
      AppleTalk, 278
      NWLink IPX/SPX Compatible Transport, 278
      NWLink NetBIOS, 278
      STREAMS, 279
   Security Handbook, 161, 178
   Server, Answer files
      AdvServerType=, 73
      AutoMode=, 74
      GopherRoot=(gopher root directory), 75
      InstallADMIN=, 75
      InstallFTP=, 75
      InstallGOPHER=, 75
      InstallHTMLA=, 76
      InstallINETSTP=, 74
      InstallW3SAMP=, 76
      InstallWWW=, 75
   Server, automated installation of, 73, 76, 78
Windows NT Workstation
   default service, 277
   disabling browser service on registry edit, 270
   installations, customizing Setup program options, 86-88, 90
   restoring, 238
      BOOT.INI file, modifying, 242
      BOOT.INI file, modifying to restore NT Workstation, 241
      BSOD errors, resolving, 241
      ERD, using, 242
      Stop Events, diagnosing, 239-240
   Server service, disabling registry edit, 270
   service, 12
   setup process, default services, 275-277
   Shutdown options, resetting, registry edit, 272
WINNT.ADM
   default computer policy options, 189
   default user policy options, 192, 195
   policy option behaviors, 195
WINNT.EXE and WINNT32.EXE
   files, 32
   startup parameters, 86-88, 90
Winreg key, security, adding to registry edit, 271
WINSPrimary=(IP Address) variable, Answer files, 62
WINSSecondary=(IP address) variable, Answer files, 62

workstations, configuring multiple, SYSDIFF.EXE, 249-250
WWWRoot=(www root directory), NT Server, 75

X-Z

Xresolution=640 variable, Answer files, 55

Yresolution=480 variable, Answer files, 55

ZAK Administration Kit, creating files, CALCS.BAT, 172

Basic Process for an Unattended Setup

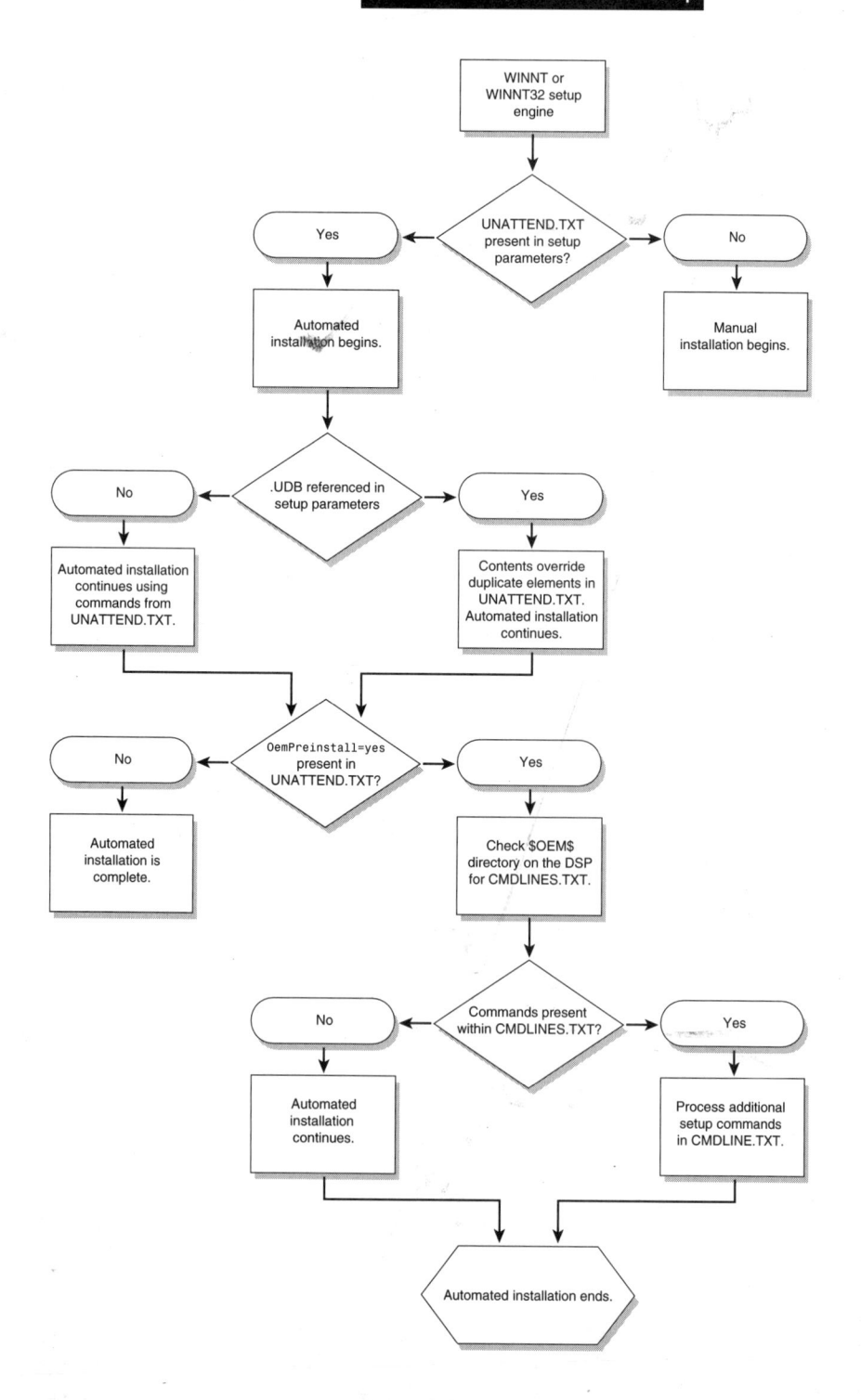

```
                    WINNT or
                    WINNT32 setup
                    engine
                         │
                         ▼
                  ┌──────────────┐
       ┌─── Yes ──┤ UNATTEND.TXT ├── No ───┐
       │          │ present in   │         │
       │          │ setup        │         │
       │          │ parameters?  │         │
       │          └──────────────┘         │
       ▼                                   ▼
  Automated                           Manual
  installation begins.                installation begins.
       │
       ▼
  ┌──────────────┐
  │ .UDB referenced in │
  │ setup parameters   │
  └──────────────┘
  No ←──┤├──→ Yes
   │           │
   ▼           ▼
Automated installation      Contents override
continues using             duplicate elements in
commands from               UNATTEND.TXT.
UNATTEND.TXT.               Automated installation
                            continues.
        │           │
        └─────┬─────┘
              ▼
     ┌──────────────────┐
  No │ OemPreinstall=yes│ Yes
◄────┤ present in       ├────►
     │ UNATTEND.TXT?    │
     └──────────────────┘
   │                       │
   ▼                       ▼
Automated              Check $OEM$
installation is        directory on the DSP
complete.              for CMDLINES.TXT.
                           │
                           ▼
                 ┌─────────────────┐
            No   │ Commands present│   Yes
         ◄───────┤ within          ├────►
                 │ CMDLINES.TXT?   │
                 └─────────────────┘
              │                       │
              ▼                       ▼
         Automated              Process additional
         installation           setup commands
         continues.             in CMDLINE.TXT.
              │                       │
              └───────────┬───────────┘
                          ▼
              Automated installation ends.
```